India: Some Aspects of
Economic and Social Development

Published by Academic Foundation
*in collaboration with*

CENTRE FOR ECONOMIC AND SOCIAL STUDIES,
(CESS), HYDERABAD

# *India*

## Some Aspects of
## Economic and Social Development

*The CESS Silver Jubilee Lectures*

EDITORS

## S. Mahendra Dev
## K.S. Babu

ACADEMIC FOUNDATION

NEW DELHI

First published in 2008
by :

**ACADEMIC FOUNDATION**
4772-73 / 23 Bharat Ram Road, (23 Ansari Road),
Darya Ganj, New Delhi - 110 002 (India).
Phones : 23245001 / 02 / 03 / 04.
Fax : +91-11-23245005.
E-mail : academic@vsnl.com
www : academicfoundation.com

*in association with :*

Centre for Economic and Social Studies
(CESS), Hyderabad
www.cess.ac.in

Cataloging in Publication Data--DK
Courtesy: D.K. Agencies (P) Ltd. <docinfo@dkagencies.com>

India : some aspects of economic and social
development / editors, S. Mahendra Dev and K.S. Babu.
    p.   cm.
Centre for Economic and Social Studies silver jubilee
lectures delivered at Hyderabad by eminent  scholars;
some were revised.
  Includes index.
  ISBN 13: 9788171886289
  ISBN 10: 8171886280

  1. India--Economic policy--1947-  2. Social problems
--India.  3. Agriculture--India.   I. Mahendra Dev, S.
II. Babu, K. S.

DDC 338.954   22

Typeset by Italics India, New Delhi.
Printed and bound in India.

10 9 8 5 4 3 2 1

# CONTENTS

# Comparison of Indian Fiscal Federalism

# Employment, Poverty and Social Dimension

# Some Recent Issues in Agriculture

# List of Tables, Figures and Appendices

## TABLES

## FIGURES

## APPENDICES

# Preface

Having completed 25 years of its existence, the Centre for Economic and Social Studies (CESS), Hyderabad has celebrated its silver jubilee in the year 2005-06. The Centre organised 14 Silver Jubilee Lectures during this year. This book contains 11 of these lectures delivered under the series. Some of the papers were revised in the light of discussions following each lecture. All the speakers are eminent scholars in their respective fields. We are grateful to them for their contributions.

The themes included in the volume are presented in five sections. The volume begins with *social development* covering issues such as higher education, trends in social science research, human development and politics of governance. The next theme is on *comparison of India and China development paths*. It examines important issues relating to comparison of economic and social development of India and China. The third theme is on *challenges in Indian fiscal federalism* while the fourth theme is on *social dimensions of globalisation and trends in employment*. The latter theme also covers a chapter on international experience of poverty alleviation programmes. The last section deals with *some issues on agriculture* covering topics such as gene revolution and the poor and small landholders and markets.

We are grateful to Prof. C.H. Hanumantha Rao and Sri B.P.R. Vithal for presiding over the silver jubilee lectures. Thanks are due to Dr. G. Ram Redy Memorial Trust for collaborating in organising the first lecture of the series. Thanks are also due to CESS faculty and administration for their help in organising the silver jubilee lectures.

India is going to celebrate 60 years of its Independence in the year 2007. There have been many achievements and failures in the last six decades. Post-reform period also witnessed achievements in terms of higher economic growth and success in external sector. However, there has been a concern regarding inclusive growth particularly on agriculture sector, social development and widening disparities across regions and social groups. Several papers in this volume discuss the issues and challenges relating to economic growth and inclusive growth. We hope this volume will be useful for researchers, policy makers, civil society and students of India's economic and social development.

S. Mahendra Dev and K.S. Babu

# Overview

S. MAHENDRA DEV and K.S. BABU

## Introduction

This book is a collection of the lectures delivered under CESS Silver Jubilee Lecture Series during 2005-06. All the invited speakers of the lecture series are nationally and internationally renowned social scientists. They spoke on key issues of India's economic and social development. Some of the lectures examine the impact of economic reforms and globalisation on India's development. The series has begun with André Beteillé's lecture on "Universities as Public Institutions." This first lecture was also in the memory of late Professor G. Ram Reddy, a founder member and former Chairman of CESS.

India is going to celebrate 60 years of its Independence in the year 2007. In the last 60 years, there have been several achievements and failures in the country's economic and social development. The development strategies followed in the last six decades also varied from time to time.

The setting at the time of Independence influenced the development strategies followed in the first three decades of independent India. The intellectual and political thinking of the period linked the economic underdevelopment of India to the British-imposed free market policies which are supposed to be motivated by imperial economic interests. As a result, there was a deep distrust of market forces and international trade. Two other factors also reinforced the distrust towards market forces.[1] First, the success of Soviet Union in achieving industrial power status through accelerated industrialisation. Second, influential intellectual opinion in Latin America argued for import substituting industrialisation.

---

1. See Ahluwalia, I.J. and John Williamson (2003). *The South Asian Experience with Growth*, Oxford University Press.

The first task of the Indian government in the immediate post-Independence period was to initiate and sustain rapid growth in a stagnant economy and to set upon a path for higher growth with social justice. The objective of India's development strategy has been to establish a socialistic pattern of society through economic growth with self-reliance, social justice and alleviation of poverty. The institutional framework of a mixed economy has been used where both public and private sectors coexist. Politically India opted for democratic form of government. The spirit of the Constitution adopted by Independent India is reflected in the Preamble itself. India was also among the first countries to include legislation aimed at affirmative action in the form of reservations for socially oppressed sections such as Scheduled Castes (SCs) and Scheduled Tribes (STs). Later experience shows that in spite of these reservations, SCs and STs are still socially disadvantaged classes. The caste system in India could be one of the reasons for the socio-political and economic problems of the country. The contradictions in political, social and economic equalities were well articulated by Dr. B.R. Ambedkar, the Chairman of the Constituent Assembly Drafting Committee. He concludes his work with a warning: "On the 26th January 1950, we are going to enter into a life of contradictions. In politics we will have equality and in social and economic life we will have inequality."[2]

The average growth rate in GDP in these three decades was around 3.5 per cent. In spite of low growth, there were some achievements such as creation of institutional capacities, development of social institutions and legal framework for a market economy, priority to science and technology, establishment of capital goods sector, etc.[3]

In the decade of 1980s, there were attempts at deregulation particularly during Rajiv Gandhi regime more or less coinciding with Seventh Five-year Plan. The decade of 1980s witnessed the highest growth as compared to previous decades. However, there were

---

2. See Dreze, Jean and Amartya Sen (1995). *India: Economic Development and Social Opportunity*, Oxford University Press, New Delhi and Oxford.

3. See Nayyar, Deepak (2006). "Economic Growth in Independent India: Lumbering Elephant or Running Tiger?", *Economic and Political Weekly*, April 15.

problems in the balance of payments and fiscal situation by the end of 1980s. The current account deficit was nearly three per cent of GDP. Expansionary policies of Central and State governments led to high fiscal deficits and inflationary pressures were building up. Foreign exchange reserves were limited to cover one or two months of imports. In other words, macro-economically the situation was unsustainable and it was argued that a correction was needed.

In India, economic reforms were initiated in mid-1991 due to problems such as insurmountable external debt, unmanageable balance of payments situation, high possibility of acceleration in the rate of inflation and the underlying fiscal problems. With a view to tide over the unprecedented economic crisis and ensuring the sustainability of the growth process, it was considered necessary to introduce certain major policy reforms on industrial, trade and public sector fronts, almost simultaneously with measures of stabilisation for reduction in fiscal and current account deficits. These reforms tried to consciously fashion as close the package developed by the two Bretton Woods Institutions (IMF and the World Bank) permitted by domestic conditions. The reforms aimed at fundamental shift towards greater reliance on the market mechanism to allocate resources and influence decision making.

In the post-reform period, Eighth Plan recorded a growth of 6.7 per cent per annum while it declined to 5.5 per cent during Ninth Plan period. However, it rose to 7.3 per cent in the first four years of the Tenth Plan period. The Eleventh Plan aims to achieve 9 per cent to 10 per cent growth per annum.

Thus, there is lot of optimism regarding the long-term economic growth of 8 to 9 per cent per annum. In the last two decades, India was among 10 to 12 highest growing countries in the world. The *Goldman Sachs Report*[4] gave a very optimum scenario on India's medium and long-term growth prospected. The report pointed out that Brazil, Russia, India, and China—the BRICs economies—could become a large force in the world economy by 2050. The optimism of the above three studies are based on four factors: India's relatively young population due to demographic changes, productivity

---

4. Wilson, D. and R. Purushothaman (2003). "Dreaming with BRICs: The Path to 2050", *Global Economics Paper* No. 99, Goldman Sachs.

increases, country's institutional strengths and optimism about economic reforms.[5]

Some of the other macro variables have also performed well in the post-reform period. Rate of inflation which was 8.7 per cent per annum during 1992-1998 declined to 4.9 per cent during Ninth Plan period (1997-2002) and to 4.8 per cent during Tenth Plan period. Gross domestic savings as per cent of GDP increased from 23.1 during Ninth Plan to 28.2 per cent during Tenth Plan (GoI, 2006). Gross domestic investment as per cent of GDP rose from 23.8 per cent to 27.5 per cent while current account balance as per cent of GDP increased from -0.7 per cent to 0.7 per cent during the same period. Combined fiscal deficit declined marginally from 8.8 per cent in Ninth Plan to 8.4 in Tenth Plan. Foreign Direct Investment (FDI) increased from an average of $ 3.7 billion in the Ninth Plan period to average of $ 5.4 billion in the first four years of the Tenth Plan. Foreign exchange reserves rose from $ 5.3 billion in September 1991 to $ 165.3 billion in September 2006. Similarly growth rates of exports and imports have also risen in the post-reform period.

In spite of the relatively satisfactory performance in some of the macroeconomic variables, post-reform period witnessed slow rate of reduction in poverty, low quality of employment growth, increase in rural-urban disparities, inequalities across social groups and, regional disparities. Agriculture growth was low in the last 10 years. Farmer's suicides are more evident now than before. Although there has been some progress in education, the rate of growth in health indicators (e.g., infant mortality) was lower in the post-reform period as compared to pre-reform period.

Since Independence the Government of India has claimed that it wanted to work towards social sector development. A lot has been achieved in the past half century. The literacy rate has increased from less than 20 per cent in 1951 to 65 per cent in 2001. According to the *Human Development Report 2006* of UNDP, the present rank of HDI index for India is 126. The performance of India in the social sector is far from satisfactory, and could have been much better. Particularly

---

5. Acharya, Shankar (2004). "India's Growth Prospects Revisited", *Economic and Political Weekly*, October.

in rural areas, the levels of education and health are much lower than those for urban areas.

In the first few years of this decade, there was a feeling that 'India was shining'. It was, however, realised that the 'feel good factor' was only in some indicators such as growth in services, IT and communication revolutions, balance of payments, foreign exchange reserves, booming stock market, etc. On the other hand, rural India and social sector have not been shining. Social exclusion is taking place in terms of regions, social and marginal groups, women, minorities and children.

There was an increasing feeling that only few sections of the population such as rich and middle class particularly in urban areas, corporate sector, foreign institutional investors, IT sector have benefited from the economic reforms. Fortunately, these issues of social exclusion are being discussed by politicians, bureaucracy, policy makers and civil society. The Common Minimum Programme of UPA government also stressed on, among other things, the need for focus on agriculture, rural development, employment and social sector. There is some sort of consensus now that growth should be shared by all sections of the society rather than limiting to few categories of population. The approach paper of the Eleventh Five-year Plan also stresses on the importance of faster and more inclusive growth. This is important to reduce poverty and various types of inequalities in the economy and society. There is complementarity between growth and equity. Economic growth can create opportunities for people. On the other hand, equity is important for its own sake and for raising economic growth.

To conclude, it is important to have high economic growth to improve the resources of the country. However, it is well known that GDP growth is only an instrument and necessary condition and not sufficient for raising the levels of living of the population particularly the poor. Exclusion is taking place in terms of regions, social and marginal groups, women, minorities and children. Apart from high growth in GDP, Government has to examine the conditions of the poor and the marginalised in terms of employment, agriculture, food and nutritional security, impact of petrol prices on common man, health, education, women, drinking water, housing and sanitation.

The topics covered in the lecture series are: i) Social issues such as higher education, trends in social science research, human development and politics of governance; ii) comparison of India China development paths; iii) challenges in Indian fiscal federalism; vi) protection of the poor, various social dimensions in globalisation and trends in employment; and v) some recent issues in agriculture. Although we could not include the papers of Pranab Bardhan, Ashwani Saith and Rammanohar Reddy in this book, excerpts of their lectures are briefly mentioned in this chapter. Given below is a summary of the chapters in each section.

## Social Issues—Higher Education, Human Development and Governance

André Beteillé's lecture indicated that the democratisation of Indian Universities in terms of more social classes accessing higher learning was not a smooth process. He was also critical of this process. During the 19th century, institutions of higher learning witnessed a number of changes and some innovations took place in this process. These changes were basically in the form of displacing the hierarchical structures which existed earlier. The process of change was rapid in France and Germany, and it is slow and gradual in case of England. He further said:

> The hierarchical structures of universities such as Cambridge, Oxford and Paris reflected the values of the medieval societies in which they had originated and grown. From the end of the 18th century onwards those societies began to change in the direction of greater equality. What I wish to emphasise is that in England, France and Germany the universities responded to changes in attitudes and values that first began elsewhere in the wider society. In India it was the opposite. The wider society began to respond, slowly and not always effectively to changes that were initiated in the colleges, universities and a small number of other modern institutions. In other words, in India the universities were in advance of society whereas in the west they had fallen behind. In contrast to the universities of the past, which were socially exclusive, the modern university is socially inclusive. The Indian university admits students and appoints teachers generally without consideration of race, caste, creed or gender. This is by and large true today of most modern universities. The emergence of modern institutions has been a slow and in many places a painful process. But they constitute the core of civil society and are essential for the creation and sustenance of universal citizenship on the one hand and the constitutional state on the other.

Universities should be vigilant to discharge its responsibilities to the society by maintaining and improving academic standards. Lot of disparities exist among universities in terms of infrastructure or human resources. It is difficult to expect the same quality in a small university located in remote area compared to the wealthy private universities like Harvard or Stanford. It is meaningless to start a new university without adequate resources citing that there is a social need. Unfortunately, a large number of undergradute colleges, post-graduate departments and universities have been opened simply to accommodate new classes and communities. He further says:

> The building of open and secular institutions that are socially inclusive and at the same time functionally effective is not an easy undertaking. The undertaking cannot be successful if we wish out of existence the deep and pervasive tensions between the demands of social inclusion and those of academic discrimination.

Rammanohar Reddy (lecture not included in the volume) spoke on recent trends in social science research in India. He said that there was not enough research on how our developmental policies are getting implemented. Hence government is facing difficulty in framing appropriate and effective policies and programmes. Similarly, there are a number of research studies on various aspects of reforms. Unfortunately, it is very difficult to get a clear picture comprehensively, about the reform process in India from these studies. The present liberalisation process has not generated enough or intensive deliberations. So far, there are no good in-depth sector specific research studies. During 1950s-1970s, research findings were intensively debated in academic journals by then young and senior researchers. Now that type of spirit in research is missing.

While examining inequalities in Human Development, Bhanoji Rao was of the opinion that the inequalities were created at primary level itself in India as the poor go to government schools and better-offs go to private or convent schools. He indicated that the government policies should be framed in such a way that they reduce visible inequalities in education, health and housing to improve human capabilities. He advocated that the government should provide the best school infrastructure, recruit qualified teachers (with better pay) and better school health programmes which include regular health check-ups and preventive care. Similarly on health side, government should establish best government polyclinics and universal health insurance schemes. Thus, government should ensure the provision of every facility which helps increasing human capabilities without any discrimination. Enhancement of capabilities would result in higher economic growth and acceptability of our man power internationally. He further said:

> One should keep hoping that just as the world is moving fast towards free movement of goods, services and capital, it will also evolve and allow the free movement of people.

Pranab Bardhan (lecture not included in the volume) said that the left parties in West Bengal and Kerala had good track record in implementing land reforms compared to any other state in the country. Due to lack of transparency in land reform process, Naxalism is spreading in Nepal, Andhra Pradesh, Bihar. As soon as left parties came to power in 1978, around 75 per cent of the land was distributed. Later another 16 per cent of land was distributed. Followed by land distribution, farmers are given agricultural implements, fertilisers and pesticides. Moreover, some public works were undertaken, especially, to create employment among rural poor.

Farmers are supplied with agriculture kits which help them to understand improved farming practices. Bardhan indicated that the land reforms had significant ramifications in reducing poverty and promoting agricultural growth. Referring to land reforms in West Bengal, he said decentralisation of local *panchayat* system, election to local level administration with five-year term, helped in hastening the reforms. These local bodies were of help in recording the rights of sharecroppers.

Bardhan sought to examine which of the two factors—political ideology or political competition contributed more to the success of land reforms in the West Bengal countryside based on a survey conducted in 90 villages of the state in 1978-79. According to him, it is political competition rather than ideology which contributed to successful implementation of land reforms in the state.

In his paper, Jaya Prakash Narayan expressed concern about the deterioration of values in the Indian polity. In order to achieve faster and equitable growth, government should improve the efficiency of the government. Despite the fiscal and political constraints, it would be possible with the sectoral reforms like providing better education and healthcare, reducing corruption and speeding up delivery of justice. In India, corruption is rampant at higher levels. In polity, executive should be kept away from political favours and influences. China made considerable progress in all the spheres. Their reforms in health, education, rural development and decentralisation have influenced world. The Chinese development is largely due to small-scale industries in rural areas.

## Comparison of India and China Development Paths

While comparing Indian and Chinese development paths, Jayati Ghosh said that the Chinese development success could be analysed from different angle. Economic growth in China is mainly attributed to the large-scale investment by the state. This investment is as high as 44 per cent (fluctuated between 35 and 44 per cent) as a share of GDP over the past 25 years; in India it is just ranged between 20 to 26 per cent. In fact, the aggregate ICORs (Incremental Capital Oriented Ratios) have been around the same in both economies. There is huge gap in case of infrastructure investment. In China it is about 19 per cent of GDP against just 2 per cent in case of India. China could attract large quantum of Foreign Direct Investment (FDI). In fact, it is the second largest destination for FDI in the world. Since 1990, the FDI accounted for 3-5 per cent of GDP in China; in its peak it reached up to 8 per cent. In fact, FDI has accounted for 6 per cent of domestic investment. Therefore, naturally it can afford to have such a large investment in infrastructure development. China has made considerable progress in terms of poverty reduction. According to official statistics, only 4 per cent of the Chinese population live below poverty line. Even official figures suggest, the percentage of the poor is as low as 12 per cent. On the other hand, the poverty ratios in India are much higher. According to NSS 2000 data, the poverty ratio ranged between 26 to 34 per cent.

Though India also started liberalisation its performance is miserable in industry. In China availability of cheap labour helped the growth of industry; low wages were made possible due to the subsidised food, housing and transport.

Taking this argument further, Ashwani Saith (lecture not included in the volume) has examined the role of institutions in both China and India. He said that there were less inequalities among Chinese people compared to Indians. India and China were at equal stage of development until 1950s. It is interesting to know how these two Asian giants were performing in various economic and social indicators. China's performance was quite impressive in almost all development indicators. China's per capita income was at twice the level of India in 2003. China's adult literacy was 91 per cent whereas in India it was 65 per cent. In China, industry contributes 53 per cent of its GDP; in India it was only 26 per cent.

In case of infrastructure availability in IT sector, China's performance is quite remarkable. During 2003, there were 424 fixed lines and mobile phone subscribers per 1000 people in China; in India there were just 71 persons. Similarly, during 2002, 28 persons possessed personal computers per 1000 persons; in India only 7 persons found having personal computers. Ashwani Saith felt that in China, corruption in higher places was turning out to be a recent problem and that the ongoing reforms have increased the gap between cities and villages.

## Comparison of Indian Fiscal Federalism

M. Govinda Rao's lecture was on fiscal federalism. According to him, Tamil Nadu and Haryana were the two states which performed well in containing their revenue deficit. With the exception of West Bengal, middle income states also did well in this respect. The performance of West Bengal and Punjab is worse in containing revenue deficit. In fact, Gujarat also recorded high deficit in 2000-01 due to earthquake. Interestingly, poor states are doing well in minimising revenue deficit, but it is done by diverting the funds meant for developmental programmes which is also not a desirable step. He stated that the states which had a strong marketing base and well developed market institutions have benefited immensely in the liberalisation. In this inter-state competition, the states which primarily depend on agriculture are badly affected.

The main objective of the fiscal federalism is to develop efficient nationwide common market. Unfortunately, there are a number of instances of violation of common market principles in terms of fiscal and regulatory policies. The predominant responsibility of every state is to provide better social services and physical infrastructure to enable domestic manufacturers to be more competitive. But it needs large investments which can be made possible only through private-public partnerships. States alone can not afford large investments due to their bad fiscal position.

The globalisation process calls for structural changes to face the new challenges. Of late, there is substantial loss of revenue due to liberalisation of import duties. This, of course, is a challenge faced all over the world. In India, VAT is levied to compensate this revenue loss partially, if not fully. Nowadays there is substantial international mobility of capital and skilled labour. The activities have increased in e-commerce. Now the challenge is to augur revenue by taxing these services in a scientific way.

At political level, it is becoming increasingly difficult to forge consensus on major policy issues due to emergence of coalition governments particularly with their differing ideologies. Some regional parties always tend to exert political and economic concessions which are discretionary rather than rule based pattern. He cautioned that this tendency would have long-term implications on the stability of Indian federalism.

## Employment, Poverty and Social Dimension

T.N. Srinivasan advocated that shifting of work force from primary activities (employed in lower productivity area) to secondary and tertiary sectors (higher productivity areas) would result in better economic growth. He said that in the past, our policies always tried to keep the poor and marginal farmers in agriculture rather than any serious attempt to shift them to high productivity areas. He drew these conclusions by looking at, how our policies were modified in a very limited way from 1950-1980s. But when these policies were modified more systematically and extensively from 1990s (started shifting to secondary and tertiary), our economic growth accelerated particularly from the contributions of service sector. He said that India would do well in outsourcing of auto manufacturing similar to what had happened in IT sector.

Despite some changes in other sectors, still agriculture is the major source of employment (66 per cent in 2004). Though government is sincerely trying to establish Special Economic Zones (SEZs), it is difficult to achieve desired results without modifying the existing labour laws suitably. To attain complete development, India should be more and more integrated with the rest of the world. He opined that there was a need to analyse the data on employment and employment opportunities to get a feedback on development prospects of different sectors. In service sector, software is doing well. But there is a need to focus on other sectors also. In manufacturing sector, China is doing well by creating lot of opportunities.

K. Subbarao indicated that during 1990s, there was impressive economic growth. However, it has failed to create employment opportunities and better livelihoods. In India, the poor as usual continued to face the age-old vulnerabilities such as health shocks. In this globalisation era their situation is further aggravated with frequent/sudden loss of employment in organised and unorganised sectors. Therefore, India should emphasise on growth with equity while implementing programmes such as national employment guarantee schemes and social security measures for workers in unorganised sector.

Following are the conclusions from his lecture: (a) Safety net programmes are doing well even in the poor countries; (b) many low income and middle income countries are facing the problem of multiplicity of programmes for the same purpose; (c) moreover, these programmes suffer from poor targeting, high level of programme leakages and administrative costs; (d) even countries like Bangladesh and Mexico with diverse backgrounds also opted for safety net programmes; provides protection for the poor during distress and also ensure better school enrolments and health outcomes; (e) target errors can be minimised by involving community for identifying the appropriate beneficiaries coupled with the proxy means tests.

Deepak Nayyar examined economic development in Independent India. According to him, If we consider India during the 20th century as a whole, the turning point in economic growth was *circa* 1951. If we consider India since Independence, the turning point in economic growth was *circa* 1980. And it is clear that the turning point, in the early 1950s, was much more significant than the structural break in the early 1980s. In the first phase of growth in post-Independence India, from 1950 to 1980, India was not the lumbering elephant that it is often made out to be. In the second phase, from 1980 to 2005,

India was not quite the running tiger that some believe it has become.

The real failure, throughout the second half of the 20th century, was India's inability to transform its growth into development, which would have brought about an improvement in the living conditions of ordinary people. The actual development should be evidenced through improvement in living conditions of the people. He is critical about FDI as it may further widen the gap between the rich and the poor. India's economic development is not complete until the problems of poverty, deprivation and persisting exclusions exists.

He has expressed concern about the present rural urban divide. The economic disparity in rural-urban divide has almost doubled. It needs urgent attention. He stressed on accountability and transparency in government functioning. Power and prosperity to the ordinary people would be possible only through improving their capabilities. The present jobless economic growth is not sustainable.

Gerry Rodgers examined globalisation from social dimension angle with following issues: social inclusion and exclusion, inequality and discrimination, culture and identity, rights and responsibilities. Globalisation offers new spaces while restricting existing options. In the globalisation process, state will be more interested in attracting international investors while compromising with social goals. Moreover, ethnic groups are likely to affect by losing their traditional sources of livelihoods; the ongoing process undermine communities built around traditional production methods. On the other hand, these communities can also avail new economic opportunities if they possess required capabilities and resources. If the country is successful in integrating itself into global economy, employment opportunities of these communities will improve with better wages. Ultimately, gobalisation should respond to the expectations and aspirations of the people and the challenge is to find the policies, rules and mechanisms by which economic and social goals can be integrated in the global economy.

He cautioned that occurrence of any economic or financial volatilities would lead to economic crisis in future and also indicated that in the process of global competition, there is every possibility of further erosion of labour laws.

## Some Recent Issues in Agriculture

Prabhu Pingali examined the impact of agricultural technology on the poor. During the last four decades there are two major waves of agricultural technology development; Green Revolution and Gene Revolution. During Green Revolution, the technology (improved germplasm) was diffused smoothly to other poor countries. This was made available to all countries as a public good without any restriction. However, during current gene revolution, there are many restrictions in passing this technology to the poor countries. The genome technology is the product of heavy investments made by private agricultural research system. Hence it is being passed through market transaction.

Developed and developing countries differ largely in terms of their agricultural systems, market institutions and research and regulatory capacities. Therefore it is doubtful to expect the same benefits for the poor countries. He advocated a strong cooperation between public sector and private sector to ensure the benefits for the poor from the ongoing gene revolution. Prabhu Pingali indicated the need for gene revolution in India on the lines of green revolution to safeguard the healthy food needs of the country's population.

Ashok Gulati said that Indian consumption basket had undergone many changes due to structural changes in Indian economy. The consumption of high value commodities like fruits, vegetables, livestock and fishery and processed food has increased. Earlier, Indian staple food largely consisted of cereals. These changes could be attributed to increased urbanisation, emerging export opportunities and more female participation in the work force.

In case of marketing of agriculture produce, there is a wide gap between producer's selling price and consumer's buying price. This wide price gap could be attributed to the inefficient transportation, lack of cold storage chains and absence of food processing measures. He advocated the entry of private players in this sector. This would help in reducing the price gap between producer's and consumer's price even after private player's share of gain.

In the case of Indian food retailing industry, the share of organised retailing is just two per cent and the share of supermarkets is approximately two per cent of the organised retailing. In the near future, this share of supermarkets would go up further with the investments coming in from corporate houses like Reliance industries, Pantaloon group, etc.

In India, small landholders (less than 2 hectares) are dominating Indian agriculture and this would continue for another decade. It is largely believed that the small landholders were largely left out of modern marketing chains. He argues that the small landholders can be integrated into the modern marketing chains by having appropriate institutions and infrastructure to promote efficient delivery.

# Social Issues—Higher Education, Human Development and Governance

# 1

## Universities as Public Institutions

### ANDRÉ BÉTEILLE

It is natural for someone who has spent the better part of his life in a university to speak well of the universities, at least in public. But there was a time in India when others too spoke well of them. Pre-eminent among them was India's first Prime Minister, Jawaharlal Nehru. In a convocation address delivered at Allahabad University just after Independence, he dwelt upon the role of knowledge in human advancement and pointed to the things for which a modern university stands. He added, "If the universities discharge their duty adequately, then it is well with the nation and the people" (Nehru, 1967: 333).

Nobody can maintain that our universities have met all the expectations placed on them at the time of Independence. They have grown enormously in the years since Independence, and their growth has been disorderly and often in response to pressures that are far removed from the ideals of scholarship, humanism and civility, for which Nehru believed the universities ought to stand. It has become a matter of routine to speak of crises on the campus. Nothing will be gained by seeking to minimise the disorder that characterises our universities today, or by saying that such disorder has been a common feature of universities all over the world, in the second half of the 20th century.

However, if we are to understand the place of the university in society, we have to take a broader view of both university and society and see their relationship over a longer span of time. Universities are not only centres of learning, however badly or well they play their part in the transmission and creation of knowledge, they are also social institutions that provide the setting for a very distinctive kind of interaction among young men and women, and between the generations. Here, we will try to examine the social significance of the university as well as its contribution to the advancement of learning.

The universities may act as bastions of traditional and conservative values as they did in Europe, for much of their existence during the Middle Ages and even later; or, they may provide the setting for a new kind of social imagination and experience as they did when they were first established in India, in the second half of the 19th century. I will argue that the Indian university has played a significant part in the education for democratic citizenship although this education, which began more than a hundred and fifty years ago, has not by any means been completed.

India has a very long and a very impressive intellectual tradition. What is remarkable about this tradition is its continuity rather than its range and diversity. It had remarkable achievements in formal disciplines such as mathematics, grammar, logic and metaphysics, but gave little attention to empirical disciplines such as history and geography. Not only was the range of subjects limited, but the setting for the cultivation of knowledge and the mechanisms for its transmission were socially exclusive even in comparison with other hierarchical societies of the past.

The 19th century witnessed great change and innovation in the institutional foundations of higher learning in the different parts of the world. The changes were all associated, in one way or another, directly or indirectly, with the displacement of a hierarchical by a democratic legal, political and social order. They took place in many different countries but not all at once or in the same way everywhere. In some countries, notably France, and to some extent also Germany, the changes were rapid and dramatic, whereas in others, such as England, they were slow and gradual. Where universities had existed before, they were often overhauled; where they had not existed before, new ones were brought into being.

The reconstitution of the institutions of higher learning began in Europe at the turn of the 18th century. The reforms took somewhat different forms in France and Germany. The changes in France were more radical. Although they had their beginnings before the Revolution, the real architect of the new system was Napoleon. What he sought to do was not so much to reform the universities, which in France were then in a moribund state, as to create institutional alternatives to them. These institutional alternatives were the *grandes écoles* or 'great schools' of which, historically, the two most important were the École Polytechnique set up in 1794 to train engineers for the civil and military services and the École Normale Supérieure set up in 1795 to train teachers for state secondary schools.

In Germany, reconstitution was less dramatic. It began with the establishment under Wilhelm von Humboldt of a new type of university in Berlin in 1812, based on the principle of *Einheit der Lehre und Forschung* or the unity of teaching and research. Humboldt wanted the universities to be engaged not only in the assimilation, criticism and transmission of existing knowledge but also to become centres for the creation of new knowledge. Under his inspiration, the German universities became the most advanced universities in the world. In course of time, the German model extended its influence to the United States where the first 'research university', Johns Hopkins was established in 1876.

Although they were not universities in the true sense of the term, the *grandes écoles* introduced principles of institutional organisation that were radically new in their time, but have now come to be accepted widely, if not universally. They were open and secular institutions and in that sense different from the universities of the past and in advance of the universities of their time, including the German ones.

The *grandes écoles* were designed to give effect to Napoleon's ideal of 'careers open to talent'. It cannot be too strongly emphasised that the idea of careers open to talent, whether in education or in employment, was a radically new one, even in Europe two hundred years ago. It permeated all kinds of institutions in the course of the 19th and the 20th centuries and gradually became a commonplace in one country after another. In the past, recruitment in both education and employment was governed to a far greater extent by birth and patronage than by merit or ability. Napoleon set out to change all this, and achieved success, though only in the long run.

In earlier times, the universities such as those at Paris, Oxford and Cambridge, were regulated largely by religious rules and religious authority. The dissociation of the European universities from the church was a slow and long-drawn process. The *grandes écoles* were pioneers in being largely secular in their orientation and organisation. The universities in Europe and elsewhere, gradually began to follow the course charted out by them. Today, if we take it for granted that the modern university should be a secular institution, we must not forget that the idea was even in the 19th century, a new one.

Education and employment came to be linked together through the idea of career. Napoleon set a very high value on education and training in the formation of public servants. Along with the great schools there grew the 'great services' or the *grands corps*, recruitment to both of which came to be based on open, national competition. All of this began at a time when the universities of Oxford and Cambridge were still closely tied to the hierarchies of the church, and recruitment to the civil and military services in England was still largely through patronage. This was to change in the 1850s with the Trevelyan-Northcote reforms, which created a new type of civil servant known in the Indian Civil Service as the 'competition wallah' (Trevelyan, 1964). The universities too began to change in England at about the same time.

Even though there is a long tradition in India of the cultivation and transmission of specialised and systematic knowledge, what we know as the universities today had their beginnings only in the middle of the 19th century. It was pointed out by the Education Commission of 1964-1966 that the universities with which it was concerned had very little genealogical or historical connection with India's 'ancient and medieval centres of learning' (Education Commission, 1971: 8). The first modern universities were established in Calcutta, Bombay and Madras in 1857, and they did not carry with them the hierarchical baggage of medieval institutions. As we have seen, this was a time of major reconstitution in the institutions of learning in the West. The Indian universities were almost from the beginning, open and secular institutions. They were among the first such institutions in the country, and as such have had a social and not just an intellectual significance far in excess of their size and material resources.

I believe that the new universities made a bigger break in the organisation of knowledge in 19th century India than they did anywhere in the West. The type of knowledge they cultivated was new, and the social setting in which it was cultivated was also new. Very little research was done at first in the new universities and for some time also very little teaching. The main centres of teaching were in the colleges, which began to be established a little before the first universities. The universities were set up initially to conduct examinations and confer degrees, and to approve and oversee the courses of study on whose basis teaching was done in the colleges and examinations conducted by the university.

Indians who entered the colleges and universities in the 19th century encountered a whole new world of ideas to which access was mainly through a new language. Educated Indians had been used to operating through more than one language. If they were upper caste Hindus, it would not be unusual for them to know some Sanskrit and a little Persian in addition to the language of the home. But exploring the world through the English language was a new kind of experience. The Indian intellectual tradition, which had once been active and vibrant, had become stagnant and moribund by the end of the 18th century. The encounter with Western ideas in the new centres of learning released a flood of dormant intellectual energy.

A whole array of new subjects and new approaches to them came into view. It is a characteristic of modern universities, in contrast to traditional centres of learning, that new branches of knowledge are continuously added and explored in them. It has sometimes been said that the fascination with Western learning led to the neglect and even the denigration of traditional forms of knowledge including much that was of value in it. While this may be to some extent true, no deliberate attempt was generally made to abolish the study of classical languages, classical philosophy or ancient and medieval history in the new centres of learning.

The Brahminical tradition of learning was not only narrowly focused intellectually, it was also socially very exclusive. Women and members of the lower castes had little or no access to it. The new centres of learning—the colleges and the universities—opened up new fields of knowledge, and also opened their doors to excluded sections of society.

Sir Henry Maine, one of the early vice chancellors of the University of Calcutta, said in his convocation address of 1866, "The fact is, that the founders of the University of Calcutta thought to create an aristocratic institution; and in spite of themselves, they created a popular institution" (Banerjee *et al.*, 1957: 127). It is not altogether clear what the founders of the university had in mind, but it is well to remember that the period in which it was founded was a time of great transition in the universities of the West. Oxford and Cambridge were only beginning to move out of the hierarchical mould in which they had been set for centuries.

Family background had an acknowledged place in the classification of students in Oxford, and the following categories were officially used: *baronis filius* (sons of noblemen), *equitis filius* (sons of knights), *armigeri filius* (sons of esquires), *generosi filius* (sons of gentlemen), *plebei filius* (sons of commoners), and *clerici filius* (sons of clergymen). In keeping with traditional distinctions of status, sons of bishops were listed with sons of noblemen, not of clergymen. Those of inferior social status paid smaller fees, but those of superior status were entitled to take the first degree after 9 instead of 12 terms of residence. It is noteworthy that these categories were used until as late as 1891 when the Registrar of Oxford began to record the father's occupation instead of his status. In Cambridge, the privilege whereby sons of noblemen were excused from taking examinations (the *jus natalium*) was abolished only in 1884 (Rashdall, 1936: 470).

The marks of invidious social (as opposed to academic) distinction were visible also in the internal structure of the college. There were the distinctions, first, between master, fellows and students. 'Students' themselves were of various categories. The core consisted of the 'scholars' who, like the fellows, were supported by the foundation: the college provided them with education as well as bed and board. But there were others who had to pay for what the college gave them: these included 'pensioners' who were ordinary fee paying students in residence, and 'fellow commoners' who paid extra and had the privilege of dining with the fellows. At the bottom were the 'sizars' who, in Cambridge, were granted the benefits of college life, including college education, in return for menial services rendered to the more privileged members of the college (Stone, 1974: Vol. 1, Chaps. I and III).

The hierarchical structures of universities such as Cambridge, Oxford and Paris reflected the values of the medieval societies in which they had originated and grown. From the end of the 18th century onwards those societies began to change in the direction of greater equality. What I wish to emphasise here is that in England, France and Germany the universities responded to changes in attitudes and values that first began elsewhere in the wider society. In India it was the opposite. The wider society began to respond, slowly and not always effectively to changes that were initiated in the colleges, universities and a small number of other modern institutions. In other words, in India the universities were in advance of society whereas in the West they had fallen behind.

In contrast to the universities of the past, which were socially exclusive, the modern university is socially inclusive. The Indian university admits students and appoints teachers generally without consideration of race, caste, creed or gender. This is by and large true today of most modern universities. The emergence of modern institutions has been a slow and in many places a painful process. But they constitute the core of civil society and are essential for the creation and sustenance of universal citizenship on the one hand and the constitutional state on the other.

In the past, universities restricted admission on grounds of religion. This was natural in a world where the institutions of learning were regulated by religious rules and religious authority. Until the second half of the 19th century, Oxford and Cambridge required students as well as teachers to subscribe to the 39 Articles of the Church of England. It is well known that both Herbert Spencer, the most famous British sociologist of the 19th century and E.B. Tylor, widely regarded as the father of British anthropology, went without a university education as they were religious dissenters.

The most striking change in the social composition and character of the university came when they opened their doors to women. Until well into the 19th century, universities and other institutions of higher learning were male preserves. As far as such institutions went, women were largely invisible, except occasionally as servants. Even the *grandes écoles* in France, which were undoubtedly ahead of their time, remained male preserves throughout the 19th century: careers open to talent meant careers open to male talent only.

Resistance to the entry of women took much time and effort to wear down in the older European universities. Cambridge provides a good example. Permission was granted for the opening of two colleges for women, Girton and Newnham, only in the second half of the 19th century. But, although women were allowed to study in these colleges, they were not allowed to take examinations of the University of Cambridge. Then they were allowed to take the examinations but not admitted to the degrees of the university. It was only in the 20th century that women were enabled to acquire full membership of the university as both students and teachers.

Whereas it took Cambridge and Oxford several centuries to open their doors to women, the University of Calcutta was producing its first women graduates within a couple of decades of its establishment. Maine was right in saying that it had become a popular institution even though in his time there were still no women in it. Whereas in England, the universities followed in the train of changes initiated elsewhere, in India they were trendsetters.

In the late 19th and early 20th centuries women came to the universities in very small numbers and mainly from well-to-do upper caste families. Now they come in larger numbers and from a variety of castes and communities although they are still outnumbered by men, and all castes and communities are not equally represented among them. If anything, there is a larger upper caste bias among women than men and this is true for students as well as teachers.

In India, the university and the college have played a more significant part in the social emancipation of women than any other public institution. Women have by now competed successfully for the best prizes in university examinations and the highest positions in faculty appointments, not in every university or in every faculty perhaps, but in a sufficient number of places for them to be able to feel secure about their academic achievements within the university. The success of women is particularly visible in the better metropolitan universities whether we take the Universities of Calcutta and Bombay among the older ones or Delhi University and Jawaharlal Nehru University among the newer. All of this has been accompanied by a marked change in the social participation of women in the universities whether as students or as teachers. For women, even more than for men, the university is not only a place of work, it is also a place of recreation, and, for some women, perhaps the only place of recreation. There is more equality between men and women in both performance and participation in the university than anywhere outside. But we must see this transformation for what it is: it is largely a middle class phenomenon although the middle class has been expanding steadily and continuously in recent decades.

The very idea of the career woman would be impossible without the college or the university. To be sure, women worked in the household and on the farm in the past. But household work was confining and women's work on the farm was generally both onerous and degrading. It is in the modern office, more than anywhere else, that college or university educated women are able to work with men as their equals and sometimes as their superiors.

Young men and women unrelated by ties of kinship and community can interact more freely in the university than perhaps in any other domain in society. If this has done nothing else, it has at the very least created a new basis for the relationship between men and women in contemporary India. In the past, whether among Hindus or Muslims, the life led by women was either hard or confined, or both, and that is probably true for most women even today. It is mainly in the college and the university that, as a young adult, a woman can enjoy a little freedom to explore new social relations and to construct a new social identity. In the past, in all social classes, a woman was already burdened by the cares of domestic life by the time she was 16 or 17; today, if she has the luck to enter a university, a new life might open up for her at that age. The university has provided a new ideal of womanhood even if only a handful of women are able to give shape and substance to that ideal.

The modern university provides a setting for a new kind of interchange not only between men and women but also among persons belonging to different castes and communities. The barriers of language, religion and caste can be overcome relatively easily in such a setting, although here identity politics can also reinforce the boundaries between communities instead of softening them. It is far from my intention to suggest that because modern institutions provide opportunities for individuals to interact on a new basis, those institutions can be guaranteed to operate without friction. No large and complex society can reconstitute itself without experiencing conflict and disorder, and if the universities appear embattled it is partly because they are in the forefront of this reconstitution.

While a modern university must strive actively and continuously to be socially inclusive, it must be academically discriminating in the treatment of its members. A university or college which is indifferent to the quality of its teachers and the performance of its students cannot be said to fulfil its obligations as a centre of learning. In a university, the objective of social inclusiveness cannot be promoted without consideration of success or failure in academic performance. In looking at our universities today, we cannot wish out of existence the real and pervasive tensions between the demands of social inclusiveness and those of academic excellence.

The Commission on University Education under Dr. S. Radhakrishnan observed: "Intellectual work is not for all, it is only for the intellectually competent" (Government of India, 1950: 98). Today, on an occasion like this, it is important to remember not only Mr. Nehru but also Dr. Radhakrishnan, for those who are responsible for the governance of universities are often willing to compromise academic standards for fear of being denounced as elitists. We can hardly discuss the responsibilities of universities as public institutions in a serious way if we fail to distinguish between unwarranted exclusion on social grounds and justifiable discrimination on academic grounds.

Napoleon's ideal of 'careers open to talent' was frankly meritocratic in its orientation and he would not fight shy of creating an elite, provided it was an elite based on merit and not birth. Many changes in outlook and orientation have taken place in the two hundred years since Napoleon's time. Social scientists (Arrow *et al.*, 2001) and philosophers (Rawls, 1973) have raised serious questions about the costs as well as the benefits of meritocracy. Rawls has associated the principles of careers open to talent with what he has called a "callous meritocratic society." In this view, the single-minded pursuit of merit at the expense of all other values is detrimental to the health and well-being of the society.

It has been pointed out by more than one author that the concept of 'merit' is ambiguous and difficult to define. A meritocracy may be viewed as a system which carries the meritarian principle to its extreme limit by excluding all other social principles such as amity, compassion, moderation and tolerance. But one does not need to be an advocate of meritocracy in order to appreciate and support the principle of selection by merit rather than some inherited attribute. It is true that there is no agreed definition of merit and that it means different things to different persons; but that hardly settles the issue. Most things that are of value are difficult to define, but that does not mean that we cannot take them into account in the operation of institutions. Critics of the meritarian principle often say that what should count in the distribution of benefits and burdens is not merit but need (Sen, 1973). Need should indeed be a consideration of first importance; but then it is no more easy to define need than it is to define merit, for different people have different conceptions not only of merit but also of need.

One does not require a general, formal and abstract definition of merit in order to grade MA examination papers in history or to select lecturers in physics or economics without fear or favour and in accordance with academic criteria agreed upon in advance. If merit is given short shrift in such cases, as it often is in India, it is not always in order to meet some higher social objective but for the pettiest and the most mundane of reasons. A public institution, whether it is a university, a hospital or a bank, has specific functions to perform and appointments to such institutions cannot be made without consideration of ability and performance in the discharge of particular responsibilities. It is in this context that discrimination has to be applied in admissions and appointments in a university, no matter how socially inclusive it may aim to be.

A university cannot discharge its responsibilities to society unless it remains vigilant in maintaining and improving its academic standards although these need not be the same everywhere. Universities differ enormously in their material as well as human resources. Such disparities exist not only between different countries but also between different universities in the same country. It would be foolish to expect a small university in a remote part of India to have the same material and intellectual capital as a wealthy private university, such as Harvard or Stanford, in a rich country. But again if there are no resources or if the resources are manifestly inadequate, it may be imprudent to start a university simply because there is a 'social' need for it, and hope that it will somehow run itself.

Every university need not be assessed by the same standards of academic excellence. Indeed, it is of the essence of a university as an autonomous institution that it should, within a broad understanding of what universities should do, set its own academic standards. To apply the same standards mechanically in every case, without consideration of the disparities in resources between 'institutions would hardly be reasonable. A university should be free to set its own academic standards after due consideration of the resources available to it; but having set those standards, it cannot suffer them to be treated with indifference or neglect in evaluating the performance of its students and teachers.

Given the variations and changes in the resources with which they have to work, universities cannot adopt a rigid and inflexible attitude to academic standards whether in teaching or in research. Even the balance between teaching and research need not be the same in every university. The manner in which teaching is conducted will depend on the ratio of students to teachers in the college or university concerned, and the scale on which research is undertaken will depend on the funds at its disposal for research. There is nothing wrong if a university with limited resources decides to devote more of those resources to teaching than to research, provided it is recognised that teaching itself suffers in the long run if research is completely neglected.

Flexibility in the determination by a university of its own academic standards should not lead to laxity in the application of the standards it has adopted for itself. A university with limited resources which adopts modest academic standards to which it adheres scrupulously, is to be much preferred to one which has larger resources and adopts elevated standards which its members persistently disregard with impunity.

Thus, academic standards are neither invariant nor unalterable. They change with changes in the volume and diversity of knowledge and also with changes in the size and composition of the institutions of learning. In the last 200 years universities have grown in number and size and have become increasingly diverse in their social composition.

As I have already indicated, the tendency for universities to become socially more and more inclusive is a secular one, and it is probably also irreversible. The tendency began to manifest itself about 200 years ago, although in most countries it began to gather momentum less than a hundred years ago. Where it started late, it was often driven by political pressure and by state policy.

A policy to make the universities fully inclusive socially may not lead to an immediate and significant change in their actual social composition, particularly in a society with many classes and communities whose individual members are very unequally endowed with social, cultural and intellectual capital. India at the time of Independence provides a clear example of this. Dalits, Muslims and women were not debarred from entering the universities, as their counterparts would have been in early 19th century Cambridge or Oxford, but they did not in fact enter them in sufficient numbers. This happened either because they lacked the formal qualifications for entry or because they stayed away from them due to social pressures from the family and the community. After Independence, the government began to play a more direct part in opening up the universities to all sections of society and pressures from below began to make themselves felt towards the same end. This came to be viewed in a broad way as the democratisation of the universities. Maine had only spoken of the university being a popular institution. After Independence, government and politics began to take a hand in making them actually so but they did not always pay heed to the academic costs that this imposed on the universities.

The democratisation of the Indian university has not always been a smooth and orderly process, and its consequences, at least in the short run, have not always been beneficial. Pressure to accommodate new classes and communities has led to rapid and sometimes reckless expansion of the institutions of learning. New undergraduate colleges, new postgraduate departments and new universities have been opened without due consideration of the resources available for their successful functioning. Academic standards have been relaxed, sometimes abruptly and even arbitrarily, in the name of equality and justice.

It is probably true that when universities become socially more inclusive, they also gain academically, at least in the long run. This is what happened in the European universities between the middle of the 19th century and the middle of the 20th. Much depends on the process of becoming socially inclusive and the forces by which that process is driven. Where the drive to become socially inclusive leads to a sudden and dramatic increase in numbers without a proportionate increase in material and intellectual resources, academic standards are bound to become unsettled and be placed in jeopardy. No one can deny that this is what happened in one Indian university after another in the sixties, seventies and eighties of the last century.

The ideal of the university as an ivory tower is no longer viable in the modern world. No university can in a democratic country insulate itself fully from the social and political currents that swirl around it. The process of rigorous academic selection affects members from some sections of society more adversely than those from others. Those who are adversely affected find it natural to believe that they have been made victims not of academic but of social discrimination. The political articulation of that belief persistently and aggressively can undermine the university's confidence in its own moral integrity. It will be idle to maintain that in this atmosphere the authorities of the university can exercise academic judgement calmly, and without fear or favour.

The building of open and secular institutions that are socially inclusive and at the same time functionally effective is not an easy undertaking. The undertaking cannot be successful if we wish out of existence the deep and pervasive tensions between the demands of social inclusion and those of academic discrimination.

# References

Arrow, K., S. Bowles and S. Durlauf (eds.) (2001). *Meritocracy and Economic Inequality*, Oxford University Press, Delhi.

Banerjee, Pramathanath *et al.* (1957). *Hundred Years of the University of Calcutta*, University of Calcutta Press.

Education Commission (1971). *Education and National Development*, Vol. 1, NCERT, New Delhi.

Government of India (GoI) (1950). *The Report of the University Education Commission, 1948-49*, Vol. 1, Ministry of Education, Government of India, New Delhi.

Nehru, Jawaharlal (1967). *Speeches, 1946-49*, Vol. 1, Government of India, New Delhi.

Rashdall, Hastings (1936). *The Universities of Europe in the Middle Ages*, Vol. 1, Oxford University Press, London.

Rawls, John (1973). *A Theory of Justice*, Oxford University Press, London.

Sen, Amartya (1973). *On Economic Inequality*, Basil Blackwell, Oxford.

Stone, Lawrence (ed.) (1974). *The University in Society*, Two Volumes, Princeton University Press, Princeton.

Trevelyan, G.O. (1964). *The Competition Wallah*, Macmillan, London.

# 2

# Minimal Visible Inequality is Human Development

BHANOJI RAO

The index of human development combines standardised measures of health, education and purchasing power. It is easy to see that a morbidity free long life is a major component of human capability. The other essential component is education, for a minimum of 12 years and more, if possible. Together, health and education provide the capability with which one has to derive purchasing power. Lacking in such capabilities, one is pushed to depend on society one way or the other. There is a significant uncertainty in converting capability into cash; some win a lot and many are in the middle, while others languish at low levels of income.

I seek the understanding of the reader for indulging in a few personal reflections.

Just a few days ago on the 6th of March, I entered the ranks of relatively more senior citizens as I completed 65 years. The average expectation of life for those born between 1941 and 1951 was an estimated 32 years. I am grateful to my parents, the society and the Almighty for this gift of a fairly healthy and relatively long life.

I did well on the education front also. The general population born in the 1940s, on the average, could at best hope for two or three years of completed education. In comparison, I had a long span of educational experience.

Teachers of the 1940s and 1950s used to derive a lot of joy in transforming ordinary students into intellectuals. They have done so despite little or no monitory incentives. A mathematics teacher by name Seshachalam Pantulu at the Municipal High School at Vizianagaram worked on me—yes, worked on me like the sculptor would on a log of wood—and lo and behold my usual passing mark of 30 in mathematics had shot up to 80 at the 10$^{th}$ grade public exam.

At the Maharajah's College, when I was just under 15 and studying grades 11 and 12, a lecturer in calculus and another in chemistry initiated me to thinking beyond the usual learning. Respectively they made me read and enjoy Collected Papers of Srinivasa Ramanujan and a book on inventors known as Out of the Test Tube. In my subconscious, they must have injected a researching mindset in me.

Society of the 1950s had the dignity and decency to ensure that those with just above average achievement in the 12$^{th}$ grade were not intimidated and subtly discriminated by entrance tests and heavy tuition fees for undergraduate and postgraduate education. While tuition fee was not very high and not the problem, my father sent me his entire take home pay of Rs. 100 for my hostel and mess charges at Visakhapatnam. He never revealed to me that he had to borrow against his accumulated provident fund for his monthly household expenses at Vizianagaram.

It is one thing to have the human capability through health and education, but there is the issue of converting the capability into cash. Two developments in the post-1950 period have generally been in my favour: one, India getting rid of the history of little or no economic growth and moving on to planned development and positive growth; and two, the rest of the world being hospitable to movement of skilled personnel from India. I request all of you to kindly underscore the importance of both processes, more so now in the context of growing international economic integration.

Despite the two facilitating factors on the domestic and global fronts, it was a long struggle to move from one step to the other on the career ladder. Throughout, however, the Almighty was on my side providing the best and shielding me from the rest. I am bursting with enthusiasm and eagerness to speak about the interactions with and interventions by that wonder called God, but this is not the forum for such an excursion. I shall not bother you with even minimal details about the way the divine has taken care of me relatively directly for over four decades since 1962.

The fact that one person has done well on all three constituents of human development is of little national value since the country as a whole is nowhere near the top ranks in terms of human development. The UNDP index for India rose at snail's pace from 0.416 in 1975 to 0.59 in 2001, at an average annual growth of 1.4 per cent for the quarter century of the last millennium. The rate is far too low to make much difference in the lives of those in the bottom half of the pack.

Pushing up the general averages by a notch or two or celebrating the victories of a few in cricket or music or nuclear energy is not the same thing as lifting the vast majority of our people to heights of knowledge from depths of ignorance, to vistas of health from the morass of morbidity, and to contentment from multiple deprivations.

Public policy has to step in and provide the wherewithal for human capability across the board. This is because even in circumstances of sustained high rates of economic growth, as long as capabilities are highly unequal among the people, income and wealth distributions will not be moderated by the forces that generate growth. In addition, neither the development of free markets nor global economic integration can make a contribution to fairness in the distribution of human capabilities. The rich as well as the upper middle class will do whatever possible to preserve their class and category: in terms of the hospitals and doctors they visit, the schools their wards attend and the homes they own or rent. It is thus utopian to think that the free markets, globalisation and economic growth resting on them will correct the imbalances in the distribution of health, education and housing.

What should be the role and content of public policy in regard to enhancing human capabilities and correcting the inequality in their distribution across people?

While considerations of equity and equality have entered the global arena and development discourse for a long time, it is only more recently that international agencies have taken the trouble to discuss policy options and initiatives at national and global levels and moved beyond the preoccupations with measurements, time trends and cross country comparisons of inequalities in income, wealth, gender, etc.

A major development at the turn of the century was the issuance of the landmark: *United Nations Millennium Declaration* on September 8, 2000. The heads of State and Government, gathered at New York affirmed, "(we) recognize that, in addition to our separate responsibilities to our individual societies, we have a collective responsibility to uphold the principles of human dignity, equality and equity at the global level." The Declaration notes that certain fundamental values are essential to international relations in the 21$^{st}$ century. These include Freedom, Equality, Solidarity, Tolerance, Respect for Nature and Shared responsibility.

The UN Millennium Declaration has also articulated the Millennium Development Goals or MDGs, which include specific targets in the areas of poverty reduction, provision of education to all children, reducing the percentage of people without access to water and sanitation, reduction in infant, childhood and maternal mortality, control the spread of diseases like HIV/AIDS and malaria and improving the lives of slum dwellers. All these are indeed important for building human capabilities.

How does one go about delivering the targets? What are the challenges globally and in individual countries? A lot can be learnt from the latest World Development Report.

World Development Report (WDR) 2006 is about addressing inequalities in opportunities. The need to address the problem arises because those inequalities contribute "to economic inefficiency, political conflict, and institutional frailty" (WDR: 14). Addressing the problem and expanding the opportunities for the poor, apart from helping them directly, will assist the development process via better institutions, more effective conflict management, and a better use of human resources, all of which help to raise the rate of economic growth in the low income countries.

The Report explicitly discusses domestic policies in terms of investing in human capacities; expanding access to justice, land, and infrastructure; and promoting fairness in markets.

In regard to investment in human capacities, the areas of policy focus include early childhood development and formal education, health and safety nets.

The Report (WDR: 16) notes that because differences in cognitive development start to widen from a very early age, early childhood development initiatives can be central to more equal opportunities. As for formal education the Report notes that access to schooling matters, which, however, must be complemented by supply-side policies (to raise quality) and demand-side policies (to correct for the possibility that parents may under-invest in the education of their children for various reasons). I am very happy that the Bank scholars endorse measures such as, "increasing teachers' incentives, enhancing the basic quality of the school's physical infrastructure, and researching and implementing teaching methods to increase the learning performance of students who do not do well when left to their own devices."

In health, the Report notes that first, there are cases where the benefits go beyond the direct beneficiary in areas such as immunisation, water and sanitation, and information on hygiene and child care. The Report says that, "Public assurance of provisioning makes sense in these areas" (WDR: 18). As for curative care and dealing with relatively high medical costs beyond the means of low income households, WDR rightly points out that relying on public hospitals works badly, especially for poor and excluded groups. Hence it suggests that some form of insurance for all needs is to be combined with incentives for providers to be responsive to all groups.

None can dispute the idea of the Report in regard to ensuring fairness of the justice system. It also gives due importance to issues pertaining to equity in access to land. While redistributive land reforms has to be resorted in some cases, in others, improving the functioning of land markets and providing greater security of tenure for poorer groups is seen as a relatively more fruitful policy (WDR: 20).

The Report acknowledges the importance of equitable access to infrastructure—roads, electricity, water, sanitation and telecoms. The authors of the World Bank Report argue, "that policymakers can improve the equitable provision of infrastructure services by expanding affordable access for poor people and poor areas—which often means working with informal providers and targeting subsidies—and strengthening the governance of the sector through the greater accountability of providers and the stronger voice of beneficiaries" (WDR: 21).

The World Development Report is a useful document to gain inspiration but not country specific policy advice, providing which is not the objective of WDR any way.

If there is something grossly missing in MDG and WDR, it is the explicit case for public housing for the low income groups with partial or full subsidisation. A dwelling unit—at a minimum one room, bathroom and kitchen—is critical for providing water and sanitation on a sustained basis and ensuring a healthy living environment. Let me once again seek your pardon and make a brief reference to my personal life.

When I was just around three, my father acquired a home with just about two rooms and a small courtyard in the front. My childhood memory was one of keeping a vessel in line before a public tap and waiting for our turn to get drinking water. By the time I entered my early teens, we had a tap connection. Finally, my first lot of savings from abroad was used to construct a latrine connected to a septic tank in our home. What is development for me ought to be development for all others. While it may make sense to have drinking water provision on a community basis, it is a disgrace to supply a toilet for groups of families.

The issue is one of fairness in the provision of education, health, housing with proper water and sanitation provision. If the distribution of these amenities is really fair, it will be there to see for one and all, it will be equality that is visible. Unfortunately, I did not come across an explicit statement on reducing visible inequalities either in the Millennium Declaration or in the WDR.

World Development Report defines equity in terms of equality of opportunity and avoidance of absolute deprivation.

The *World Development Report 2006* (Chapter 1) defines equity in terms of the following two basic principles:

- *Equal opportunity*. The outcome of a person's life, in its many dimensions, should reflect mostly his or her efforts and talents, not his or her background. Predetermined circumstances—gender, race, place of birth, family origins—and the social groups a person is born into should not help determine whether people succeed economically, socially, and politically.

- *Avoidance of absolute deprivation*. An aversion to extreme poverty, or indeed a Rawlsian form of inequality aversion in the space of outcomes, suggests that societies may decide to intervene to protect the livelihoods of its neediest members (below some absolute threshold of need) even if the equal opportunity principle has been upheld.

In contrast to the hidden profundity of the aforementioned definitions, it is best to view equality and inequality in a direct way. Inequality is most visible when some children go to the posh private school while others go to the less endowed; when some patients go to an indifferent government hospital, while others go to the caring corporate hospital; and when some live in a makeshift dwelling while others live in spacious homes.

The most crucial is the visibility of inequality in education. It is unfortunate that Indian children at the age 5 or 6 get segregated into those going to the posh private school and those going to the relatively less endowed government/municipal school. This inequality at the very inception of education, with the almost unambiguous effect of perpetuating inequalities in life outcomes, may be taken to mean an entrenched culture of inequality.

In the area of education, an urgent need, therefore, is to launch a programme to build new and identically well endowed government schools, with excellent facilities for mid-day meals and the provision of free textbooks plus uniforms for those who can't afford. On the top of them all, proper incentives should be used to attract first rate teachers. In their absence, it will simply mean the perpetuation of the culture of inequality.

In health, we need a programme to build world-class polyclinics in place of the present primary health centres and taking steps to ensure they are well staffed. Taking up such projects over a period of time is neither expensive nor difficult if only the culture of inequality does not come in our way.

I have no doubt on the importance attached to address inequalities by caste and community. We all know that our brothers and sisters from the erstwhile deprived castes and communities should be provided with the best education form KG to PG. There is thus ample justification for reservations of places for them in education. But it is not fair to take the politically expedient route of lowering required qualifications for entry at each stage of education and even in employment at times. Why did we not think of same standards for all and similar achievements for all? Is this another manifestation of the innate desire of the well-off to perpetuate the culture of inequality?

Similar comments apply in regard to our initiatives on gender inequality. In fact, the area where the culture of inequality flourishes most is the case of gender inequality—most of my generation could recall the numerous families where mothers and sisters had always had the last priority when it comes to spending on their education and other requirements. I too personally stand guilty for not encouraging my wife to study after marriage.

In an advertisement issued in the media by the Ministry of Information and Broadcasting on October 2, a few years ago, the following quote from the Mahatma was reproduced: "I shall work for an India...in which there shall be no high class and low class of people; an India in which all communities shall live in perfect harmony." Public housing and private housing with appropriate homes for the poor in and around the same cluster will go a long way in ensuring the fulfilment of the dream of the Mahatma. That housing is a nation building activity is confirmed by the breathtaking house and township development activity by the Government of Singapore.

The former Prime Minister of Singapore in his book: *From Third World to First, The Singapore Story: 1965-2000, Memoirs of Lee Kuan Yew*, (Singapore: Singapore Press Holdings, 2000), has this to say on the key role housing plays in nation-building.

"My primary preoccupation was to give every citizen a stake in the country and its future. I wanted a home-owning society. I had seen the contrast between the blocks of low-cost rental flats, badly misused and poorly maintained, and those of house-proud owners, and was convinced that if every family owned its home, the country would be more stable (p.116).

"There were enormous problems, especially in the early stages when we resettled farmers and others from almost rent-free wooden squatter huts with no water, power and modern sanitation, and therefore, no utility bills, into high-rise dwellings with all these amenities, but also a monthly bill to pay. It was a wrenching experience for them in personal, social and economic terms (p.120).

"To prevent older estates from looking like slums, I suggested to the minister for national development in 1989 that it was time to upgrade the old housing with public funds to make them approximate the quality of the new. (p.121).

More than nation-building, proper housing is a precondition to providing water and sanitation in general and toilet facilities in particular. The connection between the type of housing and the availability of sanitation facilities can be gauged from the data for 1998-99 from the *National Family Health Survey (NFHS-2), 1998–99* (Mumbai: International Institute of Population Studies, 2000).

|  | Urban | Rural | Total |
|---|---|---|---|
| Per cent of households with *pucca* house | 66 | 19 | 32 |
| Per cent of households with flush toilet | 64 | 9 | 24 |

In regard to housing provision, one should not forget the problems of the slum dwellers. It is vital not to exaggerate the need for the slum dwellers to stay put and the importance of property rights for them by 'recognising' the slums, approving them as legitimate, and so on. Such actions will surely create the moral hazard of perpetual expansion of slums and slum dwellers. Again, it will go down as the perpetuation of the culture of inequality.

The best option for improving the lives of slum dwellers is to have them relocated with as little disruption as possible to well planned homes, preferably in mid-rise housing in housing clusters in new towns, a strategy that minimises the use of land for housing and permits greenery for all and not just some. It is a sad commentary on civilised evolution of nations and its peoples if slums are allowed to persist. There are no children of a lesser God when it comes to the conceptualisation of what constitutes development. National and international development policy makers, aid agencies and NGOs should appreciate the vital need for creating a stake for people in the nations they live in.

Schools that unify children and housing estates that unify citizens are my dream for my country. I shall consider I am blessed if the general public, intellectuals and policy makers were to share the same dream.

The urgent task ahead is the reduction of the visible inequalities in education, health and housing, thus contributing to a broad-based evolution of human capabilities. As for the macroeconomic environment to assist in the cashing in of the capabilities, the higher level of equality in capabilities will help raise the economic growth rate domestically and acceptability of the manpower internationally. One should keep hoping that just as the world is moving fast towards free movement of goods, services and capital, it will also evolve and allow the free movement of people.

# Bibliography

**Books**

Rao, Bhanoji and M.K. Ramakrishnan (1980). *Income Inequality in Singapore,* Singapore University Press, Singapore.

**Chapters in Books**

Rao, Bhanoji and M.K. Ramakrishnan (1978). "Structural Changes and Change in Income Distribution: Singapore, 1966-1975", in H.T. Oshima and T. Mizoguchi (eds.), *Income Distribution by Sectors and Overtime in East and Southeast Asian Countries,* January, Tokyo, pp.67-83.

————. (1980). "Economic Growth, Employment Expansion, and Reduction in Income Inequality: The Singapore Experience, 1966-1975", in K. Ohkawa and B. Key (eds.), *Asian Socio-Economic Development,* University of Tokyo Press, Tokyo, pp.167-190.

Rao, Bhanoji (1984). "India", in W. van Ginneken and J. Park (eds.), *Generating Internationally Comparable Income Distribution Estimates,* ILO, Geneva, pp.69-74.

————. (1984). "Philippines", in W. van Ginneken and J. Park (eds.), *Generating Internationally Comparable Income Distribution Estimates,* pp.113-118, ILO, Geneva.

————. (1996). "Income Inequality in Singapore: Facts and Policies", in Lim Chong Yah (ed.), *Economic Policy Management in Singapore,* Addison-Wesley, Singapore, pp.383-396.

————. (1996). "Singapore Household Income Distribution Data from the 1990 Census: Analysis, Results and Implications", in B. Kapur *et al.* (eds.), *Development, Trade and the Asia-Pacific: Essays in Honour of Prof. Lim Chong Yah,* Prentice Hall, Singapore, pp.92-104.

————. (2006). "Gini Coefficient", *Encyclopedia of Social Policy,* Routledge, London.

Rao, Bhanoji and Habibullah Khan (1989). "Economic Growth, Poverty Alleviation, Income Inequality and Expenditure Patterns: The Singapore Case", in Helmut Kurth (ed.), *Economic Growth and Income Distribution,* Friedrich-Ebert-Stiftung Foundation, Manila, pp.172-191.

Rao, Bhanoji and P. Mukhopadhaya (2002). "Income Distribution", in Koh Ai Tee *et al.* (eds), *Singapore into the 21st Century: Issues and Strategies,* McGraw-Hill, Singapore.

**Articles in Refereed Journals**

Rao, Bhanoji and M.K. Ramakrishnan (1976). "Economic Growth, Structural Change and Income Distribution in Singapore, 1966-1975", *The Malayan Economic Review,* October, pp.92-122.

————. (1978). "A Note on the Decomposition of the Gini Ratio", *The Malayan Economic Review,* October, pp.36-39.

Rao, Bhanoji (1979). "An Analysis of Singapore Household Expenditure Distributions: 1956-57 and 1972-73", *The Philippine Economic Journal,* 4th Quarter, pp.616-629.

————. (1981). "Measurement of Deprivation and Poverty Based on the Proportion Spent on Food: An Exploratory Exercise", *World Development,* April, pp.337-355.

————. (1988). "Income Distribution in East Asian Developing Countries: A Review of the Evidence", *AsianPacific Economic Literature,* March, pp.26-45

————. (1989). "Income Inequality and Poverty in East Asia: Trends and Implications", *Indian Economic Journal,* October-December, pp.57-64.

————. (1990). "Income Distribution in Singapore: Trends and Issues", *Singapore Economic Review,* April, pp.143-160.

————. (1990). "Singapore Income Distribution Data: An Evaluation", *Singapore Journal of Statistics,* October, pp.175-198.

————. (1991). "Human Development Report, 1990: A Review and Assessment", *World Development,* October, pp.1451-1460.

————. (1993). "A Primer on Inequality", *Times Economic Link,* October-December, pp.5-11.

————. (1999). "East Asian Economies: Trends in Poverty and Income Inequality", *Economic and Political Weekly*, Vol. 34(18), May 1, pp.1029-1039.

————. (1999). "Towards an Explicit Inclusion of Core Human Values in Development Discourse", *Scima, (Systems and Cybernetics in Management)*, Vol. 26(2-3), pp.75-85.

————. (2003). "Explaining Cross-country Variation in Income Inequality Based on the Best Income Distribution Data", *Economic and Political Weekly*, Vol. 38, April 26, pp.1645-1648.

————. (2005). "Income Inequality and Public Policy: Lessons and Implications of East Asian and Global Patterns", *South Indian Journal of Social Sciences*, Vol. 3(1), pp.1-8.

Rao, Bhanoji and P. Smith (1994). "Some Issues in Income Inequality", *The Economic Review*, 11(3), February, pp.2-5.

Rao, Bhanoji and P. Mukhopadhaya (2001). "The Gini Coefficient—A Note", *The Indian Economic Journal*, 48: 4, April-June, pp.65-67.

————. (2001). "The Miracle of Low Income Inequality: Taiwan, 1976-97", *Journal of Income Distribution*.

Rao, Bhanoji, D.S. Banerjee and P. Mukhopadhaya (2003). "Earnings Inequality in Singapore", *Journal of the Asia Pacific Economy*, Vol. 8(2), pp.210-228.

**Monographs and Reports**

Rao, Bhanoji (1984). *Poverty in Indonesia, 1970-1980: Trends, Associated Characteristics and Research Issues*, January, World Bank.

————. (1985). "The Philippines: Recent Trends in Poverty, Employment and Wages", *World Bank Report* No. 5456-PH, June.

————. (1992). "Land Reforms: Recent Trends and Policy Options", *Working Paper* No. 20/1992, Institute for Social and Economic Change, December, Bangalore.

# 3

## Governance and Growth

JAYAPRAKASH NARAYAN

### Introduction: India and China—A Comparison

Despite fractious politics and short-term populism, Indian growth rate at about 7 per cent per annum, is next only to China's among major economies. This reflects the underlying strength of our economy. However, comparisons with China are inevitable, given our comparable sizes, length of history and civilisation, and somewhat parallel developments after the Second World War. Many objective observers believe that China is destined to be the next economic superpower. By contrast, India is believed to be underperforming. *Daedalus* magazine, reviewing the healthcare in the United States 25 years ago, coined the expression "Doing better, and feeling worse." That description certainly fits our economic scene. While on the one hand, when compared with earlier decades, our economy has been doing much better in terms of growth rates, the socioeconomic indicators have not changed radically.

Is this underperformance a consequence of democracy, and Chinese progress due to dictatorial policies? What is the truth? A careful analysis shows that dictatorship has been an obstacle to China's growth for decades. The infamous Great Leap Forward and Cultural Revolution led to enormous grief and vandalism. The successes of Mao's era—accessible school education, effective healthcare delivery, and transfer of technology to rural areas had nothing to do with dictatorship; they were products of sound and sensible policies.

Similarly, the Deng era successes are not a consequence of authoritarianism, but greater liberalisation and democratisation. Choice and competition in economic arena, removal of entry and exit barriers, highly decentralised economic decision making, effective local governments enjoying functional autonomy, and in recent days the experiment of deliberative democracy at local level—all these are symptoms of greater democratisation, not totalitarian control and arbitrary decision-making.

Clearly, the difference in growth rates and current GDP levels between the two countries cannot be attributed to Chinese totalitarianism and Indian democracy. Instead, sound policies and enhancement of liberty are the two key determinants of economic success. Despite our democratic system, decision making is highly centralised in India. It is said that the United States has the largest number of final decision making authorities relative to any other society. India possibly has the smallest number of final decision makers for any large society, let alone a democracy.

Not too long ago, China's spectacular advances in the field of telecommunications was a source of global wonder and admiration. But once Indian policy makers got their act together, and allowed choice, competition, technology and investment, we are now witnessing a comparable growth in this sector. The difference between the two countries is largely on account of the delayed liberalisation in India. As China, under the redoubtable Deng, changed course in 1978, we waited until the 1991 crisis to allow freedom and choice.

### Liberalisation—Not a Panacea

The economic reform process started in 1991 certainly yielded good dividends. Growth rate went up. In a country used to the Hindu rate of growth of about 3 per cent, 6-7 per cent growth rate now is widely regarded as unsatisfactory. Consumer goods are better and cheaper now, and there is greater choice on offer. Investment has gone up, and exports boomed for a decade. Contrary to fears, opening up of the economy did not lead to a deluge of foreign goods. The Indian consumer proved to be very discerning, seeking good value for money. Nor did neocolonialism or economic imperialism threaten India's freedom. The percentage of poor people is showing decline, and population is reaching replacement level in the South and the West. Removal of foreign exchange controls did not lead to flight of dollars; reserves actually went up significantly. Reductions of tax rates led to higher revenues, and not lower. Many new enterprises came up significantly, and the young people are more ready than ever before to find jobs outside the government. India saw a revolution in telecom and information sectors. Organised workers, who had enjoyed immense protection for long, now realise that their future is linked to the health of their enterprises. The person-days lost on account of industrial strife fell dramatically. The doomsayers who prophesied disaster with liberalisation proved to be wide off the mark. Most people are actually better off today than they were a decade ago. By all standards, the reform process has yielded good results.

It is now axiomatic that the government which governs the least is the best government. Public opinion has also come to accept that government has no business to run businesses. Libertarians naturally oppose high taxation or huge public expenditure. As Milton Friedman so succinctly explained, a citizen knows best how to maximise his happiness by spending, as he deems fit, the Rs. 100 in his pocket. The alternative of transferring to the State most of it and hoping that someone, somewhere will take sound decisions for him (an unsound assumption), and receiving only a small fraction of it in the form of public goods and services (after transaction costs, leakages, inefficiency and corruption) is clearly unattractive to most of us.

But closer examination of the OECD countries shows that in the real world, most States pursue economic policies that combine the libertarian principle of *laissez-faire* with expenditure for promoting social good in the form of education, healthcare and welfare. Notwithstanding Ronald Reagan and Margaret Thatcher, the public expenditure in OECD countries is about 45 per cent of GDP on an average. India's public expenditure as a share of GDP is lower than every OECD country, except the two city-states of Hong Kong and Singapore. The social expenditure alone accounts for 25 per cent of GDP, adjusting for country-variations. The high-income countries spend 5.6 per cent of GDP on public education and 6.4 per cent of GDP on public health. Medium income countries spend only 4.6 per cent and 3.2 per cent of GDP on education and health respectively, while poor countries spend a measly 2.5 per cent and 0.8 per cent on these two sectors.

What does this indicate? Limited government and political and economic freedom to citizens are vital for individual growth and national advancement. But liberty cannot be construed in a very narrow and negative sense of State not abridging individual freedoms. State is not merely a necessary evil to defend our frontiers, maintain public order, protect citizens and ensure justice. State can, and should, also be a positive institution to create basic infrastructure, develop natural resources, and most of all to provide quality school education and effective primary healthcare. Liberal think tanks and academics have been vehemently advocating rollback of the State from these areas. While State's role in business is now universally opposed, there are no realistic substitutes to State in school education, primary healthcare and the like.

It does not mean that State alone should pay for these services. Private and voluntary sectors have a significant role, and nowhere in market economies is that role more pronounced than in India. Nor does it mean that State should necessarily deliver these services. Stakeholders groups and voluntary organisations often do the job much better. But the financing has to come from the State. And, the State does not mean the centralised, remote, big-government, but localised, citizen-centred government starting with a community of stakeholders, and expanding in concentric circles to local, provincial and federal governments based on the principle of subsidiarity.

We have to recognise that social goods like school education and primary healthcare cannot be accessed by most citizens without State's intermediation or funding. And in our country, with vertical heirarchies, caste divisions and moral neutrality to social inequities, State's role is critical. With the State failing in these sectors, the bulk of our gene pool is wasted, and educational opportunities are effectively limited to a quarter of our population; poor people end up suffering and spending much more than the rich in market-driven private healthcare systems. Making education a profit-making enterprise has resulted in mushrooming of countless colleges that produce mostly literate, semi-educated, unemployable graduates. It is easy for the well-heeled and well-connected to ridicule the role of the State. But the fact remains that the future of the vast majority of our children is dictated by the circumstances of their birth. The potential of most children remains unfulfilled. Opportunities for vertical mobility are severely restricted for the bulk of the population. Paradoxically, in the 1950s and 1960s, children had better opportunities. But the decline in public education and healthcare makes the situation increasingly unacceptable. Abdication of State is no solution.

## State, Resources and Development

As pointed out, the GDP share of public expenditure in India is low compared to OECD countries. But it would be wrong to conclude that State's incapacity to deliver is a result of shortage of resources alone. Indian State was never short of resources to abstain from carrying out vital functions necessary for development. Excluding the local governments' expenditure and inter-governmental adjustments, the combined total expenditure of the Union and State governments, according to the budget estimates is a whopping Rs. 2,000 crore per day or in terms of purchasing power it is equivalent to $ 2 billion a day!

What do we get in return and what do we have to show? Eighty crore children with no access to school education, 70 crore people without access to proper toilets, shortage of teachers and excess of peons and clerks, appalling public services and woefully inadequate infrastructure. Without having to increase public expenditure, without having to seek aid from international agencies, these 8 crore children could all have access to basic school education. It just requires some reallocation of funds and commitment of the governing class. At 50 children per classroom we need to build 16 lakh classrooms. Each classroom can be built at Rs. 1 lakh or less. This will incur a one-time expenditure/investment of Rs. 16,000 crore. This is equivalent to only 8 days' government expenditure! Running the school—teachers and basic teaching aids—would incur a recurring expense of Rs. 8,000 crore; a mere four days' expenditure! A very paltry investment when you calculate the social and economic returns to the country. Similarly, all it takes to provide a safe, hygienic toilet for every household is about Rs. 12,000 crores public expenditure (half the needy households can pay from their own resources if technology and material are accessible, and a campaign is launched to promote proper hygiene and sanitation). This is equivalent to a one-time investment equal to six days public expenditure. Studies have also shown that our public health system can be completely revamped, and healthcare improved and made accessible to the poor and needy, at an additional cost of about Rs. 10,000 crores per annum.

These examples demonstrate that while resources are scarce, even the available resources are not properly deployed. The Indian State has increasingly become a stumbling block to our economic growth prospects. The State guzzles vast resources and produces very little in return. We have, in all, about 2.7 crore workers in the organised sector, or about 8 per cent of the total work force in the country. Of them, an astonishing 2 crore, or nearly three-quarters, are in government! About 1.3 crore are directly employed by the government at various levels, and about 70 lakh are in public sector undertakings. This number in the last decade has actually increased by nearly 10 lakhs. The problem is not the size of government employment in absolute terms. Many nations have a larger proportion of population employed by government. Therefore, the solution does not lie in mindless downsizing. What we need is redeployment and greater productivity. Take a large state like Andhra Pradesh with 900,000 employees in government. About 180,000 or 20 per cent are unproductive for the people, as they are engaged as peons and drivers! Another 30 per cent (270,000) are support staff (clerks, etc.) whose only purpose is to allegedly help the decision makers. There are about 40,000 officials with decision-making power at some level or other, and they could perform far more efficiently and economically with a well-trained support staff of a total of 60,000. But we have 450,000 of them employed as clerks, drivers and peons! We have about 310,000 teachers, but the State probably needs another 300,000 teachers of good quality to sustain a credible school education infrastructure. The healthcare system is inadequately staffed. We have a total of about 15,000 judges in India. Germany, with a population of 8 crore, has 30,000 judges! We have far fewer police personnel than needed in modern times. All this demonstrates that it is not merely the size of the government, what matters most is the productivity of the government. If government is productive, it creates conditions for economic growth, which in turn promotes employment in private sector. The ratio of government workers then comes down in time.

## Fiscal Rigidities and Indian State

The other important aspect that is curtailing productivity of Indian State apparatus is the rigidities that characterise the fiscal planning in India. One of the recurring themes of Indian public expenditure and budget making in the last decade is the fiscal rigidities making it difficult for governments to change policies and priorities. In the Union Budget, interest payments, defence expenditure, transfer of resources to States and wages are more or less inflexible, and there is no room for manoeuvring. It is now axiomatic that subsidies cannot be removed without incurring high political and social costs. Similarly, in States too, repayment obligations, wages, administrative costs, expenditure on ongoing schemes and projects, State's share in centrally-sponsored schemes, etc. are inflexible, leaving little room for innovation. Again, subsidies are hard to cut. The result is less than adequate social expenditure and poor quality infrastructure.

As early as in 1992, Dr. Manmohan Singh as Finance Minister lamented the shackles imposed by these fiscal compulsions. The only two changes subsequently are, defence expenditure shot up significantly in recent years, and wage expenditure of both the Union and State increased greatly with the acceptance of Fifth Pay Commission recommendations. Economists, analysts and politicians owe it to the country to evolve mechanisms to break this logjam.

However, there are realistic and effective options still available. But we need courage and skill to exercise them and achieve tangible results. Let us take subsidies as an example. For fiscal year 2002-03, major Union subsidies account for Rs. 37,392 crore. Food subsidy alone will cross Rs. 21,200 crore. Power subsidies and losses (which will eventually be subsidised) in States will probably account for Rs. 40,000 crore. And there are other subsidies in States too. Is there a way of reducing these subsidies, retargeting them without inviting massive social unrest and political opposition?

But there are ways of reducing subsidies in a politically acceptable way. Let us suppose the administration of food subsidy (the consumer part of it) is transferred to local governments. We can actually quantify the amount of subsidy based on the food grain offtake and price differential at the local level. Then the Union or

State can ask the local government to re-target the subsidies to reach the deserving poor and cut down on leakages. This will work if the subsidy amount so saved is made available to the local government for other desirable activities, say infrastructure building or social expenditure. Once local government is assured of additional resources based on performance (cut in subsidies), it will have an incentive to reduce subsidies and unlock these resources. The money saved can thus be used for schools, drains, water supply, roads, health centres and sanitation. Since there is a clear link between subsidy reduction and alternative public goods and services, a powerful local constituency will be built favouring reduction in subsidies. In centralised administration, there are only losers in subsidy reduction, and no corresponding gainers. But once it is decentralised, and savings are alternatively deployed, the same family which loses a subsidy will gain directly through better public goods and services. Or there will be as many or more gainers as losers. We will then have achieved two objectives. Subsidies would be reduced, and expenditure is directed towards more desirable goals. This principle can be applied to several subsidies—food, agricultural power, irrigation, etc.

## Public Sector Management and Indian State

The third important question pertaining to the productivity of government is the role of government in running enterprises, and the plight of infrastructure sector. It is by now well-recognised that public sector is often a euphemism for political patronage and private aggrandisement. Politicians, in power or out of it, and career bureaucrats as a rule have no respect for economic logic or wealth creation. A few more jobs to cronies, promise of illusory gains to constituents, cushy rehabilitation for favoured sidekicks, luxurious jaunts, and kickbacks in contracts and purchases are the golden eggs which make PSUs so attractive. In this anxiety to make a killing while the going is good, if the golden goose itself perishes, well, it's too bad! In any case, that is the problem for successors.

This cynical approach has been the hallmark of management of public enterprises. For decades, State monopoly in telecom sector held back services and growth and caused misery to hapless consumers. All this in the name of protecting the revenues of inefficient State monopolies and private oligopolies. Airlines have been managed as private fiefdoms of the presiding ministers. Any attempt to inject competition and efficiency, and invite investment is resisted fiercely with predictable invocation of pride in national carriers. Oil sector has suffered decades of loot by meddlesome politicians, and even now monopolies continue despite the facade of opening up. Steel plants were once the favoured trophies. But again, decades of wasteful practices and sloth led to disastrous consequences. And when a competent manager makes valiant efforts to improve efficiency and profitability, he is often victimised.

The analysis so far has demonstrated that the resources are not a vital constraint and yet the State apparatus regularly fails to provide basic services. Centralised governance has made it increasingly difficult to control fiscal profligacy and the State apparatus has become a dispenser of patronage, resulting in institutionalisation of corruption. Most Indians share a sense of unease and disquiet. Our potential remains unfulfilled even today. Impressive as they are by global standards, our growth rates are insufficient to make a significant dent in poverty, or to absorb the millions of youngsters joining the work force. Fiscal deficits stubbornly remain at the 10 per cent GDP level. Government continues to be wasteful, inefficient and corrupt. As a consequence, there are many who ask: how come our political class is not displaying courage and skill to achieve tangible results? But political skills of individual leaders alone is not sufficient. There are large numbers of politicians who have consistently displayed courage in taking decisions that are bold and imaginative. Yet the crisis of bad governance persists due to distortions in our political process. What are these distortions? Huge, illegitimate election expenditure has resulted in money power becoming dominant in elections. The social divisions and the electoral system have facilitated rise of fiefdoms and legislator to become a disguised executive. The centralised governance system and vast bureaucracy are having pernicious impact on fiscal health of States and the Union. With these distortions, the State apparatus can never function in a productive manner. And an inefficient State apparatus will act as an impediment to economic prosperity. Hence, an exploration into causes of distortions in political process and reasons for absence of good governance will provide us with the keys to economic prosperity and political transformation of India.

Leadership in modern world provides a great contrast to that in India. In a remarkable speech to European Parliament recently, Tony Blair exhorted politicians to respond to the challenges of today. Emphasising the need for keeping pace in a changing world, he reminded OECD countries, "The USA is the world's only superpower. But China and India in a few decades will be the world's largest economies, each of them with populations three times that of the whole of the EU...(European social model) is allowing more science graduates to be produced by India than by Europe. India will expand its biotechnology sector five-fold in the next five years. China has trebled its spending on R&D in the last five..." Outlining the challenges of today, he called for renewal of the idea of Europe, and said, "Now, almost 50 years on, we have to renew. There is no shame in that. All institutions must do it. And we can. But only if we remarry the European ideals we believe in with the modern world we live in." That is the stuff of true politics and great leadership rooted in genuine soul-searching, passion and spirit of public service.

## The Problem of Our Politics

Does our politics measure up to the challenges of today? Four unhappy characteristics dominate our political landscape. First is the patronising attitude to people: citizens know nothing and are parasitic; and they need regulation, protection and doles. As a corollary we need centralised administrative apparatus, as large number of citizens are ignorant and are incapable of participating in local governance structures. The notion that citizens have no capacity to understand their self-interest and are incapable of taking charge of their own lives at local level is absurd in a democracy. And yet, we extol the virtues and wisdom of voters when they exercise their franchise in electing state and national governments. Many of us admire China's rapid economic growth in recent years. But we often ignore the fact that the employment and exports in China are powered by the millions of town and village enterprises (TVEs) with the support and active participation of local governments. One of the ironies of contemporary history is authoritarian and communist China is far more decentralised than liberal democratic India! When the British argued that we were not fit for freedom, our leaders pointed out that good government was no substitute to self-government. They had to grudgingly admit that the British did give good government, and yet we fought for our freedom. Today, centralised government has become a repository of corruption, incompetence and misgovernance. What we have in the name of governance is constitutional brigandage and legal plunder and yet we continue with highly centralised administrative apparatus, which does not facilitate peoples' participation in governance apparatus.

### Unceasing Fervour of Failed Ideologies

This patronising attitude towards people also manifests itself as ideological populism. Witness the quality of debate on BHEL disinvestment. Every perceptive citizen knows that public sector in India is largely private sector of those in public office. We only need better goods and services at least cost, and it does not matter who produces them. We all know, during the past 50 years, in the name of socialism, we undermined true entrepreneurship. And we became control freaks. I vividly remember that only 20 years ago we had cement control and dual pricing, and people had to beg for cement permits to build homes! We had bureaucrats controlling steel sales and seeking bribes and exercising patronage. On the other hand, the state's failure in education, healthcare, rural technologies and infrastructure have been too well documented to need elaboration. In short, the State failed in its core areas of legitimate functioning, and did everything possible to undermine our self-esteem and enterprise. And yet, even today we hear arguments for increased State intervention in non-critical areas.

Let us compare and contrast the efficiency and competitiveness of public sector *vis-à-vis* private sector. Disinvestment ministry has quoted a NCAER study to conclusively establish that public monopolies cannot effectively respond to changed conditions. Comparisons of factor productivities, profitability and cost structure—all show the dynamism of private management and inertia of State control. As the total factor productivity in private sector recorded 3.4 per cent growth since 1985, in public sector there is a negative growth of -1.1 per cent. Manufacturing PSEs continue to show losses, while manufacturing private sector shows decent profits. From resource utilisation point of view and competitiveness, the most critical comparison relates to cost structure of power and fuel, wages and interest as a ratio of net sales. In 1990-91, the public sector (minus oil sector) spent 37.7 per cent of net sales on these three heads, as opposed to private sector's cost of 21.7 per cent, with a net saving of 16 per cent. Amazingly, by 1997-98, this difference in cost incurred has increased to 38.3 per cent of net sales, with public sector spending 54.5 per cent of net sales on these three items, and private sector 16.2 per cent! Increased competition and open markets forced private sector to reduce costs to a tune of 5.5 per cent, whereas public sector costs went up by almost 17 per cent! There cannot be a more severe indictment of public sector management. The managers are not at fault; the same personnel in private environment produce excellent results. We must recognise that even if all else is equal, public sector culture does not foster the best management practices. With the economy opening up, and competition growing, continued insistence on government controlling PSEs will only erode their assets, and eliminate them from the market.

The champions of State control must answer a fundamental question. Have people elected them to govern, or to run a business? Socialism took roots as a moral philosophy based on compassion and concern for equity at a time when predatory capitalism of robber baron variety led to extreme degrees of oppression and misery. But today's market economy adapted the best features of humanism, welfare and sustainability. Resorting to outdated arguments and shibboleths, and criminal waste of scarce public resources at the cost of justice, rule of law, education, healthcare and decent infrastructure is cruel to the poor and disadvantaged. Quality schooling, accessible healthcare, speedy justice and security net for the indigent are the best anti-poverty programmes. A government, which cannot provide these, has no moral authority to take upon itself other burdens, and discharge them incompetently. Ministerial office and bureaucratic sinecures have become private fiefdoms, and loss of patronage and control unnerves those in authority. But equating self-interest of those in power with public interest is an insult to the intelligence of the long-suffering people of the country, and a cruel irony in a society impoverished by bad policies and worse governance. Moreover, unnecessary and inefficient State interventions, and imprudent economic polices are pushing our governments into fiscal crisis. And yet, public interest is sacrificed at the altar of failed ideologies. Or take the fears of globalisation stoked with unceasing fervour. Mighty US and Europe are showing signs of anxiety with the increasing competitiveness and growing market share of China and India, and our antiquated politics can only see dangers in every opportunity! Or take the labour markets: the world over, rigid markets and overregulation led to large-scale unemployment; and yet we want to perpetuate *status quo* at the cost of the millions of job seekers. And of course the politicians' eternal preference of doles and subsidies over empowerment and liberation of productive potential is too well known to require elaboration.

## Politics of Plunder and Rent-seeking

The second dangerous feature of our politics is its predatory nature. Politics of plunder and rent-seeking have become the norm, and public-spirited politicians are increasingly marginalised. Distortion of markets, kleptocracy, and shameless display of unearned wealth have created a culture of illegitimate plutocracy. Power and ill-gotten money acquired by abuse of power have become ends in themselves. Politics has in a large measure ceased to be a means to public good. Obsession with power at any cost has created a class of criminals and crooks dabbling in politics, and decent citizens are increasingly shunning public life. For instance, after the elections to Maharastra Assembly, a one-time mafia don, Arun Gawli, and a few others with notorious record of crime, have become lawmakers. Arun Gawli did not even need a major party support—he was elected as an independent! In India's poorest state of Bihar too, Pappu Yadav, who strikes terror in the hearts of rival gangs and law-abiding citizens, won with massive majority and is now a Lok Sabha member, a privilege denied to Dr. Manmohan Singh in 1999. And Pappu Yadav won against the combined opposition of Samata, BJP, Communists and Lok Janshakti!

Wringing our hands in despair at this increasing criminalisation of politics, and politicisation of crime will do no good. We need to understand the economic and institutional imperatives that increasingly legitimise crime and violence in society and public life. These criminals have not come out of a vacuum. Our malfunctioning governing institutions created fertile conditions for their rise. Any one who has an unresolved civil dispute with a business partner or customer understands how tough it is to run a business ethically in India. For instance, if an honest entrepreneur produces high quality products at competitive price, and if the government is the monopoly buyer of his product, the travails he faces are unbelievable. If he cooperates with the CBI or other anti-corruption agencies to trap the errant officials, then his troubles multiply. The whole organisation suddenly gang up against him and makes his life miserable.

If such are the problems faced by asset-rich, resourceful and well-connected entrepreneurs, the pain and suffering inflicted on lesser mortals in getting civil contracts enforced, or receiving reparation for the damages sustained have to be seen to be believed. A house-owner who cannot get her property vacated even for self-occupation, and the owner of a small plot of land who cannot evict a land-shark have no realistic legal recourse in our society. With 25 million cases pending in courts, and with most litigations taking decades for resolution, people have no realistic hope of justice through formal mechanisms. As a result, millions of cases never reach the courts. Like 'missing' girl children on account of female foeticide, there are millions of such 'missing' cases in India every year. These missing cases, and not merely pending cases, reflect the appalling failure of due process and rule of law in our country. Most people prefer to swallow injustice and suffer silently. A few who have means, or are desperate, seek rough and ready justice through brutal methods. The neighbourhood 'bhai', or the local mafia don is supplying his services to meet this unmet demand. In a civil court, even if you are lucky to get a decree in your favour after decades of struggle, your problems continue. To enforce a decree, an execution petition has to be filed, and another prolonged, excruciating process begins! But the local don will ensure settlement of dispute for a price within a few days, and his 'verdict' is enforced instantly. No wonder, many people see crime lords not as villains, but as saviours!

It is no secret that many banks and other financial institutions are now deploying musclemen to recover debts. If formal, organised businesses feel the need to resort to use of force to run legitimate businesses, it is no surprise that ordinary people treat criminals with deference. In such a twilight zone, the distinction between 'hero' and 'villain' is erased. Brute force becomes the only effective arbiter. We can set things right only when it is possible to do business or protect rights through peaceful and lawful means. Rise of criminals is a consequence, not the cause, of breakdown of rule of law. This is particularly true of urban India.

A similar process is at work in government too. The spectacle of helpless citizens, in Andhra Pradesh, and at times influential persons and officials, queuing in front of the Maoist Communists ('Naxalites'), petitioning for redressal of their grievances says it all. There is no greater indictment of the functioning of our governing institutions than the public display of faith in armed revolutionary groups in the midst of the peace negotiations with government. In general, people have lost faith in the system, and have come to believe that nothing is accomplished through peaceful efforts, or due process.

Is it a surprise then that voters have no qualms in electing notorious gangsters as their representatives? People do know the difference between right and wrong, and good and evil. But they have realised that an honest, peaceful representative cannot really deliver results in this unhappy milieu. That is why a Manmohan Singh, whose assumption of office as Prime Minister was universally hailed, is not elected as a mere MP in a Lok Sabha constituency. And the decent men and women who do get elected are helpless in getting things done. We have created a system of alibis in which authority is delinked from accountability, and stake-holding is divorced from power-wielding. In such a situation, honest legislators have very little capacity to influence events for public good. But a mafia don enforces iron discipline, and makes the bureaucracy comply. The very criminal reviled by the media and middle classes is perceived as a saviour by the common man! And once a gangster makes money, he spends lavishly for 'good causes', styles himself as the leader of his caste or religious group, and can muster the muscle power required to navigate through the political and bureaucratic minefield. Witness the rise of Arun Gawli!

Once a legislator gets elected by deploying illegitimate and unaccounted money power, he converts politics as business. While constituents are kept relatively happy by 'good' deeds and selective intervention, the legislator's influence is largely deployed for postings of pliable bureaucrats and transfers of inconvenient officials; distorting market forces and undermining fair competition in contracts, tenders and public procurements; and endless interference in crime investigation. This is the 'dangerously stable equilibrium' Robert Wade described in his authoritative studies 25 years ago. The situation is even more complex in some ways now, but is by no means intractable. However, as Yeats lamented, "The best lack conviction, and the worst are full of passionate intensity." In the process, very few new and powerful ideas are vigorously pursued to improve the conditions of the bulk of our people or to accelerate our growth rate.

*Medieval Politics*

Third, politics continues to be medieval in nature. Much of the debate on education is centred around rewriting history or detoxification of textbooks. The 'great' debates are about the location of a temple or a mosque, or past insults and private injuries, or perpetuation of barbaric practices and shunning of modern, humanistic vision. Obscurantism is zealously guarded, and the clear stream of reason 'has lost' its way into the dreary desert sand of dead habit.

The medieval character of our polity is also reflected in the way political recruitment is done. In India, traditionally parties have been seen as pocket boroughs of those at the helm. Often there are entry barriers to members. Those who pose a potential threat to entrenched leadership are denied access to a party, or expelled even for faintest criticism or dissent. The parties, which exhibit such authoritarian tendencies in protecting the privilege of those in power and nipping in the bud any potential threat to individual dominance have not shown the slightest sense of shame or remorse in assiduously cultivating and recruiting known criminals, corrupt persons and those with a dubious record. Such shady elements are courted and welcomed, while decent and dignified citizens are shunned and often rejected. There are no published membership rolls, and spurious membership has become a common feature. There are no internal democratic norms and procedures in leadership choices at various levels. There are no mechanisms for open debate or dissent, and for influencing the views of members. Finally, the choice of candidates nominated by a party for elective public office is left entirely to the discretion of the party bosses with members having little say. With this, the control of party bosses and coteries is complete—they are often unelected, and unaccountable, and they perpetuate themselves with illegal funding and a culture of nominations to all party posts and elective offices. All this has created political fiefdoms resembling ancient monarchies or medieval *zamindaris*. Little dynasties have spawned all over the country and these oligarchies have a vice-like grip over our legislatures. A careful analysis of the nearly 5000 legislative offices in States and Lok Sabha will reveal that probably two-thirds of them are controlled by about 10,000 well-connected political families. No matter which party wins, power alternates between members of these families. Politics has become big business. Big investments are made in elections, and much bigger profits are reaped once elected to office. A legislator is more a disguised and unaccountable executive than a public representative. This prevalence of medieval culture in political parties is the root cause of the increasing failure of parliamentary democracy.

*Incompetent Policies: A Case of Education and Healthcare*

Finally, incompetence and laziness have become virtues in our political domain. Even now, our vision of education is merely increasing enrolment of school children and reduction of dropouts. Quality of education, high productivity of citizens, and seizing opportunities that modern world offers do not even enter our public discourse. Our universities languish despite the undoubted potential of our youngsters and the civilisation strength we enjoy. Statistically education sector in India looks impressive. We have over 5 million scientists, engineers and technicians in India now. About 300,000 of them (6 per cent) are engaged in research and development. We can boast of 450,000 allopathic physicians, 200,000 agricultural graduates and 40,000 veterinarians. The stock of other postgraduate degree holders is about 4.5 million in liberal arts, and a million each in sciences and commerce. In addition, we have about 9.5 million graduates in liberal arts, 4.5 million in sciences and 5 million in commerce. Our engineers alone exceed a million now, with 1,100 colleges producing 350,000 technologists every year, 60 per cent of whom graduate from the four southern states alone!

All these are impressive numbers by any standards. India certainly has a vast higher education infrastructure, which can be the envy of any developing country. But these numbers hide a grave crisis in our higher education. Out finest scholars—about 5 per cent—are a match for the brightest and best in the world. But many of them are migrating to the US and West. Recent reports say that the 75,000 Indian students constitute the largest foreign contingent in American universities! These are products of the few good institutions, backed by exceptional talent, family support and conducive environment. But most of our colleges and universities produce graduates of indifferent quality. A culture of rote learning, lack of application of knowledge, and poor examination system have undermined our higher education. Most graduates lack basic communication skills, nor do they exhibit problem solving capacity. Educated unemployment is very much on the rise, largely because most graduates cannot promote wealth creation and are therefore unemployable. And yet, our society faces acute shortage of problem solvers, and capable workers in various fields like healthcare, education, justice delivery and law and order. This is a classic case of a mismatch between our needs and human resources. As Coleridge lamented in his immortal poem, "Water, water everywhere; but not a drop to drink!"

Clearly, the main function of higher education system is to add real value to human resources, and produce wealth creators and leaders in all fields—business, professions, politics, administration, and creative pursuits. Even the crisis in school education is compounded by the failure of higher education. Most problems in our schools—curriculum, textbooks, teaching methods, examination system—can be overcome by innovative efforts and sensible public policy. But there is phenomenal shortage of good teachers. And only university graduates can be teachers! Millions of graduates are hunting for jobs, and yet, most of them cannot be trusted with our children's education. A classic vicious cycle has set in: poor school education has weakened university standards; and collapse of higher education denies good teachers to schools! All of us face this dilemma in our schools.

Given this, most households are petrified at the thought of a kid to be admitted to school, or a sick person seeking medical attention.

Quality education and healthcare are simply inaccessible and unaffordable to most Indians. Let's take healthcare. There is ample evidence to demonstrate that delivery of public health services in India is insufficient and iniquitous. India's allocation for public health is indeed pitiful—0.9 per cent of GDP. Shamefully, our public health expenditure at 17 per cent of total health expenditure is comparable to that of failed societies like Cambodia, Burma, Afghanistan and Georgia. Many studies reveal that on an average, s/he spends 60 per cent of the annual income towards medical costs for a single episode of hospitalisation—whether in private facility or in government hospital. Consequently, 40 per cent of hospitalised Indians are forced to sell their properties or borrow at high interest rates. This results in a good 25 per cent falling below the poverty line. Most of this burden is borne by the poor, unorganised sectors of population.

China may run medical schools to educate Indians at moderate costs; US and Europe may attract bright Indian youngsters to their universities; India may have the potential to create world-class facilities to meet our growing needs and become the hub of global education and health services. But our politicians are oblivious to the challenges of today, and frame lazy policies and execute them incompetently.

## Vicious Cycles

The distortions of our political process have significantly eroded the State's capacity for good governance. First, the positive power to promote public good has been severely restricted; while the negative power of undermining public interest is largely unchecked. Authority is delinked from accountability at most levels, and in respect of most functions. As a result, most State functionaries have realistic and plausible alibis for non-performance. Second, while the electoral system has demonstrated great propensity to change governments and politicians in power, the rules of the game remain largely unchanged. Increasingly, honesty and survival in political office are incompatible. Third, all organs of State are affected by the malaise of governance. Political executive, legislature, bureaucracy and judiciary—no class of functionaries can escape blame. For instance, 2.5 crore cases are pending in courts, and justice is inaccessible, painfully slow and costly. Fourth, at the citizen's level, there are no sufficient incentives for better behaviour. Good behaviour is not rewarded sufficiently and consistently, and bad behaviour is not only not punished consistently, it is in fact rewarded extravagantly. As a result, deviant and socially debilitating behaviour has become prevalent, and short-term individual interest has gained precedence over public good.

## Interlocking Vicious Cycles

In a well-functioning democracy, the political process ought to find answers to governance problems. Every election holds a promise for peaceful change. People in India have been voting for change, time and again. But the political process is locked into a vicious cycle, and has become a part of the problem. There are several factors complicating the political process, perpetuating the *status quo*.

First, election expenditures are large, unaccounted and mostly illegitimate. For instance, expenditure limit for Assembly elections in most major States was Rs. 6 lakh until recently, when it has been revised to Rs. 10 lakh. In reality average expenditure in most states is several multiples of it, sometimes exceeding Rs. 1 crore. Most of this expenditure is incurred to buy votes, bribe officials and hire musclemen. Sadly, the southern states, which are hailed for better governance, have the dubious distinction of being the worst offenders in this regard. The expenditure incurred in Andhra Pradesh in the current Assembly and Lok Sabha polls is estimated to be about Rs. 800–1000 crores. On an average, the leading candidates for Assembly spend Rs. 1 to 1.5 crores each, and those for Lok Sabha about Rs. 3–4 crores each. The expenditure in the Kanakapura by-election (in Karnataka) for Lok Sabha held in 2003 was estimated by knowledgeable people at about Rs. 20 crores! The eventual winner was reported to have been heavily outspent by his nearest rival. Curiously, the stakes in that by-election were limited: only a few months of Lok Sabha membership was at stake, and both the leading contenders would have to sit only in opposition! Saidapet by-election in Tamil Nadu Assembly too was said to have broken records, with expenses exceeding Rs. 10 crores!

There are three features of such skyrocketing election expenses. First, large expenditure does not guarantee victory; but inability to incur huge expenses almost certainly guarantees defeat! There are a few candidates who win without large expenditure, but such constituencies are limited. Also in great waves, expenditure is irrelevant. The Lok Sabha victory of Congress in 1971, Janata in 1977, NTR's victory in Andhra Pradesh in 1983—these are among the many examples when money power had no role. But in the absence of ideology, and increasing cynicism, large expenditure has become necessary to win. Desperate to win at any cost, parties are compelled to nominate mostly those candidates who can spend big money. Such large, unaccounted expenditure can be sustained only if the system is abused to enable multiple returns on investment. The economic decision-making power of the State is on the wane as part of the reform process. But as the demand for illegitimate political funds is not reduced, corruption is shifting to the core areas of State functioning, like crime investigation. Robert Wade studied this phenomenon of corruption, and described the dangerously stable equilibrium, which operates in Indian governance. This vicious chain of corruption has created a class of political and bureaucratic 'entrepreneurs' who treat public office as big business.

Second, as the vicious cycle of money power, polling irregularities, and corruption has taken hold of the system, electoral verdicts ceased to make a difference to people. Repeated disappointments made people come to the conclusion that no matter who wins the election, they always end up losing. As incentive for discerning behaviour in voting has disappeared, people started maximising their short-term returns. As a result, money and liquor are accepted habitually by many voters. This pattern of behaviour only converted politics and elections into big business. As illegitimate electoral expenditure skyrocketed, the vicious cycle of corruption is further strengthened. With public good delinked from voting, honesty and survival in public office are further separated.

Third, this situation bred a class of political 'entrepreneurs' who established fiefdoms. In most constituencies, money power, caste clout, bureaucratic links, and political contacts came together, perpetuating politics of fiefdoms. Entry into electoral politics is restricted in real terms, as people who cannot muster these forces have little chance of getting elected. While there is competition for political power, it is often restricted between two or three families over a long period of time; parties are compelled to choose one of these individuals or families to enhance their chances of electoral success. Parties thus are helpless, and political process is stymied. Absence of internal democratic norms in parties and the consequent oligarchic control has denied a possibility of rejuvenation of political process through establishment of a virtuous cycle.

Fourth, in a centralised governance system, even if the vote is wisely used by people, public good cannot be promoted. As the citizen is distanced from the decision making process, the administrative machinery has no capacity to deliver public services of high quality or low cost. Such a climate which cannot ensure better services or good governance breeds competitive populism to gain electoral advantage. Such populist politics have led to serious fiscal imbalances.

Fifth, fiscal health can be restored only by higher taxes, or reduced subsidies or wages. The total tax revenues of the Union and States are of the order of only 15 per cent of GDP. Higher taxation is resisted in the face of ubiquitous corruption and poor quality services. De-subsidisation is always painful for the poor who do not see alternative benefits accruing from the money saved by withdrawal of subsidies. A vast bureaucracy under centralised control can neither be held to account, nor is wage reduction a realistic option.

Sixth, elected governments are helpless to change this perilous situation. As the survival of the government depends on the support of legislators, their demands have to be met. The legislator has thus become the disguised, unaccountable executive controlling all facets of government functioning. The local legislator and the bureaucrats have a vested interest in denying local governments any say in real decision making. The vicious cycle of corruption and centralised, unaccountable governance is thus perpetuated.

Seventh, the first-past-the-post (FPTP) system exacerbates our social divisions as it tends to over-represent geographically concentrated social groups and underrepresent the scattered minorities. This representational distortion leads to ghettoisation and marginalisation of the excluded social groups, which then indulge in strategic voting. This gives rise to vote-bank politics in which obscurantists become interlocutors of the group drowning the voice of reason and modernity. For instance, religious symbolism and not education and job opportunities become dominant issues of public discourse. This pandering of fundamentalism leads to competitive mobilisation of various groups based on primordial loyalties, leading to communal polarisation and social strife.

Eighth, the need for money power and caste clout to win a plurality of votes in FPTP system precludes political participation of men and women of integrity and competence. With their exclusion, bad public policy and incompetent governance become endemic, deepening the crisis.

Ninth, under FPTP system, only a high threshold of voting ensures victory. Usually a party needs 35 per cent vote or more to get reasonable representation in legislature, or social groups with local dominance get elected. As a significant but scattered support pays no electoral dividends, reform groups and parties below the threshold tend to wither away. Voters prefer other 'winnable' parties and candidates. This tends to marginalise reform parties, and national parties in many states. It is no accident that the main national parties, Congress and BJP, are directly competing for power in only a few major states. In most states, one or two regional parties are dominant. FPTP thus tends to lead to oligopoly of parties.

## Social infrastructure and Good Governance: A *Sine Qua Non* for Growth

Given this complex nature of our crisis, we need a multipronged strategy to improve the efficiency of governance machinery in order to have a faster and equitable growth. However, can something be done to accelerate growth within the stated fiscal and political constraints? In other words, are there painless, low-cost solutions? Happily, there are at least four areas of improvements which will raise growth rates spectacularly. All these are politically feasible, win-win solutions, which can be implemented within the present or projected budgetary allocations.

First, delivery of education—at both school and university level. Allocations for schools have gone up, and the recent education cess is universally accepted. But even in this day and age, our focus is merely on enrolment and retention, and not on quality. As a result, much of our education is futile. Functional literacy, communication skills, conceptual clarity, skill promotion, and creation of meaningful knowledge and its application form the essence of education.

Except for a few elite schools and colleges, and a small proportion of gifted children, most of our education is unproductive. As a result, millions of unemployable school and college graduates are churned out every year. Happily, there is phenomenal demand for quality education. Even the poor are willing to spend considerable sums for education, in the hope of a better future for their children. Sensible policies and non-monetary inputs based on best practices will improve the quality of human power, and enhance growth rate by at least one per cent.

Second, our healthcare system is in shambles. The government's record in public health is appalling. A few correctives are being applied in recent years, and the Prime Minister launched the Health Mission in April, 2005. But more allocations and better infrastructure alone are not sufficient. Avoidable hospital costs and sickness are the chief causes of poverty, indebtedness and low productivity. Decentralised management, accountability to the community, integration of various health programmes and nutrition, water supply and sanitation at the grassroots level, and most of all, choice, competition and altered incentives in hospital management are the critical changes in trajectory in healthcare delivery. If there is a genuine change of course, even the projected modest enhancements in allocations for public health will ease the suffering of the bulk of our people, raise their productivity and incomes, and substantially accelerate growth.

Third, rule of law is the bedrock of market economy and growth. Proper land surveys, assured property titles, speedy and fair adjudication of disputes, swift punishments for violation of law, quick and effective enforcement of contracts and non-discriminatory treatment are all critical requirements to ensure predictability and encourage investment, risk-taking and hardwork. While normatively we have an independent judiciary and institutions of rule of law, in reality they are moribund and ineffective. As a result, there is a growing market demand for criminals in society, and mafia and musclemen have become the undeclared judges dispensing rough and ready justice by brutal means for a price. There are reports of even a few foreign banks in India hiring musclemen to enforce recovery of overdues. Clearly such a climate inhibits economic activity and retards growth. There are many low cost, politically acceptable, popular mechanisms to improve justice delivery and rule of law. This alone will enhance growth by at least one per cent per annum.

Fourth, extortionary corruption and arbitrariness in tax departments are sapping the energies of small and medium enterprises and seriously eroding the competitiveness of our manufacturing sector. The direct taxes have witnessed some measurable improvements. But the administration of central excise, service tax, customs and state-level sales tax are still largely discretionary, unpredictable and arbitrary. Rent-seeking behaviour is therefore exceedingly common, seriously undermining the competitiveness of honest tax payers, and diverting the precious time and energy of the entrepreneurs. Transparent, industry-friendly procedures will not only help the economy, but will also enhance revenues. It costs no money, and yet boosts growth.

Improvements in these four sectors cost little, make the government popular, accelerate economic growth by 3-4 per cent, promote investment and employment generation, and create several virtuous cycles of growth, savings and investment. All these are eminently feasible, but require bureaucratic accountability and delivery of services, sound, self-correcting, sustainable policies, and display of minimum level of political skills to build consensus and mobilise public opinion in favour of these improvements.

Apart from the sectoral reforms mentioned above, we need to involve civil society and ordinary citizens to improve efficiency and combat corruption in the State apparatus. There are mechanisms for involving citizens directly in the fight against corruption. In the US, there is a law called False Claims Act, which directly empowers citizens. Any citizen can file a civil suit on behalf of the Federal Government if there is corruption and loss to the public exchequer— directly in monetary terms, or indirectly by way of social or environmental costs. The court is empowered to swiftly try such cases called *qui tam* suits, and impose a penalty equal to three times the loss sustained. The citizen gets 15-35 per cent of the penalty as compensation for his initiative, depending on the degree of involvement. Over the past 15 years, nearly $15 billion was thus recovered in these *qui tam* suits.

Right to information, citizen's charters, and other people-friendly measures of accountability are powerful weapons in the fight against corruption. In Andhra Pradesh, a citizen's charter for the municipalities provides for a compensation of Rs. 50 per day's delay in a few basic services. This measure, which came about because of Lok Satta's advocacy, has had a very salutary effect in improving those services and minimising corruption. Surveys reveal that in those services, satisfaction levels now are over 90 per cent. The recently enacted Right to Information law is well-drafted and citizen-friendly. Once this is operationalised in all agencies, states and local governments, it will be a powerful tool in the hands of citizens. Civil society organisations need to seize the opportunity and educate, organise, and mobilise the public in this fight against corruption.

Finally, we must recognise that our political system itself is founded on corruption. Vast, illegitimate expenditure in elections and multiple returns in office have become a vicious cycle distorting our democracy. Politics has become big business. Increasingly, a new class of entrepreneurs who are willing to 'invest' vast sums is attracted to politics. There is thus an inexhaustible appetite for illegitimate funds in our system. Every lever of State is manipulated to get multiple returns on investment. The estimated expenditure of candidates and parties, in elections for Lok Sabha and State Assemblies in a cycle of five years is about Rs. 10,000 crore. Most of it is illegitimate and unaccounted for. The system can be sustained only if there is a ten-fold return to politicians to cover risk, return on investment, provisioning for the next election, upkeep of an army of political 'workers,' and private gain. In return, politicians created a system of rent-seeking, with corruption proceeds shared with the bureaucracy. Given that the employees extorting money vastly outnumber politicians, the actual corruption over a five-year period to sustain this corruption chain is of the order of Rs. 10,00,000 crore or Rs. 2,00,000 crore per annum. This is the burden of corruption that citizens face. The message is clear: corruption can be substantially eradicated; but it needs painstaking efforts and will, and most of all, far-reaching political reforms. In my considered judgment, there are three such reforms required.

## Political Reforms

### Mixed Compensatory Proportional Representation

The first-past-the-post (FPTP) system that India has adopted led to several distortions, given the passage of time and ingenuity of legislators. Politics of fiefdom at constituency level has forced the parties to rely on local strongmen. As a result, the political parties and independent candidates have astronomical election expenditure for vote buying and other illegitimate purposes. This has led to a significant weakening of the party platform and ideology, reducing elections to private power games. In many States, national parties have been marginalised where their voting percentage falls below a threshold. Following this, regional parties have occupied centre stage in several pockets, holding larger interests at ransom.

All these failings find expression in serious and long-term predicaments. The inability of all political parties to attract and nurture best talent is the primary issue. Difficulties of minority representation leading to ghetto mentality, backlash, and communal tension form another facet of the problem. Lastly, leadership is undermined by permanent reservation of constituencies (or regular rotation) in order to provide fair representation to excluded groups. The solution to this flawed system is adoption of proportional representation.

Pure proportional representation (PR) in India would invite three legitimate objections. First, in a caste-ridden society, PR will lead to further political fragmentation, mushrooming of parties, and greater social schism. The answer to this problem lies in having a reasonable threshold of voting requirement, of say 10 per cent of votes polled in major states, for representation in legislature. Second, party bosses will become even more autocratic in nomination of candidates in list system. This tendency can be curbed by political party reform, mandating choice of candidates for elective office by members of the party or their elected delegates through secret ballot at the local level. Third, people are used to a system of territorial representation, and PR snaps the link between the constituency and its elected legislator. This can be addressed by electing half the legislators from single-member constituencies as now, and electing the rest from party lists in a manner that the final composition of legislature is based on the principle of proportionality of votes. The key features of the suggested system are as follows:

- The overall representation of parties in legislature will be based on the proportion of valid vote obtained by them.

- A party will be entitled to such a quota based on vote share only when it crosses a threshold, say 10 per cent of vote in a major State, and more in minor States.

- Fifty per cent of legislators will be elected from territorial constituencies based on FPTP system. This will ensure the link between the legislator and the constituents.

- The balance 50 per cent will be allotted to parties to make up for their shortfall based on proportion of votes.

  e.g. 1): If the party is entitled to 50 seats in legislature based on vote share, but has 30 members elected in FPTP system, 20 more will be elected based on the party list.

  e.g. 2): If the party is entitled to 50 seats based on vote share, but has only 10 members elected in FPTP system, it will have 40 members elected from the list.

- The party lists will be selected democratically at the state or multi-party constituency level by the members of the party or their elected delegates through secret ballot.

- There will be two votes cast by voters—one for a candidate for FPTP election, and the other for a party to determine the vote share of the parties.

It needs to be remembered that PR system can be effective only after internal functioning of political parties is regulated by law. Otherwise, PR system will give extraordinary power to party leaders and may prove counterproductive. However, the PR system has one more advantage of ensuring better representation of women in legislatures.

*Political Party Regulation by Law*

Political recruitment has suffered a great deal, and bright young people are no longer attracted to politics. Centralised functioning of parties is imposing enormous burden on leadership to manage the party bureaucracy, leaving little time for evolving sensible policies or governance. Party leaders are helpless in candidate selection, and the choice is often between tweedledum and tweedledee. An important reform to improve the quality of politics and restore credibility would be a law to regulate political parties' functioning, without in any way restricting leadership choice and policy options. A law needs to be enacted to regulate political parties in the following four key aspects:

- Free and open membership with no arbitrary expulsions.

- Democratic, regular, free, secret ballot for leadership election; and opportunity to challenge and unseat leadership through formal procedures with no risk of being penalised.

- Democratic choice of party candidates for elective office by members or their elected delegates through secret ballot.

- Full transparency in funding and utilisation of resources.

## Clear Separation of Powers at the State and Local Levels through Direct Election of Head of Government

The other systemic reform that is needed to isolate the executive from unwanted influences, as has been pointed out, is to ensure direct election of head of government in states and local governments.

As election costs have skyrocketed, candidates spend money in anticipation of rewards and opportunities for private gain after election. Legislators perceive themselves as disguised executive, and Chief Ministers are hard pressed to meet their constant demands. Postings, transfers, contracts, tenders, tollgates, parole, developmental schemes, and crime investigation—all these become sources of patronage and rent-seeking. No government functioning honestly can survive under such circumstances. While the legislators never allow objective and balanced decision-making by the executive in the actual functioning of legislation, their role has become nominal and largely inconsequential. This blurring of the lines of demarcation between the executive and legislature is one of the cardinal features of the crisis of our governance system.

Therefore, separation of powers, and direct election are necessary in states and local governments. At the national level, such a direct election is fraught with serious dangers. Our linguistic diversity demands a parliamentary executive. Any individual seen as the symbol of all authority can easily become despotic, given our political culture. But in States, separation of powers poses no such dangers. The Union Government, Supreme Court, constitutional functionaries like the Election Commission, UPSC, and CAG, and the enormous powers and prestige of the Union will easily control authoritarianism in any State. This necessitates adoption of a system of direct election of the head of government in states and local governments. The fundamental changes suggested find mention as under:

The legislature will be elected separately and directly, while the ministers will be drawn from outside the legislature. The legislature will have a fixed term, and cannot be dissolved prematurely except in exceptional circumstances (sedition, secession, etc.) by the Union Government. The head of government will have a fixed term, and cannot be voted out of office by the legislature. Any vacancy of office will be filled by a due process of succession. The elected head of government will have no more than two terms of office. Even though these changes may not be panacea to all evils in the present structure of legislature and executive, they will certainly encourage more healthy and vibrant democracy and democratic processes. Further, clear and periodic delineation of functions between Union and States, and among various tiers of local governments, is also a necessary condition for a vibrant democracy. It is only a true federal structure that can ensure unity in this multi-ethnic and multi-religious society.

We need to remember that the economic growth rate of a country is not merely a product of economic policies and productive capacity of its industry and agriculture. The economic growth rate of a country is also contingent on the way it governs itself. The collapse of erstwhile Soviet Union bears testimony to this fact. This combined with the experience of the transition countries demonstrate that good governance is a prerequisite for economic growth. The above enunciated measures constitute good governance, and that is what is lacking now. Freedom is not a liability; it is a glorious asset for growth. Sound politics is about making democracy and growth compatible, not finding alibis for non-performance. We can, and should, overtake China in long-term growth. But we need to set our house in order first.

# Comparison of India and China Development Paths

# 4

# China and India

## A Comparison of Recent Development Trajectories

### JAYATI GHOSH

Academic comparisons of China and India have been around for several decades, but in recent years they have gone beyond the usual cottage industry of professionals to dominating discussions even in policy circles around the world. Even in the international press, there is almost an obsession with these two economies, and how their current growth presages the coming 'Asian century'. It is not just that they are both countries with large populations covering substantial and diverse geographical areas, and therefore, with currently large economies and even more huge potential economic size. Most of all, they are cited as the current 'success stories': two economies in the developing world that have apparently benefited from globalisation, with relatively high and stable rates of growth for more than two decades and substantial diversification. The success is defined by the high and sustained rates of growth of aggregate and per capita national income; the absence of major financial crises that have characterised a number of other emerging markets; and substantial reduction in income poverty.

In India too, the obsession with China is now well-developed, mostly in the form of a longing eastern gaze. The rapid economic growth and structural transformation in China are not just eyed with envy; they are typically invoked to justify the economic policy of choice. Thus, there are those who argue that the recent Chinese economic success is because of liberalisation and openness to foreign trade and investment. By contrast, others point out that the early Communist history of land reforms and egalitarian policies formed the essential basis upon which all subsequent change has depended.

In the outside literature, these economies are often treated as broadly similar in terms of growth potential and other features, and this even infects some Indian analyses. But in fact, there are crucial differences between the two economies which render such similarities very superficial, and which mean that individual policies cannot be taken out of context of one country and simply applied in the other to the same effect. This chapter dwells upon the differences, of which there are at least 10 that are significant.

The first relates to the nature of the economy itself, the institutional conditions within which policies are formulated and implemented. India could be described until recently, as a traditional 'mixed economy' with a large private sector, so it was and remains a capitalist market economy with the associated tendency to involuntary unemployment. Even during the period of the 'dirigiste' regime of the 1950s and 1960s, the emphasis was dominantly on the regulation of private capital rather than actual determination of levels of production by the state. The neoliberal reforms undertaken in the phase of globalisation have, however, substantially expanded the scope for private activity and reduced regulation. Essentially, macroeconomic policies in India have been designed and implemented in contexts similar to those in other capitalist economies, where involuntary unemployment is rampant and fiscal and monetary measures have to be used to stimulate effective demand. This need for macroeconomic policies to stimulate demand operated, in addition to the usual 'developmental' role of the state.

China, by contrast, has been for the most part a command economy, which until recently had a very small private sector, and only recognised the legal possibility of homegrown capitalists a few years ago. Throughout the period of 'liberalisation', that is the 1990s and later, there have remained important forms of state control over macroeconomic processes that have differed from more conventional capitalist macroeconomic policy. Even in 2004, public enterprises accounted for more than half of GDP and more than two-fifths of exports.

The control over the domestic economy in China has been most significant in terms of the financial sector, which describes the second big difference between the two economies. In India, the financial sector was typical of the 'mixed economy' and even bank nationalisation did not lead to comprehensive government control over the financial system; in any case, financial liberalisation over the 1990s, has involved a progressive deregulation and further loss of control over financial allocations by the state in India.

But the financial system in China still remains heavily under the control of the state, despite recent liberalisation. Four major public sector banks handle the bulk of the transactions in the economy, and the Chinese authorities have essentially used control over the consequent financial flows to regulate the volume of credit (and therefore, mange the economic cycle) as well as to direct credit to priority sectors. Off-budget official finance (called "fund-raising" by firms) has accounted for more than half of capital formation in China even in recent years, and that together with direct budgetary appropriations have determined nearly two-thirds of the level of aggregate investment.[1] This means that there has been less need for more conventional fiscal and monetary policies, although the Chinese economy is now in the process of transition to the more standard pattern.

The third difference is quite apparent to all—the dramatically high rate of GDP growth in China compared to the more moderate expansion in India. The Chinese economy has grown at an average annual rate of 9.8 per cent for two and a half decades, while India's economy has grown at around 5-6 per cent per year over the same period. Chinese growth has been relatively volatile around this trend, reflecting stop-go cycles of state response to inflation through aggregate credit management. The Indian economy broke from its average post-Independence annual rate of around 3 per cent growth to achieve annual rates of more than 5 per cent from the early 1980s. The most recent period has witnessed even higher rates, although these are still well below the Chinese averages over the same period.

This higher growth in China essentially occurs because of the fourth major difference, the much higher rate of investment in China. The investment rate in China (investment as a share of GDP) has fluctuated between 35 and 44 per cent over the past 25 years,

---

1. In 2003, for example, direct state budgetary appropriation accounted for less than 5 per cent of the financing of total fixed capital formation, but "fund-raising" accounted for 54 per cent and bank loans from the government-controlled banking system accounted for another 20 per cent (*China Statistical Yearbook*, 2004).

compared to 20 to 26 per cent in India. In fact, the aggregate ICORs (incremental capital-output ratios) have been around the same in both economies). Within this, there is the critical role of infrastructure investment, which has averaged 19 per cent of GDP in China compared to 2 per cent in India from the early 1990s.[2]

It is sometimes argued, that China can afford to have such a high investment rate because it has attracted so much foreign direct investment (FDI), and is the second largest recipient of FDI in the world at present. But FDI has accounted for only 3-5 per cent of GDP in China since 1990, and at its peak was still only 8 per cent. In the period after 2000, FDI has accounted for only 6 per cent of domestic investment. In fact in recent times, the inflow of capital has not added to the domestic investment rate at all, macroeconomically speaking, but has essentially led to the further accumulation of international reserves, which have been increasing by more than $ 100 billion per year.

In terms of economic diversification and structural change, China has followed what could be described as the classic industrialisation pattern, moving from primary to manufacturing activities in the past 25 years. The manufacturing sector has doubled its share of work force and tripled its share of output, which, given the size of the Chinese economy and population, has increasingly made China 'the workshop of the world'. In India, by contrast, the move has been mainly from agriculture to services in share of output, with no substantial increase in manufacturing, and the structure of employment has been stubbornly resistant to change. The share of the primary sector in national income has fallen from 60 per cent in the early 1950s to 25 per cent between 2001 and 2003, but the share of the primary sector in employment continues to be more than 60 per cent, indicating a worrying persistence of low productivity employment for most of the labour force. The higher rates of investment in India over the past two decades have not generated more expansion of industry in terms of share of GDP, but have instead been associated with an apparent explosion in services, that catch-all sector of varying components. The recent expansion of some services employment in India has been at both high and low value-

---

2. *China Statistical Yearbook*, various years.

added ends of the services sub-sectors, reflecting both some dynamism and some increase in 'refuge' low productivity employment.

The sixth major difference, relate to trade policy and trade patterns. Chinese export growth has been much more rapid, involving aggressive increases on world market shares. This export growth has been based on relocative capital, which has been attracted not only by cheap labour but also by excellent and heavily subsidised infrastructure resulting from the high rate of infrastructure investment. In addition, since the Chinese state has also been keen on provision of basic goods in terms of housing, food and cheap transport facilities, this has played an important role in reducing labour costs for employers. In India, the cheap labour has been because of low absolute wages rather than public provision and underwriting of labour costs, and infrastructure development has been minimal. So it is not surprising that it has not really been an attractive location for export-oriented investment, its rate of export growth has been much lower, and exports have not become an engine of growth.

There is another issue relating to trade policy. In China, the rapid export growth generated employment which was a net addition to domestic employment, since until 2002, China had undertaken much less trade liberalisation than most other developing countries. This is why manufacturing employment grew so rapidly in China, because it was not counterbalanced by any loss of employment through the effects of displacement of domestic industry because of import competition. This is unlike the case in India, where increases in export employment were outweighed by employment losses, especially in small enterprises because of import competition.

The seventh difference is in terms of poverty reduction. China has been much more successful in this regard—official data suggest that 4 per cent of the population now lives under the poverty line, unofficial estimates suggest around 12 per cent. The poverty ratio in India is much higher, between 26 per cent and 34 per cent depending upon how one interprets the 1999-00 NSS data. The Chinese success in this regard can be related to several features, but it must be borne in mind that fundamentally we are talking of two very different economic systems under which poverty reduction occurred. To begin with, the basic issues in terms of asset redistribution and basic needs provision were the focus of the Chinese Communist State until the late 1970s. This also assisted in economic growth: because of the more egalitarian system, there was a larger mass market for consumption goods, which has allowed producers to take advantage of economies of scale.

Subsequently, poverty reduction in China has been concentrated into two main phases: 1979-1982 and 1994-1996, which were both phases of higher crop prices and rising agricultural incomes. In the first phase, institutional change in the form of allowing peasant production in diversified crops played a great role in increasing productivity and allowing peasants to benefit from rising prices. Also, since Chinese economic growth has been more employment generating, this has also operated to reduce poverty.

Until recently, there was much more focus on 'human development' in China, and public provision of health and education. This included universal education until Class X, as well as better public services to ensure nutrition, health and sanitation. However, in recent years, this emphasis has been much reduced and there is greater privatisation of such services in China, which has also led to worsening conditions, especially in particular areas. In India, the public provision of all of these has been extremely inadequate throughout this period and has deteriorated in per capita terms since the early 1990s.

In terms of inequality, in both economies the recent pattern of growth has been unequalising. In China the spatial inequalities—across regions—have been the sharpest. In India, vertical inequalities and the rural-urban divide have become much more marked. In China recently, as a response to this, there have been some top-down measures to reduce inequality, for example, through changes in tax rates, greater public investment in western and interior regions and improved social-security benefits. In India, it is political change that has forced greater attention to redressing inequalities, though the process is still very incipient.

This brings into focus the tenth big difference: that of political systems. It can be argued that the political democracy in India, which now appears deeply entrenched even though it has not translated into universal economic enfranchisement, has played some role in creating more confused but less extreme patterns of economic growth. Certainly, the historic and potentially transformatory economic legislation such as the National Rural Employment Guarantee Act which was enacted in 2004, could only come about because of impact of political changes. Perhaps, the ability of the economic system to force at least some change of direction in economic policies in India can serve as an important example to the rest of the world, and one of which Indian can justly be proud.

However, in terms of the future prospects, surprisingly both economies end up with very similar issues despite these major differences. There are clear questions of sustainability of the current pattern of economic expansion in China, since it is based on a high export-high accumulation model, which requires constantly increasing shares of world markets and very high investment rates. Similarly, the hope in some policy quarters in India that IT-enabled services can become the engine of growth for the entire economy is one which raises questions of sustainability, quite apart from questions about whether it will be enough to transform India's huge labour force into higher productivity activities.

The most important current problems in the two economies are also rather similar—the agrarian crisis and the need to generate more employment. In both economies, the social sectors have been neglected recently by public intervention. In both countries, therefore, despite the very different institutional conditions and the dissimilarities even in the way that recent economic trends have played out, the policy message appears to be the same, and may be what the rest of the developing world also should note. This message is that the most basic issues of food, livelihood and employment security, as well as of basic needs for the population, are those that require to be addressed first, and if these can be dealt with successfully, the other areas of expansion will probably look after themselves.

---

This lecture draws on joint work with C.P. Chandrasekhar.

# References

Chandrasekhar, C.P. and Jayati Ghosh (2006). "Macroeconomic Policy, Inequality and Poverty Reduction in India and China", in Andrea Cornia (ed.), *Pro-poor Macroeconomic Policies: A Consideration of Developing Country Experiences*, Macmillan-Palgrave, London. (Further references cited therein.)

# Comparison of Indian Fiscal Federalism

# 5

## Fiscal Federalism in India

*Emerging Challenges*

M. GOVINDA RAO

### Introduction

I have chosen to write on a subject in which I presume I have some comparative advantage namely, challenges in Indian fiscal federalism in the emerging political and economic environment. Some of the challenges arise from inherent shortcomings of the policies and institutions of the fiscal system evolved over the years. Others are exogenous, they arise from changing economic and political environment. Any forward looking reform agenda has to recognise not only the basic shortcomings in the system but also should examine and identify the challenges that are faced in the emerging political and economic environment.

### Challenges

Discussion on the emerging challenges on Indian fiscal federalism is important for a number of reasons. First, the changing role of the state and market on the one hand and opening up of the economy and internationalisation of economic activities on the other, call for significant changes in inter-governmental policies and institutions.[1] Second, declining fiscal health of the states and the focus of fiscal adjustment on reducing fiscal deficits during the last decade and a half has compressed allocations to physical infrastructure and human development and the problem is particularly severe in poorer states (Rao and Chakraborty, 2006). Third, transition from plan to market involves many difficult reforms in both policies and institutions. These relate to pricing and output policies, removal of regulations,

---

1. For a detailed analysis of challenges of federalism in a globalising environment in a number of countries developed and developing, see, Wallack and Srinivasan (2006).

promotion of nationwide common market, changes in policies relating to regional resource allocations and replacing enterprise revenues with taxes (Rao, 2006). Fourth, changing political environment poses significant challenges for Indian fiscal federalism as well. The emergence of coalition government at the centre, regional parties in states and the latter becoming 'pivotal' members of the ruling central coalition have important implications for the functioning of the multilevel fiscal system. In addition, declining time horizon of political parties and politicians have led to 'competitive populism', vitiated political competition and have posed serious challenges to the system of 'checks and balances'.[2] Finally, despite the constitutional recognition of the third tier of government, much remains to be done to make them effective. With *Gram Panchayats* assigned an important role in the implementation of Rural Employment Guarantee Act, the challenge of capacity building in them and instituting the system of peoples' participation in decision making to prevent elite capture is also formidable. Let me discuss each of these challenges.

### Deterioration in State Finances

A major challenge to Indian fiscal federalism arises from the steady deterioration in fiscal health of the states. These have macroeconomic implications as the aggregate revenue deficits of the states during 2000-03 averaged over 3 per cent of GSDP and aggregate fiscal deficits was estimated at over 5 per cent of GSDP. In addition, there are deficits in the public enterprise account and power sector deficits alone amount to about 1.4 per cent of GSDP. The severity of fiscal stress can have microeconomic implications as well. It can constrain allocations for the maintenance of physical infrastructure and social development.

The increasing fiscal imbalances at the state level has been a matter of concern and every Finance Commission subsequent to the Ninth has been asked to draw up fiscal restructuring plan to reduce deficits and create surpluses in the revenue account and reduce fiscal deficits. In fact, the Twelfth Finance Commission (TFC) was asked to

---

2. A detailed analysis of political influencing intergovernmental fiscal outcomes is available in Rao and Singh (2005).

draw up a restructuring "...plan by which the governments, collectively and severally, may bring about restructuring of public finances restoring budgetary balance, achieving macroeconomic stability and debt reduction along with equitable growth." While the focus of all these attempts has been to reduce revenue and fiscal deficits, the fiscal stress manifests itself in different ways depending on their response to the situations. This includes, besides increase in deficits, reduction in spending on basic public services itself.

This is amply illustrated by the fact that from the yardstick of deficits, the two poorest states, Bihar and Uttar Pradesh have performed reasonably well. However, this should not be taken to mean that severity of their fiscal problems is any less. In fact, low deficit situation in them is due to cutting down of developmental expenditures. In fact, an important fiscal outcome of prevailing system is the high positive correlation of per capita development expenditures with per capita incomes of the states with significant implications for further accentuation of inter-state disparities.

The two worst case scenarios of fiscal and revenue deficits are those of West Bengal and Punjab. Gujarat too had high level of revenue and fiscal deficits in 2000-01 due to the earthquake, but since then it has come down. In general, the middle income states except West Bengal have shown a better performance in containing their deficits than other states. On the whole, the performances of Tamil Nadu and Haryana were better than other states. Interestingly, there is no association between the per capita income levels and revenue and fiscal deficits. The correlation coefficients of revenue and fiscal deficits with per capita GSDP in non-special category states are not significant.

The evidence that the poorer states tried to contain their deficits by cutting developmental expenditures may be seen from the fact that per capita development expenditure in 2002-03 in Bihar at Rs. 1075 was lower than the average of non-special category States (Rs. 2035) by 48 per cent and in Uttar Pradesh (Rs. 1187) it was lower by 42 per cent. In general, it is seen that while revenue and fiscal deficits had no significant correlation with per capita GSDP, per capita expenditure was significantly lower in states with low per capita GSDP with a correlation coefficient of 0.813.

*Increasing Inequalities in States*

It is by now well recorded that acceleration of growth in the aftermath of economic reforms in 1991 was accompanied by widening inter-state disparities. The analysis shows that correlation coefficient between the level of per capita incomes and their growth rates was 0.331 during the 1991-2001 and if the two agricultural states, Punjab and Haryana are excluded, it is 0.77. Economic liberalisation and opening up of the economy during the 1990s seems to have benefited the states with a stronger manufacturing base and with more developed market institutions than the states which are predominantly agricultural.

Another interesting feature of the pattern of growth is that, the relative positions of the lowest and highest per capita income States have not changed. Bihar continues to be the lowest per capita income state and Punjab has continued to hold the top spot among the non-special category states (excluding the small state of Goa). In the case of Bihar, in particular, per capita GSDP has steadily deteriorated in relation to that of the all-India average, the position of Punjab has improved, particularly after the mid-1990s. Thus, there has been increasing divergence in the per capita income levels between the states with the lowest and the highest per capita GSDP. Low levels of per capita development expenditures in poorer states in the context of sharply accentuating disparities in income levels present a serious challenge to Indian federalism.

*Transition from Plan to Market*

Another important challenge of Indian federalism is to gear up to the changing requirement of transition from plan to market. The transition from plan to market involves applying market principles for allocating resources. This calls for changes in fiscal federalism practices. This, in itself, is a major challenge that has to be undertaken to ensure that market based liberalisation has accommodating inter-governmental policies and institutions. The detailed changes in the principles of federalism required for developing and transitional economies are discussed elsewhere and here some of these are summarised.

Centralised planning involves controls on prices and outputs. This causes transfer of resources between different states in unintended ways. Besides, planning also involves regional allocation of resources according to plan priorities, which may not be efficient, but are sustained in a closed economy. As the economy is liberalised and resources are allocated according to the market principles, it will minimise such implicit transfers and distortions, the production structure and the stock of capital created by past investments will continue to impact on future resource allocations.

Equally worrisome are the resource distortions caused by restrictions placed on the free movement of goods and factors. Ensuring a nationwide common market is an important objective of fiscal federalism. In India, violation of common market principles have also arisen from both fiscal and regulatory policies. The taxes on inter-state sale of goods, octroi are the important examples of the former. The restriction placed on the movement of goods under the Essential Commodities Act is the prime example of the latter. The consequence of all these is to segment the economy into several tariff zones within the country with unintended resource distortions the estimates of which are not available.

## Globalisation and Fiscal Federalism

Closely related to the above is the challenge arising from globalisation. Liberalisation of international trade and flow of international capital entails a number of important initiatives and they impact adversely on the fiscal systems of the states. Given the predominance of states in providing social services and coequal role in providing physical infrastructure, ensuring a level playing field in terms of competitiveness to domestic manufacturers requires large investments. The prevailing fiscal situation constrains this and the only feasible alternative is to forge private public partnerships. Promoting such partnerships requires significant changes not only in policies but setting up entire edifice of regulatory system.

Another aspect of liberalising imports is the loss of revenue from customs. This is a challenge faced all over the world and although not entirely adequate, the levy of VAT has been the often employed, to substitute revenue loss from reducing import duties. In Indian context, however, the power to levy VAT rests with the states. Not surprisingly, liberalisation of imports and reduction in customs tariff since 1991 has resulted in the loss of revenue and the ratio of GDP, the revenue declined by more than 2 percentage points from 3.6 per cent in 1990-91 to 1.5 per cent in 2004-05. Further liberalisation of imports will entail decline in the ratio even more. Improving the revenue productivity of domestic tax system to replace revenue loss from customs, therefore, remains an important challenge.

Globalisation brings with it, a greater international mobility of capital and skilled labour and the challenges of taxing them can be really daunting. The problems of transfer pricing, difficulties in taxing e-commerce are only some of the examples. As it is, the tax system in India suffers from narrow base with several exemptions and tax preferences and tax administration will have to gear up to meet greater complexities in taxing mobile capital and labour.

*Substituting Enterprise Revenues with Prices*

Another important policy issue involves replacement of public enterprise revenues with taxes. Much of the profits of public enterprises arise due to physical restrictions on imports and high tariffs—a part of import substituting industrialisation regime, and administered prices. Despite dismantling of administered price regime to a large extent, many of the prices continue to be determined through government fiat. When the administered prices are at work, particularly on commodities that are price inelastic, there is a very thin line dividing taxes and public enterprise profits. In fact, in India, over 40 per cent of indirect taxes including customs, excises and sales taxes are collected from petrol and diesel. Developing diversified tax base and improving the revenue productivity of the tax system is a major challenge for ensuring successful transition to the market.

A related issue pertaining to public enterprises is the way they have been used to soften the budget constraints at sub-national levels. In Indian context, the central government has been rescheduling and writing of the loans to them from time to time. The states too, found several means to soften their budget constraints by borrowing through their enterprises and borrowing through special purpose vehicles. Replacing central lending to states with market loans is a major challenge. Although the TFC has recommended this, the primary market for state government securities is yet to be developed. So far the Reserve Bank has played the role, but the imposition of market discipline in this area requires changes in policies, development of effective rating system, mechanism to deal with extremely poor and strategically located states.

### Challenges to Fiscal Federalism from Changing Political Environment

The most important challenge to Indian fiscal federalism, however, comes from the changing political environment. The dominance of single party in power at the centre and in the states for over a quarter century after Independence did not help to evolve the rules and conventions in conflicting situations. With the polarisation of political parties and competitive relationships between the centre and many of the states, both vertical and horizontal conflicting relationships have become real. The resolution of these conflicts will continue to be a major challenge in the years to come as has been demonstrated in the case of river water disputes in India.

An important political development is the emergence of coalition governments at the centre and regional parties at the states. The coalition of disparate parties with differing ideologies makes it difficult to forge consensus on major policy issues. When the regional parties become 'pivotal' members of the coalition, they tend to extract various concessions—political and economic and this can result in discretionary rather than rule based system of inter-governmental system. The asymmetric treatment could have long term implications for the stability of Indian federalism.

The discussion on political environment is not complete without referring to the declining time horizon of political parties and politicians. In the last Lok Sabha elections, only 32 per cent of the candidates were reelected. With low probability of getting re-elected, the political parties develop a short term rather than a long-term horizon. This has an adverse effects on long-term reforms in policies and institutions.

## Reforming Intergovernmental Policies and Institutions

I have tried to present some of the important challenges of federal fiscal arrangements in India in the changing political and economic environment. Some of the problems are inherent in the multilevel fiscal system itself, and others are due to methods and working of institutions.

There are two opposing forces at work on fiscal decentralisation. On the one hand, economic liberalisation and greater role for the market requires sub-national governments to assume larger role in creating the enabling environment for the private initiative to prosper. On the other hand, improvement in information technology has tended to reduce the transaction cost of central governments in providing sub-national public services. Yet, there is considerable lag in the adoption of technology by the governments and given the diversity in India, fiscal decentralisation will continue to be pursued. Therefore, reforms in fiscal federalism will continue to be a central theme in ensuring efficient public service provision and in creating an enabling business environment.

*Reforms in Tax Systems*

The starting point of reform is in the tax assignment system itself. For many reasons, it makes sense not to separate tax powers on incomes on the basis of their origin. At the same time, it makes a lot of sense to allow the state concurrent tax powers to taxes such as personal income taxes by allowing them to piggyback their levies on central levies. This will provide an important tax handle to the states. Of course, the transfer mechanism will have to take account of the skewed resource distribution arising from this and provide corrective.

Another major issue in overlapping tax powers is in consumption taxes. From the viewpoint of tax harmonisation, the levy on goods and services tax at the central level with separate central and state components worked out would seem appropriate. However, this has to be achieved with willing cooperation of the states and that does not seem feasible in the medium term. Therefore, the feasible solution would be to allow for dual VAT—the central VAT on goods and services up to the manufacturing stage and the state VAT up to the retail stage. This would also call for reassigning the taxation of services—to enable the states to levy the destination based retail VAT on goods and services. There are problems of assigning services with inter-state scope to states, but resolution of this may not be entirely satisfactory. Nevertheless, solution for this has to be found. Equally, if not more important is the issue of phasing out the taxes on inter-state sale without which the VAT can not acquire the character of destination based.

Phasing out inter-state sales tax is important also from the viewpoint of removing impediments to internal trade and establishing a common market in the country. On the same note, it is also possible to abolish octori and empower the urban local governments to levy an additional rate on the VAT on purchases within the municipal jurisdictions by different municipalities. These could be collected by the state tax administration and the proceeds could be appropriated by municipalities. This will further remove the impediments and provide the much needed resources to municipalities. Reforms are also necessary to remove restrictions on the movement of goods within the country under the Essential Commodities Act.

*Reforms in the Transfer System*

The most important reform in inter-governmental fiscal arrangement that is required is in the transfer system. To begin with it is necessary to have clarity in the roles of Finance and Planning Commissions. This was the recommendation made by the Administrative Reforms Commission almost 40 years ago. Given the constitutional position of the Finance Commission, the reform could be to convert it into a professional body with a qualified permanent secretariat and entrust the grant giving function entirely to it. The Planning Commission, on the other hand, could be entrusted with the task of developing the physical infrastructure in the country and until such times as the primary debt market develops, could provide concessional loan assistance to poor and smaller states in the North-east and Jammu and Kashmir. This measure will result in, among other benefits, looking at the budgets of the states in a holistic manner than in a compartmentalised way.

The Finance Commission, too, will have to change its approach and methodology. It will have to evolve a formula based transfer system which is simple, equitable and does not involve disincentives. One way to go about is to have the tax devolution based on disability in taxable capacity and provide larger amount of grants to equalise standards in primary education and healthcare and get rid of the gap filling grants altogether. The TFC has initiated equalising grants and this should be substantially augmented to ensure minimum standards within a reasonable time period. Reducing inequalities in education and healthcare would reduce inequalities in human development and pave the way for productivity and improved governance in poorer states.

Indeed, the reforms in centrally sponsored schemes should focus on rationalising them and consolidating them from the prevailing over 200 schemes to just about a dozen. Rationalisation of schemes will help to ensure minimum levels of these services in all the states. It is important to have matching requirements to impart a sense of ownership of these schemes by the states, but in order the matching ratio from different states could be varied to take account of their differential capacities (Feldstein, 1975).

While it is important to design an equitable transfer system, the problem of ensuring that the transferred resources are spent productively is a major challenge. Ensuring productive transformation of expenditures into outputs and the outcomes has been a problem particularly in states receiving larger transfers. In some of the states, there are serious problems of governance which has hindered efficient implementation of expenditures. This has raised questions on the desirability of giving larger transfers to these states. This calls for not only restoring proper incentives for fiscal management in the transfer system but also immediate measures to improve governance in these states.

*Fiscal Consolidation*

One of the important reasons for the fiscal stress at the state level during the 1990s was the decline in the ratio of central transfers to GDP. A large part of the decline of over one per cent of GDP was in tax devolution and that was mainly due to declining customs revenue. Although the Finance Commissions will consider the sharing of taxes every five years afresh, the difficult fiscal situation at the center constrains any appreciable increase in transfers in the near future. There will be further decline in the revenue from import duties as the economy is opened up and more importantly, taxing mobile capital and skilled labor in globalising environment will pose severe difficulties. The introduction of VAT is expected to bring in improvement in revenue productivity, but it is doubtful whether it can completely offset the revenue loss from customs.

The ultimate solution to the fiscal problems lies in fiscal consolidation at both central and state levels. The TFC has worked out the magnitude of adjustment required to achieve sustainable fiscal situation and this requires increasing tax revenue—GDP ratio by about two percentage points, non-tax revenues by about one percentage point and reducing the revenue expenditure by about 1.5 percentage points. This is a priority area and unless overall fiscal consolidation is made, reform of inter-governmental finance will not be meaningful and effective.

## Local Government Reform

An important area that has concerned the policy makers in India is the poor and declining standards of service delivery. The constitutional amendments to empower the local governments have failed to make them effective, and lack of people's participation in the functioning of local governments, particularly in rural areas, a major concern. Empowerment of local governments is meaningful only when people have sustained interest in them and this is possible only when their stake in local governments is enhanced. One important way is to make concerted efforts to reform their tax system to raise larger amounts of local resources for development. Equally important is the need to consolidate the various schemes administered by the local governments to release larger volume of untied funds for development. Also, it is necessary to make the employees accountable to the *panchayats*. Reform in this area is possible only when the information on revenues, expenditures and other economic variables in different *panchayats* are collected and used for policy. This is necessary also to design an appropriate transfer system at the local level. Policy and institutional reform in this area has to be carefully calibrated to make the local governments effective institutions of democratic polity and public service delivery.

## Making The Inter-governmental Institutions Effective

One of the major problems confronted by Indian fiscal federalism is the absence of an effective mechanism for conflict resolution as conflicts are likely to intensify in an environment of more intense inter-governmental competition. This has been amply demonstrated by the river water disputes. Conflicts can be vertical—between different levels of government or horizontal—between different units within the same level. While institutions such as National Development Council (NDC) and the Inter-State Council are extremely important, the domination of single party in power for a long period has not helped to draft the 'rules of the game' and a framework for bargaining to evolve effective conflict resolution mechanism in Indian fiscal federalism. The issue has gained further importance with the emergence of coalition government at the centre, regional parties in power in states and the regional parties becoming the 'pivotal' members of coalition at the centre.

While both the NDC and Inter-State Council have done commendable work in the past, it is necessary to bring them to the center-stage in regulating inter-governmental competition. In fact, there is a tendency not to use the constitutional institutions in resolving inter-state issues. The most important example is the introduction of VAT. The entire reform is calibrated by the 'Empowered Committee of State Finance Ministers' totally outside the Inter-State Council. Legitimately, the Empowered Committee should have functioned under the Inter-State Council. The issue of resolving inter-state conflicts will intensify with the phasing out of the inter-state sales tax, and introduction of the system to relive the tax paid at the state of origin as goods are taken to the destination state. We have also referred to the conflicts relating to river water sharing between the states and the lack of an appropriate institutional mechanism to deal with this contentious issue.

Notwithstanding the weaknesses, it must be noted that the system of inter-governmental fiscal arrangements in India has served well for over 50 years. It has achieved a significant equalisation over the years, instituted a workable system of resolving the outstanding issues between the Centre and the States and among the States *inter se*, and adjusted to the changing requirements and thus has contributed to achieving a degree of cohesiveness in a large and diverse country. No doubt, the analysis brings out several areas of reform; what is however important is that it is eminently possible to reform the system.

# Reference

Eallack, Jessica and T.N. Srinivasan (2006). *Federalism and Economic Reform*, Cambridge University Press.

Feldstein, Martin (1975). "Wealth Neutrality and Local Choice in Public Education", *American Economic Review*, Vol. 65(1), pp.75-89.

Rao, M. Govinda (2006). "Fiscal federalism in Planned Economies", in Ehtisham Ahmad and Georgio Brosio (eds.), *Handbook on Fiscal Federalism*, Edward Elgar, Cheltanham; U.K.

Rao, M. Govinda and Pinaki Chakarborty (2006). "Multilateral Adjustment Lending to States in India: Hastening Fiscal Correxction or Softening the Budget Constraint?" *Journal of International Trade and Economic Development*, Vol. 15(3) (September), pp.335-358.

Rao, M. Govinda and Nirvikar Singh (2005). *Political Economy of Federalism in India*, Oxford University Press.

# Employment, Poverty and Social Dimension

# 6

## Trends in Employment, Unemployment and Wages in India since the Early Seventies

### T.N. SRINIVASAN*

### Introduction

An overwhelming majority of India's population depend on their own labour as the dominant source of livelihood, through its productive use, either in self-employment or in work for others. Labour and issues of employment and its security, productivity and wages have been at the centre of attention in pre- and post-Independence plans for national development. Moreover, India's Constitution, adopted in 1950, has a set of articles on Directive Principles of State Policy as its Part IV. Although not judiciable (i.e., cannot be enforced through the judicial system), these articles cover many aspects of livelihood and employment: a guarantee of the right to livelihood for all citizens (Article 39a); equal pay for equal work (Article 39d); right to work, to education and to public assistance in cases of unemployment, old age, sickness and disablement, etc. (Article 41); humane conditions of work and maternity relief (Article 42); living wage for workers (Article 43), and participation of workers in management of industries (Article 43a). Over more than five decades, these rights and guarantees have remained as aspirations rather than concrete achievements.

The report of the National Commission on Labour (NCL, 2002) rightly traces the origins of the contents of these articles farther back to the principles that Gandhiji had articulated in the monumental

* Revised text of the lecture with the title "Trends in Employment, Unemployment and Wages in India: A Conceptual Framework and an Assessment of Findings", delivered on March 23, 2006 at The Centre for Economic and Social Studies, Hyderabad, India.

struggle for Independence and also to the plans for development put forward by various groups as the Second World War was about to end. These groups spanned the political spectrum from the Indian Federation of Labour (with its People's Plan) on the left, the National Planning Committee for the Indian National Congress (chaired by Jawaharlal Nehru) in the middle, and captains of Industry (with their "Bombay Plan") on the right. Even earlier, Sir M. Viswesvaraya, the engineer statesman, had published his book entitled: *Planned Economy for India* in 1934 (See Srinivasan, 2000 for further discussion of and references to these plans).

It is, therefore, not surprising that there was then a political consensus on a planned economy with the state playing a dominant role. It was in no small part driven by commonly held belief that the Soviet Union and Nazi Germany were successful in transforming their economies in a short span of time through planning. Of course, lack of individual freedoms and persecution of minorities in both states were deplored by leaders in India. However, they were not then aware of the horrors of the Soviet system and of the holocaust, since information about them became common knowledge only after the conclusion of the Second World War. The NCL (2002: 22) quotes K.T. Shah, Honorary General Secretary, National Planning Committee, as having said that, "enterprise cannot be left to profit making individuals; employment cannot be left to be the plaything of demand and supply; national economy, social justice and public welfare cannot be entrusted to *laissez faire*. They must be the concern of the state." Given the Fabian Socialist persuasion of Nehru and many of his colleagues on the National Planning Committee, their mistrust of markets and belief in the state is not surprising. What is surprising is that the authors of the Bombay Plan, namely, the captains of Indian industry, who could be presumed to be champions of the market mechanism of free enterprise and capitalism, also envisioned extensive state intervention in the economy. Such intervention in their view was needed to "secure to every person, a minimum income essential for a reasonable standard of living and to prevent gross inequities in the incomes of different classes and individuals...control by the state, accompanied in appropriate cases by State ownership or management of public utility, basic industries, etc. will also tend to diminish inequalities of income" (NCL: 24).

What is more, they advocated land and tenancy reform, and the establishment of multipurpose cooperatives in part as a means for achieving full employment and as a step towards the goal of instituting a comprehensive scheme of social insurance. They recognised that such a scheme has to wait until "a policy of full employment has had time to work itself out and some approximation is made to a position of stable employment for the greater part of the population, i.e. until the risks of insurable are reduced to manageable proportions and until the average individual income has risen sufficiently to meet the contributions necessary under a scheme of insurance" (NCL, 2002: 26).

The authors of the Bombay Plan, besides advocating unemployment insurance, wanted the state to take a step towards the establishment of a basic minimum wage for 'all' occupations by establishing minimum wages in certain well established industries like cotton textile, sugar, cement, engineering, jute, mining, etc., as essential components of a comprehensive employment policy. In what seems like an afterthought, the authors added, "as a general rule, these rewards, namely wages, interests and profits, should continue to be determined on the basis of demand and efficiency [presumably through the market mechanism]...subject to the overriding consideration that wages should not fall below a certain minimum and that interest rates 'should be controlled' with a view to maintaining full employment. Profits *should be* kept within limits through fixation of prices, restriction of dividends, taxation, etc. But care should be taken to 'leave sufficient' incentives for improvement in efficiency and expansion of production" (NCL, 2002: 27, emphasis added). In retrospect, it is odd that the distortion that the plethora of controls on prices, profits, interest rates, dividends would have on basic incentives, to work, save, invest and allocate resource efficiency is raised obliquely almost *en passant* by champions of industry! They apparently could not resist the temptation of being 'two-handed' economists who start every public policy analysis with 'On the one hand', only to qualify it heavily in the next sentence starting with 'On the other hand'! That such a well-informed, successful and obviously intelligent group did not recognise the adverse consequences of extensive state controls on the economy is very surprising.

I need not remind the reader that the political consensus of pre-Independence days on planning for development, and for the state playing a dominant role in the economy, was reflected not only in the Directive Principles of State Policy but also, importantly, in the establishment of the Planning Commission in March 1950, within two months after the adoption of the Constitution. We all know that soon after the ambitious Second Five Year Plan ran into a shortage of foreign exchange and other critical resources, a system of controls that the authors of the Bombay Plan had advocated was introduced, thereby giving birth to the license-permit *raj*.

I cannot resist reproducing here my description in Srinivasan (2000: 3-4) of the reach of the control system and its crippling effects on incentives:

> At its most expansive and inclusive, the system involved the following: *industrial licensing* under which the scale, technology, and location of any investment project other than relatively small ones were regulated and permission from the government was needed to expand, relocate, and change the output or input mixes of operating plants; the *exchange control system* which required exporters to surrender their foreign exchange earnings to the Reserve bank of India at the official exchange rate, and allocated the exchange earnings to users through *import licensing; capital issues control* under which access to domestic equity markets and debt finance was controlled; *price controls* (complete or partial) on some vital consumption goods (for example, foodgrains, sugar, vegetable oils) and critical inputs (for example, fertilizer, irrigation water, fuel); *made-to-measure* protection from import competition, granted to domestic producers in many 'priority' industries, including in particular the equipment producers. The agricultural sector was insulated from world markets, subjected to land ceiling and tenancy legislation, and forced to sell part of the output at fixed prices, but it was also provided subsides on irrigation, fertilizer, and electricity. Large commercial banks, which were nationalized in 1969, were subject to directed and selective credit controls, controls on deposit and lending rates, and in effect had to lend more than half of their loanable funds to government through the operation of reserve requirements of various kinds.
>
> The controls taken together were far more restrictive than each of them individually. For example, grant of an industrial license did not imply grant of a capital goods import license so that the capacity licensed could not be operational if the intended imports were essential. Besides the crucial aspect of all the regulations is the uncertainty about their fair implementation because they were essentially *discretionary* rather than *rule-based* and *automatic*. Although some principles and priorities were to govern the exercise of these regulatory powers, these were largely non-operational for two reasons. First, it was impossible, even in theory, to devise a set of principles or rules for all the myriad categories of regulations that were mutually consistent and in consonance with the multiple goals of the industrial

policy framework, which in themselves were not entirely consistent. Second, the problem of translating whatever rules there were into operational decisions was one of Orwellian dimensions. The allocative mechanism was largely in the form of quantitative restrictions unrelated to market realities. A chaotic incentive structure and the unleashing of rapacious rent-seeking and political corruption were the inevitable outcomes. Indeed, the discretionary regulatory system instituted in the name of planning for national development instead became a cancer in the body politic.

Another dimension of the exercise of regulatory power was that it was *anticipatory* in nature-that is, the regulations were meant to *prevent* the occurrence of any prospective deviation from the objectives of policy by firms or other regulated entities rather than to *punish* or cure any deviant behavior that actually occurred. While preventive, rather than curative, medicine is often preferable in health care systems, clearly it is not appropriate in industrial regulations. But in India a system of *curative* health care and *preventative* industrial regulations has been in existence since the 1950s!

One of the critical elements of the control system that is relevant for this paper is the set of labour laws enacted after Independence. These made it costly for large enterprises to hire workers for long term employment. Once hired, workers could not, in effect, be dismissed for economic reasons, because of the costly and time consuming procedure for dismissal. The potential deleterious effects of these laws on economic growth and income inequalities was noted long ago by no less a person than Professor P.C. Mahalanobis (1969: 442 and 1961: 157):

...certain welfare measures tend to be implemented in India ahead of economic growth, for example, in labour laws which are probably the most highly protective of labour interest in the narrowest sense, in the whole world. There is practically no link between output and remuneration; hiring and firing are highly restricted. It is extremely difficult to maintain an economic level of productivity or improve productivity...the present form of protection of organised labour, which constitutes, including their families, about five or six per cent of the whole population, would operate as an obstacle to growth and would also increase inequalities...it would seem better to try to attain the highest possible efficiency of labour and increasing productivity, and use the additional value obtained in this way to create more employment rather than lower the industrial efficiency by slack or restrictive practices through overstaffing.

Mahalanobis not only made a prescient diagnosis of the deleterious effects of our labour laws, but also prescribed an alternative way of assuring the legitimate interests of workers and their families while at the same time preserving the right incentives for efficient employment and increasing productivity. It consisted of creating a Labour Reserve (LR) "to absorb such industrial workers as may be considered surplus and be 'laid off' by existing industrial enterprises at their discretion, and also to serve as a pool for other enterprises to draw upon, again, at their own discretion. The Labour Reserve Service (LR) would then act as a buffer against unemployment and would serve as a (perhaps socially more useful and psychologically more preferable) form of or substitute for unemployment insurance....The LR would provide training of various kinds and would continually try to use the men for productive purposes. Workers in the LR would have an incentive to find better jobs at the earliest opportunity" (Mahalanobis, 1961: 157-158).

Considerations of efficiency, rightly emphasised by Professor Mahalanobis appeared to have played no role in the small-scale sector reservation policy. This policy not only failed to deliver its employment objectives but also crippled India's competitiveness in world markets, since many of the reserved products were major export items. Nearly a decade ago, a committee headed by Mr. Abid Hussain concluded that, "...the case for reservations is fundamentally flawed and self-contradictory...the policy crippled the growth of several industrial sectors, restricted exports and has done little for the promotion of small scale industries" (p.130, as quoted in World Bank, 1998: 27). Although some products (including most importantly, garments, which are one of our major exports) have been recently de-reserved, there are many that still are reserved.

The fact that Indian labour laws are highly protective of labour, noted long ago by Professor Mahalanobis, has at last received official recognition by the Ministry of Finance (MoF). The latest economic survey (MoF, 2006: 209) notes, "these laws apply only to the organised sector. Consequently, these laws have restricted labour mobility, have led to capital-intensive methods in the organised sector and adversely affected the sector's long run demand for labour." Interestingly, the survey notes that, "perhaps there are lessons to be learnt from China in the area of labour reforms. China, with a history of extreme employment security, has drastically reformed its labour relations and created a new labour market, in which workers are highly mobile. Although there have been many lay-offs and open unemployment, high rates of industrial growth especially in the coastal regions helped their redeployment." However, it fails to point out that in the Special Economic Zones (SEZs) in the coastal areas of China, employers were free to hire and fire workers and 100 per cent foreign ownership was allowed.[1] Our recently legislated SEZs are neither exempted from labour laws nor from sectoral caps on foreign ownership.

The overall performance of the Indian economy under more than three decades of planning, state control and direction is described at best as modest. It delivered an average rate of growth of real GDP of around 3.5-3.75 per cent per year during 1950-1980, the infamous Hindu rate of growth. Rapid industrialisation, one of the prime objectives of our development strategy did not happen: the share of industry in real GDP increased from 14 per cent in 1950-51 to 22 per cent in 1980-81. In the next 25 years it has glacially moved to 24 per cent in 2004-05 (MoF, 2006, Table 1.3), even though the rate of GDP growth increased to nearly 6 per cent a year on an average between 1980-81 and 2004-05. Even more disappointingly, the share of manufacturing industry in GDP rose from 11 per cent in 1950-51 to 16 per cent in 1980-1987 and it was still at 16 per cent in 2004-2005. Although these trends depict the dismal failure to industrialise the economy in more than five decades, still to be fair, it must be said that the industrial policy with its emphasis on heavy industry, chemicals and other intermediates, created a diversified, though costly and uncompetitive by international standards.

What about employment? Unfortunately, it is virtually impossible to document the trends in total employment since Independence. The National Sample Survey Organisation (NSSO) began its systematic surveys of employment and unemployment only from the 32nd Round in 1977-78, although some earlier rounds included data on both. The decennial population censuses collect data on work force participation. However, as (NCL, 2002: 57) noted:

---

1. There are some studies (Roy, 2004; Nagaraj, 2000, 2004; Deshpande, Standing and Deshpande, 1998) claiming that India's labour laws have not adversely affected growth. These are not entirely persuasive for the reason that they either ignore completely or do not carefully account for the fact that the regulations critically affect the entry and exit dynamics of firms. As such any analysis based on establishments or firms in existence has to allow for selection effects to be valid. The firms in existence represent those who chose to enter at various points of time earlier and have not exited as yet. After all, firms that anticipate their being able to either comply with or evade labour laws at a cost would enter if it is profitable for them to do so taking into the cost of compliance. Having entered, they would stay unless unanticipated events (such as for example, an increase in costs of corruption for evading labour laws or changes in product prices and non-labour costs make staying unprofitable.

"economic data from the successive censuses are beset with problems of comparability (at least up to 1981) due to varying concepts." The unorganised sector of the economy, which accounted for 59.2 per cent NDP in 1999-2000 (a fall from 63.1 per cent in 1993-94), is still the dominant sector in terms of net value added and even more so in employment (NAD, 2004: Appendix 1.1). As NAD (2004) notes that there is no flow of current data on the unorganised non-agricultural segment of the economy either for official sources or through annual surveys. Table 6.1 presents the data on employment in the organised sector.

First, it is evident from Table 6.1 that compared to a work force on January 1, 2000 of 393 million (NCL, 2002: Table 2.10) total employment in the organised sector in 2001 was only around 28 million or roughly 7 per cent of the work force. Second, employment in the organised manufacturing sector of the economy has been stagnant for more than two decades, hovering between 6.0 and 6.4 million.[2] Third, the public sector has accounted for more than two-thirds of total employment during this period. The GDP growth acceleration since 1980-81, and the shift away from public ownership in the economy since systematic economic reforms were initiated in 1991, are yet to be reflected in terms of employment in the organised sector.

### Table 6.1

*Employment in the Organised Sector*

|                                        | 1981 | 1991 | 2001 | 2003 |
|----------------------------------------|------|------|------|------|
| Private Sector Total (millions)        | 7.4  | 7.7  | 8.7  | 8.4  |
| of which manufacturing                 | 4.5  | 4.5  | 5.0  | 4.7  |
| Public Sector Total (millions)         | 15.5 | 19.1 | 19.1 | 18.6 |
| of which manufacturing                 | 1.5  | 1.9  | 1.4  | 1.3  |
| Private and Public Sectors (Total)     | 22.9 | 26.8 | 27.8 | 27.0 |
| of which manufacturing                 | 6.0  | 6.4  | 6.4  | 6.0  |

*Source:* MoF (2006), Tables 3.1–3.3 Appendix.

---

2. Abhijit Banerjee in a private communication suggests that this stagnation during the period of reforms and rapid growth of the service sector needs a disaggregated analysis. In particular, he asks: which sectors experienced a decline in employment or output as services grew. Such a causal analysis though, beyond the scope of this descriptive paper, is very much needed.

It is evident that the employment generation process in the Indian economy, both before and after the reforms, calls for an in-depth analysis. It is also clear that the available data are not adequate for the task. In what follows, I will comment on concepts and definitions used in various sources of data on employment with emphasis on those used by NSS, in Section 2. Section 3 is devoted to a description of trends in employment, unemployment and wages. I will confine myself to the trends for India as a whole. Interstate differences are important both from the perspective of positive analysis and of normative policy formulation. But their description has to wait for another occasion.

## Concepts for Employment, Unemployment and Work Force Participation

### Sources of Data

The two of the main sources of data on workers and their distribution across economic activities in the economy as a whole are the decennial population census (PC) and the Employment and Unemployment Surveys (EUS) of the NSS. Other sources include the Directorate General of Employment and Training (DGET) which publishes data on the organised part of the economy under its Employment Market Information (EMI) Programme. The Annual Survey of Industry conducted by the Central Statistical Organisation (CSO) is another source of employment data. With some exceptions and changes over time, its coverage its restricted to the establishments listed as factories under Section 2m (i) and 2m (ii) of the Factories Act of 1948.

Another important source is the Economic Census, initiated in 1977 as a countrywide census of all economic activities (except crop production and plantation) and followed by detailed sample surveys of unorganised segments of different sectors of non-agricultural economy in phased manner during the intervening period of two successive economic censuses. These "Economic Census Follow-up Surveys" also called Enterprise Surveys (ESs), produce estimates of production, inputs, employment, factor income, capital formation etc.

The definitions used are not the same in all sources and has even varied over time, in the same source, as in the population censuses.

Also, some of the sources such as the Economic Census are of recent origin, while the population census goes back to 1881! Although, the first EUS was carried out by the NSS in its 9$^{th}$ Round (May-September 1955), and also in the 17$^{th}$-20$^{th}$ Rounds (September '61 through June '66) for the urban sector, only from the 32$^{nd}$ Round (1977-78), EUS became part of the National quinquennial household surveys of NSS using essentially identical concepts of employment and unemployment. Apart from the large quinquennial surveys, NSS also collects data annually from a smaller sample of households distributed over the same number of first stage units as its normal socioeconomic survey.

It is believed that estimates of employment and unemployment from the rounds other than quinquennial rounds in which EUS is conducted, particularly those meant for Enterprise Surveys (ESs), besides being subject to larger sampling errors because of smaller sample size (particularly at the state and regional levels), are suspected to be biased as well. It is suggested that in such rounds:

> The selection procedure of first stage units is designed to produce efficient estimates of enterprise-related parameters or other households and individual characteristics. *As a result, the work force estimates based on the data collected in these rounds are not only subject to higher sampling error but are also suspected to be biased owing to the lesser attention paid to the employment-unemployment component of the survey.* Nevertheless, from the data collected in these rounds, it is possible to generate distribution of workers over the activity-groups that deserve to be considered, albeit critically (NAD, 2004: 10, emphasis added).

Since, no concrete evidence has thus far been adduced in support of suspected biases in estimates from smaller-sample rounds, I will assume that there are no biases but only higher sampling errors in these estimates. Since in Section 3, I will be reporting only the estimates for India as a whole based on fairly large samples in all rounds, even the fact of higher sampling errors is less of a problem for them. The coverage of sources of data other than PC and EU is limited either in geographical area or sectors or in other ways. The Economic Censuses and ESs exclude crop production and plantation activities in which a large proportion of the rural work force is employed. Even PC and EUS which are supposedly national in coverage, some states (Jammu and Kashmir and Northeastern states) have been excluded on occasions for various reasons including primarily civil disturbances and insurgencies.

The methods of coverage by PC and EUS differ as well. As noted earlier, Annual Survey of Industries covers only establishments covered by Factories Act of 1948. DGET data "covers all establishments in the public sector (except the defense establishments and armed forces) and those establishments in the private sector that employ 25 or more persons on the last day of the quarter under reference. Apart from this, since 1966, the establishments employing 10 to 24 persons are also covered on a voluntary basis" (NAD, 2004: 11-12).

There are many other sources of partial data on employment, unemployment, wages and other aspects of labour, sources of which are based on reports required to be submitted by employers under various acts. The report of the National Commission on Labour (NCL) (the Second Labour Commission), has a comprehensive discussion of sources and limitations of labour statistics (NCL, 2002). The very first Royal Commission on Labour in 1931 had already identified the need for reliable and representative data on labour related markets.

There has been significant progress in the 75 years since the Royal Commission reported in meeting the need it underlined, such as, for example, the start of regular EUSs by the NSS. Yet as the NCL (2002) laments: "We regret to say that the Labour Statistics as it stands today is not dependable. The industries do not have an obligation to submit the returns prescribed under the law. The collectors of data do not have any obligation to publish the data on time. In some cases there is a gap of more than 32 months in the publication of the data. Some State Governments have a gap of three to four years before the data is released. As a result of this poor quality and unreliable frequency of data, policy makers do not find it easy to rely on them or make use of them" (NCL, 2002, Chapter XII, Part IV: 28). I do not wish to underplay the importance of accurate and timely reporting by public agencies and of the need for incentives for those who are to provide the agencies with the data for complying with the laws as well as penalties for non-compliance. However, many of the conceptual, measurement and data gathering problems relating to labour statistics largely arise from the complexity of the Indian labour market. From the employee or worker side, complexities arise from the fact that individuals (particularly females) move in and out of the work force within a year, not infrequently more than once. Even those who participate in the work force and are employed throughout the year could move from self-employment in their own farms in one season to wage employment in another season within the same year. Indeed, self-employment is the single largest source of employment in the economy. Although, the proportion of population living in households whose major source of income is self-employment declined from 55.6 per cent in 1987-88 to 50.9 per cent in 1999-2000 in rural areas, it increased slightly from 38.9 per cent to 39.2 per cent during the same period in urban areas (NSS, 2001, Table 4.2). Also, an individual could be engaged in more than one economic activity at the same time or at different times in a year.

From the employer side also the situation is just as complex. A farmer employs workers not only from his/her own household but also hires agricultural labourers during peak agricultural season. The same farmer would be employed as or looking for casual work outside the farm during slack agricultural season. Outside of crop production activities, as the data from the latest economic census (GoI, 2006) show, 98.6 per cent of the number of enterprises in existence in 2005 in the economy employed less than 10 workers.[3] In the earlier census of 1998, this proportion was similar at 98.1 per cent and they accounted for 76.5 per cent of the number of usually working persons. A large majority, 61.3 per cent of the enterprises operated in rural areas. Also, 20 per cent of rural and 15.5 per cent of urban enterprises operated with no premises. It is very likely that enterprises employing less than 10 workers would maintain written records of their activities. There is no way, other than by canvassing, such enterprises directly through a well designed survey or census, one could gather data on their employment. This is indeed what an Economic Census and its follow up survey, attempt to do. However, the census excludes a large share of the work force employed in crop production activities.

Given the wide differences in their concepts and definitions and the extent of coverage among sources it should cause no surprise that

---

3. Strictly speaking, the data from the economic censuses refer to the number of positions and not to workers. Thus, the same position could be held by different persons during a year.

it is virtually impossible to adjust for these differences and arrive at comparable estimates. The dissatisfaction with the then available PC and EUS statistics of unemployment led to the appointment by the Planning Commission of a committee of experts under the chairmanship of M.L. Dantwala (known as the Dantwala Committee) on Unemployment Estimates. The Committee submitted its report in 1970. The EUSs of NSS have since adopted the committee's recommendations regarding concepts of employment and unemployment.

## Work and Worker in the Population Census

### Population Census (PC)

The fact that individuals (particularly females) move in and out of the work force frequently, and that even while working could divide their work time over different economic activities is addressed in the census by making a distinction between 'main' and 'marginal' workers, with work being defined as any economically productive work. In the most recent census of 2001 the following questions were canvassed on the characteristics of workers and non-workers *(http://www.censusindia.net/census2001/qpopenu.html)*.

Q. 16: Did the person work any time last year? (includes even part time help or unpaid work on farm, family enterprise or in any other economic activity) (Categories: Main worker: If worked for 6 months or more, Marginal Worker: If worked for less than 6 months, Non-Worker: If not worked at all)

Q. 17: Economic activity of Main or Marginal Worker

Q. 17(i): Category of the economic activity of the Main or Marginal Worker

For Workers in Household Industry and for other Workers only

Q. 17(ii): Occupation of the person *(describe the actual work of the person)*

Q. 17 (iii): Describe in detail the nature of industry, trade or service where the person works/worked or of self employment

Q. 17 (iv):     Class of Worker

Q. 18:          If Marginal Worker or Non-Worker, under Q.16, record non-economic activity

Q. 19:          If Marginal Worker or Non-Worker, is the person seeking/available for work ?

Q. 20:          Travel to place of work (for Other Workers only)

Q. 20 (i):      Distance from residence to place of work in Kilometres

Q. 20 (ii):     Mode of travel to place of work

The questions relating to workers and their characteristics have varied over the census. For example, in the census of 1981 only the following were the questions (GoI, 1981):

Q. 12:          Worked any time at all last year?

Q. 13.A:        Was this your main work during last year/last season?

Q. 13.B:        Any 'other work'/'work' any time last year?

Q. 13.C:        If 'No' in 12 or 13A, seeking work?

Q. 14.A:        Worked at least one day in the last one week?

Q. 14.B:        If 'No" in 14A, seeking work?

Even though the listing of these questions took less than half a page in the manual of instructions to the census enumerators, the explanation of the questions and their intended meaning, including codes for type of workers and non-workers, took thirty eight pages, thus illustrating the complexity of the Indian labour scene.

The reference period in the 2001 census was a year whereas in the 1981 census time two reference periods, a year and a week, were used.

### Reference Periods and Concepts in EUS of NSS

NSS adopts three time frames in the EUS–a reference year for the usual status, a reference week for the weekly status, and a daily average during the reference week for the daily status (see Appendix 6.1 for details). Thus, the work force according to:

> ...'*usual status*' approach represents the number of persons engaged in some economic activity in either *principal*, or *subsidiary* capacity, or both,

during the 365 days preceding the date of survey. A person engaged in some economic activity 'more or less regularly' for a relatively shorter period during the reference 365 days is treated as having a *subsidiary-capacity* work. Engagement in work in *subsidiary* capacity arises out of the following two situations:

(i)   a person may be engaged for a relatively longer period during the last 365 days in economic/non-economic activity and for a relatively shorter period in another economic activity and

(ii)  a person may be pursuing one economic/non-economic activity almost throughout the year in the *principal usual activity* status and also pursuing along side another economic activity for a relatively shorter period in a *subsidiary* capacity.
      (NAD, 2004: 15)

NAD (2004: 16) suggests that,

Though the definition of marginal workers in PC is somewhat more liberal than the definition of *subsidiary* status workers in EUS of NSSO, those of 'main' workers of PC and *'usual principal capacity'* workers of EUS are, in principle, quite comparable. More significantly, the main and marginal workers obtained from the PC should be close to, or exceed, the usual *principal* and *subsidiary* status workers obtained from the EUS of the NSS.

## Comparison of PC and EUS

Even though in principle the 'usual status' estimates of EUS and the 'main plus marginal' marker based estimates from PC should be close to each other, there are a number of problems in comparing the two. First, for the inter-censal years there are no PC based estimates to be compared directly with the EUS estimates, but only broad population projections based on growth rates between adjacent census years. Second, the reference year for EUS is the year preceding the day on which a household is canvassed. Since households are canvassed throughout the year, the reference year ranges over a two-year period. Third, the reference year has varied from round to round, most often being July 1 to June 30, but not infrequently the calendar year. Of course the census population estimates are supposed to be for the mid point of the census year. Fourth, the geographical coverage of census and EUS are not the same. NSS (2005a: 16) points out:

Compared to the census population or the projections thereof, population estimates from the NSSO surveys are, in general, on the lower side. This difference arises mainly due to the differences in methods and coverage adopted by the NSSO in comparison with the census operation. However, the ratios obtained from the survey are much closer to the ratios obtained using census figures. Usually the estimates on employment-unemployment are presented as ratios. To estimate an absolute number in any category, it is advisable to apply the survey estimates of ratios to the census population or projections thereof, for that category.

The recommendation that census figures or projections can be used in combination with 'ratios' from EUS to obtain absolute numbers, though plausible, is valid only under the strong assumption that the estimated ratios in the states covered by EUS are the same in those not covered in the EUS, but covered in the PC. In general, there is no independent evidence to validate this assumption. Table 6.2 compares PC totals for the census year of 2001 with corresponding figures for 1999-2000 from the EUS, without making any adjustment for the growth in population between 1999-2000 and 2001.

Table 6.2 shows that EUS underestimated the total population of India by nearly 10 per cent. But the extent of underestimation was higher at 18 per cent in urban areas and lower at 7 per cent in rural areas.[4] Moreover, the share of urban population at 25.42 per cent in EUS was lower than the share at 27.7 per cent in the PC. It seems that only the sex ratios, i.e. the proportions of males in the population, are nearly the same in PC and EUS. Sundaram and Tendulkar (2005) note that, "there are significant differences between the [unsmoothed] age distribution in the survey and that in the (nearest) population census which materially affect the overall (weighted average) WFPRs/LFPRs [Work Force Participation Rates/Labour Force Participation Rates]." Thus, there are differences between PCs and EUS data, not only with respect to estimates of 'absolute numbers', but also with respect to various ratios, such as sharers of different age groups, urban residents, and so on, in the total population.

The difference between the population age distributions between the census and the EUS leads Sundaram and Tendulkar (2005) to use the census-based share of each age group as weight to the EUS based estimate of that group's Work Force Participation Rate (WFPR) and Labour Force Participation Rate (LFPR) to arrive at the overall weighted of average WFPR and LFPR. Clearly multiplying their

---

4. Strictly speaking because the comparison does not take into account the growth in population between 1999-2000 and 2001 (roughly 2.2 per cent), these figures slightly overstate the extent of underestimation.

**Table 6.2**

*Estimates of Population: PC (2001) and EUS (1999-2000)*

| | | Rural | | | Urban | | | Total | |
|---|---|---|---|---|---|---|---|---|---|
| | | Absolute | Ratio Row | Ratio Column | Absolute | Ratio Row | Ratio Column | Absolute | Column |
| Males | PC | 381.14 | 71.74 | 51.39 | 150.14 | 28.26 | 52.61 | 531.28 | 100 |
| | EUS | 350.69 | 74.15 | 51.06 | 122.25 | 25.85 | 52.21 | 472.94 | 100 |
| Ratio (EUS/PC) | | 92.01 | | | 81.42 | | | 89.02 | |
| Females | PC | 360.52 | 72.72 | 48.61 | 135.22 | 27.28 | 47.39 | 495.74 | 100 |
| | EUS | 336.19 | 75.03 | 48.94 | 111.85 | 24.97 | 47.78 | 448.05 | 100 |
| Ratio | | 93.25 | | | 82.71 | | | 89.68 | |
| Persons | PC | 741.66 | 72.21 | | 285.36 | 27.79 | | 1027.02 | 100 |
| | EUS | 686.88 | 74.58 | 100 | 234.11 | 25.42 | 100 | 920.99 | 100 |
| Ratio | | 92.61 | | | 82.04 | | | 90.38 | |

Sources: For PC: *www.censusindia.net/results/rudist.html*, accessed on March 8, 2006.
For EUS: NSS (2005b), Appendix Table 3.

weighted average WFPR by the census population total would obviously lead to a different absolute number of persons in the work force as compared to the one obtained by multiplying the weighted average WFPR based on survey-based age distribution. Should their method be preferred to the second? The answer depends on which of the following assumptions is more plausible and they are 'assumptions' and not facts. Their implicit assumption is that whatever the differences in methods and coverage there are between PC and EUS, they do not affect the WFPR/LFPR of 'each' age group. The alternative assumption is that such differences do not affect the WFPR/LFPR in the 'population as a whole', i.e., all age groups' taken together. In effect the latter assumption allows for differences in methods and coverage to affect both the age distribution and the age specific WFPR/LFPR in an off setting manner.

The implications of the two assumptions can be seen as follows, let

$N_a^M =$ number of persons in age group $a$ using method $M$, $M=PC$, $EUS$.

$R_a^M =$ work force participation rate for age group $a$ in method $M$.

$$W_a^M = \frac{N_a^M}{\sum_a N_a^M} \,, M = PC, EUS$$

$$\overline{R}^M = \sum_a W_a^M R_a^M$$

$$\overline{R}^{ST} = \sum_a W_a^{PC} R_a^{EUS} \quad \text{(ST denotes Sundaram and Tendulkar)}$$

The 'true' number of persons in the work force ($W^F$) in the population is by definition $\left(\sum N_a^{PC}\right)\overline{R}^{PC}$. Although $N_a^{PC}$ is known, we do not know $R_a^{PC}$ and hence $\overline{R}^{PC}$. There are two alternative estimates for $W^F$. The first, $W_1^F$, following the suggestion of NSS, is $\left(\sum N_a^{PC}\right) \bullet \overline{R}^{EU}$. The second, $W_2^F$ following the procedure of Sundaram and Tendulkar is $\left(\sum N_a^{PC}\right) \bullet \overline{R}^{ST}$.

Now  $W^F - W_1^F = \left(\sum N_a^{PC}\right)\left[\overline{R}_a^{PC} - \overline{R}_a^{EUS}\right]$

$= \left(\sum N_a^{PC}\right)\left[\sum W_a^{PC}\left(R_a^{PC} - R_a^{EUS}\right) + \sum\left(W_a^{PC} - W_a^{EUS}\right)R_a^{EUS}\right]$

$W^F - W_2^F = \left(\sum N_a^{PC}\right)\left[\sum W_a^{PC}\left(R_a^{PC} - R_a^{EUS}\right)\right]$

Clearly, under the ST assumption that $R_a^{PC} - R_a^{EUS}$ for each $a$, $W^F = W_2^F$. However, if $R_a^{PC} \neq R_a^{EUS}$ for some ages $a$ and also the $W_a^{PC} \neq W_a^{EUS}$ for some ages $a$, but the effect of differences in $R_a$ weighted by population census weights $W_a^{PC}$, that is $\sum_a W_a^{PC}\left(R_a^{PC} - R_a^{EU}\right)$, is 'equal in magnitude and opposite in sign' of the effect of differences in $W_a$ weighted by age specific participation ratios $R_a^{EUS}$, that is $\sum\left(W_a^{PC} - W_a^{EUS}\right)R_a^{EUS}$ then $W^F = W_1^F$ while $W^F \neq W_2^F$. Given, there is no way of judging which assumption is appropriate, unless the differences in methods and coverage between NSS and PC are probed in depth, there is no way of resolving this issue. In the meantime perhaps the average $\dfrac{\left(W_1^F + W_2^F\right)}{2}$ could be used as an estimate of $W^F$.

The analysis thus far is based on a comparison of PC and EUS data for just one year. However, growth rates implied in population projections for non-census years by the Registrar General do not equal the growth rates for the same years derived from the EUS. For example, the Registrar General (GoI, 2001) projects the population to grow from 1012.4 million in 2001 to 1094.1 million by 2006 implying an average annual growth rate of 1.56 per cent. NSS estimates the population in 1999-2000 at 921 million and in 2004 at 956 million (NSS, 2000 and 2004), implying an annual average growth rate of only 0.94 per cent! Thus, the underestimation of population from differences in method and coverage between PC and EUS is growing over time. Under the circumstances, the recommendation of blowing up EUS ratios using census population numbers needs to be reconsidered.

*Person Rate versus Person-Day Rate in EUS*

In the EUS, a person could be in one or combination of the following three broad activity statuses during the relevant reference period (year, week or day): (i) employed or working (i.e. being engaged in economic activity), (ii) unemployed or not working, but either making tangible efforts to seek work or being available for work if work is available and (iii) not working and not available for work. Statuses (i) and (ii) correspond to being in work force and status (iii) relates to being out of work force. It is possible for a person to be in all three statuses concurrently depending on the reference period. Under such a circumstance, one of the three was uniquely identified as that person's status by adopting 'either the major time or priority criterion'. The former was used in identifying the 'usual activity status' and the latter for 'current activity status'. More precisely, the principal usual activity status of a person is that status among the three in which he or she spent relatively longer time (i.e. major time criterion) during the 365 days preceding the date of survey. In addition to his or her principal activity in which he or she spent a major part of her time, he or she could have pursued some economic activity for a relatively shorter time during the preceding year. This minor time activity was that person's subsidiary activity.

The 'current weekly status' of a person during a period of 7 days preceding the date of survey is decided on the basis of 'a certain priority cum major time criterion.' The status of 'working' gets priority over the status of 'not working but seeking or available for work,' which in turn gets priority over the status of 'not working and not available for work'. A person is classified as 'working (employed)' while pursuing an economic activity, if he or she had 'worked for at least one hour during the 7 day reference period'. A person who either did not work or worked for less than one hour is classified as unemployed, if he or she actively sought work or was available for work for any time during the reference week, even if not actively seeking work in the belief that no work was available. Finally, a person is classified as not in the work force if he or she neither worked nor was available for work any time during the reference period. The current daily status of a person was determined on the basis of his/her activity status in each day of the reference week using a priority-cum-major time criterion (See Appendix A-6.1 for details).

Which of the three rates, namely 'usual status (principal and secondary capacity work combined)', 'weekly status' and 'daily status' are to be used, in, say, estimating the levels and trends in work force or the number of unemployed? The first two of the three are 'person rates', i.e., they refer to persons, for example the number of persons employed or unemployed per 1000 persons in the population. The third is a person-day rate i.e. it refers to the number of person days employed or unemployed per 1000 person-days. Thus, if a person in the sample was deemed to have worked (i.e. employed) for 3.5 days in the reference week, his employed person-days is 3.5 and total person-days is seven so that his employed person-day rate is 0.5, i.e. 500 person days of employment in the week per 1000 person days. Averaging this daily rate over all persons and multiplying it by the population figures from the census to adjust for underestimation in EUS will yield the total number of 'person-days' of employment per day.

The total number of person-days of employment is not the same as the total number of employed 'persons.' The reason is that a given total number of 'person-days' of employment could be distributed among the same number of persons in many ways so as to lead to different numbers of 'persons' employed. For example, consider a four person economy in which all four participate in the work force and together they were employed for ten person-days in the week. This yields a person-day rate of employment of 10 out of 28 or 36 per cent. If the ten person-days are distributed in a way that one person is employed for seven days, another for three days and the remaining two are unemployed, then person-rate of employment is two out of four or 50 per cent. On the other hand, if it is distributed in a way that three persons work for three days each and one person works for just a day, the person rate of employment is four out of four or 100 per cent, given the priority given to the status of employment! Unfortunately, official publications seem unaware of the distinction between persons and person-days. In other words, the heterogeneity among the population in the days worked is ignored. For example, MoF (2004, Table 20-7) purports to present the number of persons in the work force, employed and unemployed, using daily status rates that refer to person-days. Interestingly, at the top of the table, the phrase 'person-years' is used, suggesting that the numbers in the table refer, not to persons but to person-years. Apparently, MoF wants to have it both ways!

*Employment Elasticity:*
*A Concept Lacking Analytical Foundation*

The trend in absolute numbers employed (ignoring official confusion between persons and person-years) has been analyzed and policy pronouncements based on it have been made (MoF, 2004; Planning Commission (2001, 2002, 2005)). For example, MoF (2004: 207) suggests that, "In view of the declining employment elasticity of growth, observed during 1994-2000, the Special Group (constituted by the Planning Commission on targeting ten million employment opportunities per year over the Tenth Plan period) has recommended (Planning Commission, 2002) that over and above employment generated in process of present structure of growth, there is a need to promote certain identified labour intensive activities." In its Mid-term Appraisal of the Tenth Plan, the Planning commission (Planning Commission, 2005, Table 8.1) provides estimates of work force, work opportunities and persons unemployed in the Tenth Plan ostensibly on a current daily status basis again confusing persons with person–years. The text associated with the table mentions that the data on employment generated are based on observed employment elasticities and actual GDP growth, echoing MoF (2004: 209).

Unfortunately, such projections and policy pronouncements based on them have no analytical foundations. Elementary economics would suggest that the observed employment in any period represents an equilibrium between labour supply and labour demand. In principle, both supply and demand functions could shift over time. For example, GDP growth, *ceteris paribus*, would shift the labour demand function outward. Similarly, growth of the number of individuals in the prime working ages due to population growth, *ceteris paribus*, shift the supply curve outward. Depending on the relative strengths of these shifts almost any trend (up, down or no change) in equilibrium employment is possible. In other words, the so-called 'employment elasticity' is not a deep behavioural parameter and can take on any number. It is what econometricians would deem a 'reduced form' rather than a 'structural parameter'. Although it is understandable that policy makers, including the Planning Commission make their projections and policy choices on the basics of such 'reduced forms', one has to recognise their limitations.

## Trends in Employment and Unemployment and Wages

### Employment

In view of the problems associated with estimating the trends in absolute numbers of persons in the work force employed and unemployed, I will focus only on the relevant ratios from various rounds, quinquennial as well as annual, of NSS for India as a whole. Table 6.3 shows the trends in rural and urban areas of the number of persons (male and female) employed per 1,000 persons according to usual status (primary and secondary capacity) and current weekly status and number of 'person-days' of employment per 1000 'person-days' according to current daily status. The usual status employment rates of males shows remarkable stability.[5] The 20 observations covering a period of more than three decades (1972-73 to January-June 2004), cover a very narrow range, with the lowest at 53.1 per cent in 1999-2000, and the highest at 56 per cent in 1994-95, and with 12 out of 20 falling in an even narrower range of 54.1 per cent-55.0 per cent. The current weekly status employment rates, naturally varied more with the lowest being 50.4 per cent in 1983 and highest at 54.1 per cent, also in 1994-95 (still 12 out of 20 observations fell within a narrow range of 52.1 per cent and 53.5 per cent). There are only seven observations for the whole period on current daily status 'person-day' rates, and these varied between a low of 47.1 per cent in the first half of 2004, to a high of 50.4 per cent in 1993-94. Employment rates for males in urban areas varied more over time compared to rural areas. Still 14 (or 70 per cent) of the observations for usual status and for current weekly status, fell in the range of 50.6 per cent to 52.51 per cent.

---

5. Abhijit Banerjee (in a private communication) finds this stability very puzzling in view of the large demographic changes that have occurred in the past three decades. Any attempt to resolve the puzzle would have to be based on an analysis of the dynamics of the labour force participation, labour demand and labour supply. This enormous task, which is eminently worth doing, is beyond the scope of this descriptive paper.

## Table 6.3

*Employment Rate (Number of Persons/Persons-Days Worked per 1000 Persons/Persons-days) according to 'Usual Status', 'Current Weekly Status' and 'Current Daily Status' Approaches for Different Rounds*

All-India

| Round (Survey Period) | Male | | | | Female | | | |
|---|---|---|---|---|---|---|---|---|
| | Usual Status | | Current Weekly Status | Current Daily Status | Usual Status | | Current Weekly Status | Current Daily Status |
| | ps | All (ps+ss) | | | ps | All (ps+ss) | | |
| (1) | (2) | (3) | (4) | (5) | (6) | (7) | (8) | (9) |
| **Rural** | | | | | | | | |
| 60(Jan.-June'04) | 527 | 542 | 511 | 471 | 228 | 315 | 245 | 190 |
| 59(Jan.-Dec'03) | 536 | 547 | 525 | - | 235 | 311 | 236 | - |
| 58(July-Dec'02) | 537 | 546 | 529 | - | 214 | 281 | 219 | - |
| 57(July'01-June'02) | 531 | 546 | 523 | - | 241 | 314 | 241 | - |
| 56(July'00-June'01) | 532 | 544 | 525 | - | 221 | 287 | 217 | - |
| 55(July'99-June'00)* | 522 | 531 | 510 | 478 | 231 | 299 | 253 | 204 |
| 54(Jan.-June'98) | 530 | 539 | 524 | - | 207 | 263 | 202 | - |
| 53(Jan.-Dec.'97) | 541 | 550 | 535 | - | 222 | 291 | 222 | - |
| 52(July'95-June'96) | 542 | 551 | 538 | - | 234 | 295 | 233 | - |
| 51(July'94-June'95) | 547 | 560 | 541 | - | 237 | 317 | 241 | - |
| 50(July'93-June'94)* | 538 | 553 | 531 | 504 | 234 | 328 | 267 | 219 |
| 49(Jan.-June'93) | 532 | 545 | 527 | - | 243 | 311 | 232 | - |
| 48(Jan.-Dec.'92) | 541 | 556 | 536 | - | 250 | 313 | 244 | - |

*contd. ....*

...contd. ...

| Round (Survey Period) | All-India | | | | | | | |
| | Male | | | | Female | | | |
| | Usual Status | | Current Weekly Status | Current Daily Status | Usual Status | | Current Weekly Status | Current Daily Status |
| | ps | All (ps+ss) | | | ps | All (ps+ss) | | |
| (1) | (2) | (3) | (4) | (5) | (6) | (7) | (8) | (9) |
| 47(July-Dec.'91) | 538 | 546 | 534 | - | 244 | 294 | 238 | - |
| 46(July'90-June'91) | 542 | 553 | 535 | - | 242 | 292 | 230 | - |
| 45(July'89-June'90) | 537 | 548 | 528 | - | 252 | 319 | 230 | - |
| 43(July'87-June'88)* | 517 | 539 | 504 | 501 | 245 | 323 | 220 | 207 |
| 38(Jan.-Dec.'83)* | 528 | 547 | 511 | 482 | 248 | 340 | 227 | 198 |
| 32(1977-78)* | | 542 | 519 | 458 | | 331 | 232 | 194 |
| 27(1972-73) | | 545 | 530 | 503 | | 318 | 277 | 231 |
| **Urban** | | | | | | | | |
| 60(Jan.-June'04) | 531 | 540 | 525 | 504 | 121 | 150 | 136 | 118 |
| 59(Jan.-Dec.'03) | 535 | 541 | 528 | - | 119 | 146 | 121 | - |
| 58(July-Dec.'02) | 530 | 534 | 523 | - | 118 | 140 | 118 | - |
| 57(July'01-June'02) | 547 | 553 | 542 | - | 110 | 139 | 111 | - |
| 56(July'00-June'01) | 525 | 531 | 519 | - | 116 | 140 | 117 | - |
| 55(July'99-June'00)* | 513 | 518 | 509 | 490 | 117 | 139 | 128 | 111 |
| 54(Jan.-June'98) | 506 | 509 | 504 | - | 99 | 114 | 99 | - |
| 53(Jan.-Dec.'97) | 516 | 521 | 513 | - | 111 | 131 | 114 | - |
| 52(July'95-June'96) | 522 | 525 | 520 | - | 107 | 124 | 109 | - |

contd. ...

...contd. ...

| Round (Survey Period) | Male | | | | Female | | | |
| | Usual Status | | Current Weekly Status | Current Daily Status | Usual Status | | Current Weekly Status | Current Daily Status |
| | ps | All (ps+ss) | | | ps | All (ps+ss) | | |
| (1) | (2) | (3) | (4) | (5) | (6) | (7) | (8) | (9) |
| 51(July'94-June'95) | 514 | 519 | 511 | - | 112 | 136 | 117 | - |
| 50(July'93-June'94)* | 513 | 521 | 511 | 496 | 121 | 155 | 139 | 120 |
| 49(Jan.-June'93) | 506 | 509 | 504 | - | 113 | 130 | 109 | - |
| 48(Jan.-Dec.'92) | 502 | 507 | 501 | - | 125 | 146 | 122 | - |
| 47(July-Dec.'91) | 511 | 516 | 509 | - | 120 | 132 | 117 | - |
| 46(July'90-June'91) | 508 | 513 | 506 | - | 123 | 143 | 124 | - |
| 45(July'89-June'90) | 501 | 512 | 503 | - | 124 | 146 | 121 | - |
| 43(July'87-June'88)* | 496 | 506 | 492 | 477 | 118 | 152 | 119 | 110 |
| 38(Jan.-Dec.'83)* | 500 | 512 | 492 | 473 | 120 | 151 | 118 | 106 |
| 32(1977-78)* | | 508 | 490 | 472 | | 156 | 125 | 109 |
| 27(1972-73) | | 501 | 491 | 477 | | 134 | 123 | 108 |

Note: *: Quinquennial Rounds

Source: NSS (2005a), Statement 7.

## Table 6.4

*Change in Employment Rate (in per cent)*

|  | Rural Areas | | | Urban Areas | | |
|---|---|---|---|---|---|---|
|  | US(PS+SS) | CWS | CDS | US(PS+SS) | CWS | CDS |
| 1983 to 1987-1988 | -0.46 | -0.37 | 3.9 | -1.17 | 0.00 | 0.35 |
| 1983 to 1993-1994 | 1.10 | 3.91 | 4.6 | 1.76 | 3.80 | 4.86 |
| 1983 to 1999-2000 | -3.10 | -0.19 | -0.82 | 1.18 | 3.45 | 3.59 |
| 1987-88 to 1993-1994 | 2.60 | 5.35 | 0.60 | 2.16 | 3.36 | 3.78 |
| 1987-88 to 1999-2000 | -1.48 | 1.19 | -4.59 | 2.37 | 3.45 | 2.72 |

*Source*: Table 6.3.

Employment rates for females are considerably lower and vary much more compared to males both in rural and urban areas. The facts that work force participation and employment rates are lower for females are well known. Since the focus of this paper is on a factual description of the trends and not a causal analysis, I will not get into the determinants of these rates and sex-differences in them.

Table 6.3 is very useful in assessing the significance of the official finding that, "rate of growth of employment, on Current Daily Status (CDS) basis, declined from 2.7 per cent per annum in 1983 to 1993-1994 to 1.07 per cent per annum during 1994-2000" (MoF, 2004: 208). The absolute numbers of employment in MoF (2004) were derived by multiplying the relevant census population numbers (respectively for rural males, rural females, urban males and urban females) by the CDS employment rate for that category. Thus, the employment trends combine the effect of trends in CDS 'person-day' employment rates and of the growth of population in the relevant category.

Let us ignore, albeit inappropriately, the distinction between 'person-day' rates, and person rates as discussed in Section 2.2.3 and follow MoF (2004). Then, if we compare the changes in rate of employment per 1000 persons using current daily status (CDS) 'person-day' rates, usual status (primary+secondary) person rates (US(PS+SS)), and current weekly status (CWS) person rates, for the four years considered in MoF (2004), we get the following picture for males who constitute the overwhelming majority (in excess of 75 per cent) of those employed (Table 6.4 derived from Table 6.3). First, the changes in employment rates over a 20 year period, however measured, are relatively modest, the maximum increase being 5.35 per cent for the changes in CWS rate for the period 1987-88 and 1993-94 and the maximum decrease being 4.59 per cent for the longer period 1987-88 to 1999-2000. Second, the signs of the changes, though not their magnitudes, are the same according to the three rates, except during 1983 to 1987-88 and 1997-98 to 1999-2000 in rural areas and 1983 to 1987-88 in urban areas, when the sign of one of the rates was the opposite of the signs of the other two.

While using the census absolute numbers as multiplicants of NSS rates, if instead of CDS rates, one uses CWS employment rates, aggregate employment growth between 1983 and 1999-2000 would have been faster in rural areas, slower in urban areas and faster overall. But between 1983 and 1987-88 on the other hand, the use of CWS would lower the growth of employment both in rural and urban areas. The point is that it matters which of the three employment rates is used for projecting aggregated employment. It is the unfortunate use of this inappropriate rate by MoF (2004) and the Planning Commission that has led to a pessimistic assessment of employment trends since the early eighties. I have already argued that the CDS rate, being a person-day rate is inappropriate.

The fact that the underestimation of total population in the NSS relative to the census is increasing over time is a cause for concern. One cannot rule out the possibility that whatever is causing the increasing under estimation could also affect the estimated employment and unemployment rates as well as many other ratios in EUS. Moreover, the sampling design of the NSS changes from round-to-round, sometimes in a major way, and often in minor ways. Except for the controversy confronting poverty estimates because of changes in the reference period for consumption of some commodities, the impact of design changes on the means and variances of estimates of other characteristics, and hence their comparability over time, has not attracted much attention. It is high time that the NSS examines this issue in depth.

*Unemployment*

Turning to unemployment rates in Tables 6.5.A-6.5.D, once again there is no evidence of any noticeable time trends regardless which

## Table 6.5.A

### Unemployment Rates (number of persons (or person-days) Unemployed per 1000 Persons (or person-days) in the labour force) for Different Rounds

| Rural Round | Male | | | | Female | | | |
| | | | | | All-India | | | |
| | Usual Status | Usual Adjusted | Current Weekly Status | Current Daily Status | Usual Status | Usual Adjusted | Current Weekly Status | Current Daily Status |
| (1) | (2) | (3) | (4) | (5) | (6) | (7) | | |
| 60 | 24 (13) | 18 (10) | 47 (25) | 90 (47) | 22 (5) | 13 (4) | 45 (12) | 93 (19) |
| 59 | 19 (10) | 15 (9) | 28 (15) | - | 10 (2) | 6 (2) | 16 (4) | - |
| 58 | 18 (10) | 15 (8) | 28 (15) | - | 10 (2) | 6 (2) | 16 (4) | - |
| 57 | 14 (7) | 11 (6) | 26 (14) | - | 20 (5) | 14 (5) | 26 (7) | - |
| 56 | 16 (9) | 14 (8) | 23 (12) | - | 6 (1) | 4 (1) | 18 (4) | - |
| 55 | 21 (11) | 17 (9) | 39 (21) | 72 (37) | 15 (4) | 10 (3) | 37 (10) | 70 (15) |
| 54 | 24 (13) | 21 (11) | 29 (15) | - | 20 (4) | 15 (4) | 27 (6) | - |

contd. ..

...contd. ..

| Rural Round | All-India | | | | | | | |
|---|---|---|---|---|---|---|---|---|
| | Male | | | | Female | | | |
| | Usual Status | Usual Adjusted | Current Weekly Status | Current Daily Status | Usual Status | Usual Adjusted | Current Weekly Status | Current Daily Status |
| (1) | (2) | (3) | (4) | | (5) | (6) | (7) | |
| 53 | 16 (9) | 12 (7) | 20 (11) | - | 9 (2) | 7 (2) | 18 (4) | - |
| 52 | 15 (8) | 13 (7) | 18 (10) | - | 8 (2) | 7 (2) | 9 (2) | - |
| 51 | 12 (7) | 10 (6) | 18 (10) | - | 5 (1) | 4 (1) | 12 (3) | - |
| 50 | 20 (11) | 14 (8) | 30 (17) | 56 (30) | 14 (3) | 8 (3) | 30 (8) | 56 (13) |
| 45 | | | 26 | | | | 21 | |

*Note:* Figues within brackets indicate the proportion of unemployed per 1000 persons (person-days).

*Source:* NSS (2005a), Statement 16R.

## Table 6.5.B

### Rural Unemployment Rates during 1972-73 to 1999-2000 in Different NSS Rounds

Rural Unemployment Rates (Number of Persons (or Person Days) Unemployed per 1000 Persons (or Person Days) in the Work Force) for Different Rounds

| All-India Round (year) | Male | | | Female | | |
|---|---|---|---|---|---|---|
| | US (adj.) | CWS | CDS | US (adj.) | CWS | CDS |
| 43 (1987-88) | 18 | 42 | 46 | 24 | 44 | 67 |
| 38 (1983) | 14 | 37 | 75 | 7 | 43 | 90 |
| 32 (1977-78) | 13 | 36 | 71 | 20 | 41 | 92 |
| 27 (1972-73) | 12 | 30 | 68 | 5 | 55 | 112 |

*Source:* NSS (2000).

## Table 6.5.C

Unemployment Rates (Number of Persons (or Person-days) Unemployed per 1000 Persons (or Person-days) in the Labour Force) for Different Rounds

| Urban Round | All-India | | | | | | | |
| --- | --- | --- | --- | --- | --- | --- | --- | --- |
| | Male | | | | Female | | | |
| | Usual Status | Usual Adjusted | Current Weekly Status | Current Daily Status | Usual Status | Usual Adjusted | Current Weekly Status | Current Daily Status |
| (1) | (2) | (3) | (4) | | (5) | (6) | (7) | |
| 60 | 46 (25) | 40 (22) | 57 (32) | 81 (45) | 89 (12) | 67 (11) | 90 (14) | 117 (16) |
| 59 | 43 (24) | 40 (23) | 51 (28) | - | 44 (5) | 35 (5) | 49 (6) | - |
| 58 | 47 (26) | 45 (25) | 55 (31) | - | 61 (8) | 47 (7) | 57 (7) | - |
| 57 | 42 (24) | 39 (22) | 46 (26) | - | 49 (6) | 38 (5) | 48 (6) | - |
| 56 | 42 (23) | 39 (22) | 48 (26) | - | 38 (5) | 29 (4) | 39 (5) | - |
| 55 | 48 (26) | 45 (24) | 56 (30) | 73 (38) | 71 (9) | 57 (8) | 73 (10) | 94 (12) |

contd. ...

...contd. ...

| Urban Round | All-India | | | | | | | |
| | Male | | | | Female | | | |
| | Usual Status | Usual Adjusted | Current Weekly Status | Current Daily Status | Usual Status | Usual Adjusted | Current Weekly Status | Current Daily Status |
| (1) | (2) | (3) | (4) | | (5) | (6) | (7) | |
| 54 | 53 (28) | 51 (27) | 54 (29) | - | 81 (9) | 68 (8) | 78 (8) | - |
| 53 | 37 (21) | 39 (21) | 43 (23) | - | 51 (6) | 44 (6) | 58 (7) | - |
| 52 | 40 (22) | 38 (21) | 41 (22) | - | 36 (4) | 31 (4) | 35 (4) | - |
| 51 | 37 (20) | 34 (18) | 39 (21) | - | 41 (5) | 34 (5) | 40 (5) | - |
| 50 | 45 (24) | 40 (22) | 52 (28) | 67 (36) | 83 (11) | 62 (10) | 84 (12) | 105 (14) |
| 45 | | | 45 | | | | 40 | |

*Note:* Figues within brackets indicate the proportion of unemployed per 1000 persons (person-days).

*Source:* NSS (2005a), Statement 16U.

## Table 6.5.D

*Urban Unemployment Rates During 1972-73 to 1999-2000 in Different NSS Rounds*

| All-India Round (year) | Urban Unemployment Rate (Number of Persons (or Person-days) Unemployed per 1000 Persons (or Person-days) in the Work Force) for Different Rounds | | | | | |
|---|---|---|---|---|---|---|
| | Male | | | Female | | |
| | US (adj.) | CWS | CDS | US (adj.) | CWS | CDS |
| 43 (1987-88) | 52 | 66 | 88 | 62 | 92 | 120 |
| 38 (1983) | 51 | 67 | 92 | 49 | 75 | 110 |
| 32 (1977-78) | 54 | 71 | 94 | 124 | 109 | 145 |
| 27 (1972-73) | 48 | 60 | 80 | 60 | 92 | 137 |

*Source*: Same as for Table 6.5.b.

of the three rates are used. As is to be expected, US and CWS person rates are lower than the person-day CDS rates. Also, female unemployment rates fluctuate more than the male rates.

### Some Characteristics of the Usually Employed

**Current Weekly and Current Daily Status**

The next set of tables looks at different aspects of those who are 'usually' employed, taking together their principal and secondary activities. Since their unemployment rates are low (i.e. less than 50 for 1000 persons), and they cover nearly 95 per cent of those who participate in the work force, let us focus on usually employed (ps + ss), Tables 6.6.A and 6.6.B present their distribution according to their employment status as measured by CDS and CWS. The usually employed, by definition "are working in an economic activity for more than 183 days in a year." Table 6.6.A shows that in the current week, a proportion among them, ranging between 4.3 per cent in 1993-94 and 6.8 per cent in 1987-88 of rural males, and from 16.9 per cent in 1990-2000 and 32.5 per cent in 1987-88 of rural females, did not work (i.e. were either unemployed or out of work force). Corresponding proportions in urban areas for males as well as females are lower compared to rural proportions.

NSS (2001: 154) views these proportions as "underemployment rates," without defining what exactly they mean by underemployment.

## Table 6.6.A

*Per 1000 Distribution of Usually Employed (Principal and Subsidiary Status Taken Together) by their Broad Current Weekly Status (All India)*

| Current Weekly Status | Rural | | | | | | | | Urban | | | | | | | |
| | Male | | | | Female | | | | Male | | | | Female | | | |
| | Jan-Jun 2004 | 1999-2000 | 1993-94 | 1987-88 | Jan-Jun 2004 | 1999-2000 | 1993-94 | 1987-88 | Jan-Jun 2004 | 1999-2000 | 1993-94 | 1987-88 | Jan-Jun 2004 | 1999-2000 | 1993-94 | 1987-88 |
| (1) | (2) | (3) | (4) | (5) | (6) | (7) | (8) | (9) | (10) | (11) | (12) | (13) | (14) | (15) | (16) | (17) |
| Employed | 440 | 956 | 957 | 931 | 769 | 832 | 807 | 675 | 972 | 977 | 976 | 967 | 848 | 900 | 884 | 768 |
| Unemployed | 28 | 22 | 15 | 23 | 28 | 21 | 14 | 8 | 17 | 11 | 11 | 17 | 13 | 9 | 9 | 17 |
| Not in Work Force | 32 | 22 | 28 | 46 | 209 | 148 | 179 | 317 | 11 | 12 | 12 | 16 | 89 | 91 | 107 | 215 |
| All | 1000 | 1000 | 1000 | 1000 | 1000 | 1000 | 1000 | 1000 | 1000 | 1000 | 1000 | 1000 | 1000 | 1000 | 1000 | 1000 |

*Sources:* For 1987-88, 1993-94 & 1999-2000: NSS (2001). For Jan-June 2004: NSS (2005a).

For example, even a person who is employed throughout a year would not be in the work force on holidays. Beside, they could be unemployed on days between change of longer term jobs, a category of unemployment known as 'frictional unemployment' in advanced countries. Table 6.6.A also shows, among those usually employed who were not working during the current week, a considerably larger proportion among females than males reported as being out of the work force. NSS (2001: 155) suggests that, "when work is not available, a large proportion of females withdrew from the work force rather than report themselves as unemployed." There is no basis for this inference in the data themselves. NSS offers no justification for assuming, first of all, that if a usually employed person is not working in the current week, it is because "work is not available" whatever that means! Second, the reason why females might choose to report to a greater extent than males of being out of work force, rather than as unemployed is not explained. It is more likely that the days of employment exceeding 182 that qualifies a female to be usually employed consists of several bouts of employment, interspersed with days being out of work force for reasons relating to household exigencies and little to do with 'work not being available.' On the other hand, males are much more likely to heave continuous stretches of employment and less likely to drop out of the work force for household exigencies.

Tables 6.6.B and 6.6.C respectively provide the distribution of person-days of those usually employed and those employed according to weekly status, the latter spend fewer days not being employed than the former. This is particularly the case for females.

NSS (2001: 156), asked those who were usually employed "whether they worked more or less regularly throughout the year" and tabulated the results according to the broad usual status of the nature of their employment. Unsurprisingly, a large proportion of those who were engaged in casual labour did not work "more or less regularly." Again, NSS considers the proportion not working regularly as another indicator of underemployment, and without any clear definition of what it means to be underemployed. Those above the age of 15 who were usually employed according to principal status were asked whether they sought or were available for additional or alternative work and the reasons thereof. The

## Table 6.6.B

*Per 1000 Distribution of Person-days Usually Employed (Principal and Subsidiary Status Taken Together) by their Broad Current Daily Status (All India)*

| | Rural | | | | | | | | Urban | | | | | | | |
| | Male | | | | Female | | | | Male | | | | Female | | | |
| Current Daily Status | Jan-Jun 2004 | 1999-2000 | 1993-94 | 1987-88 | Jan-Jun 2004 | 1999-2000 | 1993-94 | 1987-88 | Jan-Jun 2004 | 1999-2000 | 1993-94 | 1987-88 | Jan-Jun 2004 | 1999-2000 | 1993-94 | 1987-88 |
| (1) | (2) | (3) | (4) | (5) | (6) | (7) | (8) | (9) | (10) | (11) | (12) | (13) | (14) | (15) | (16) | (17) |
| Employed | 868 | 897 | 909 | 926 | 547 | 676 | 663 | 638 | 932 | 942 | 949 | 938 | 778 | 791 | 766 | 716 |
| Unemployed | 64 | 53 | 40 | 27 | 49 | 41 | 30 | 26 | 43 | 27 | 27 | 37 | 28 | 22 | 24 | 37 |
| Not in Work Force | 69 | 51 | 51 | 47 | 385 | 283 | 306 | 336 | 23 | 31 | 25 | 25 | 192 | 187 | 210 | 247 |
| All | 1000 | 1000 | 1000 | 1000 | 1000 | 1000 | 1000 | 1000 | 1000 | 1000 | 1000 | 1000 | 1000 | 1000 | 1000 | 1000 |

Sources: For 1987-88, 1993-94 & 1999-2000: NSS (2001). For Jan-June 2004: NSS (2005a).

## Table 6.6.C

### Per 1000 Distribution of Person-days of Current Weekly Status Employed Persons by their Broad Current Daily Status (All India)

| Current Daily Status | Rural | | | | | | | | Urban | | | | | | | |
|---|---|---|---|---|---|---|---|---|---|---|---|---|---|---|---|---|
| | Male | | | | Female | | | | Male | | | | Female | | | |
| | Jan-Jun 2004 | 1999-2000 | 1993-94 | 1987-88 | Jan-Jun 2004 | 1999-2000 | 1993-94 | 1987-88 | Jan-Jun 2004 | 1999-2000 | 1993-94 | 1987-88 | Jan-Jun 2004 | 1999-2000 | 1993-94 | 1987-88 |
| (1) | (2) | (3) | (4) | (5) | (6) | (7) | (8) | (9) | (10) | (11) | (12) | (13) | (14) | (15) | (16) | (17) |
| Employed | 923 | 936 | 949 | 995 | 774 | 808 | 819 | 945 | 959 | 963 | 970 | 969 | 964 | 873 | 860 | 922 |
| Unemployed | 43 | 32 | 26 | 4 | 35 | 25 | 21 | 26 | 25 | 16 | 15 | 22 | 18 | 15 | 17 | 29 |
| Not in Work Force | 34 | 32 | 24 | 1 | 191 | 167 | 158 | 29 | 16 | 21 | 13 | 9 | 118 | 112 | 122 | 49 |
| All | 1000 | 1000 | 1000 | 1000 | 1000 | 1000 | 1000 | 1000 | 1000 | 1000 | 1000 | 1000 | 1000 | 1000 | 1000 | 1000 |

*Sources:* For 1987-88, 1993-94 & 1999-2000: NSS (2001). For Jan-June 2004: NSS (2005b).

proportion who sought additional or alternative work was less than 10.5 per cent regardless of the sex of the individual or residence (rural/urban). The prime reason for seeking additional or alternative work unsurprisingly was to earn additional income or higher remuneration. Since the terms 'additional and alternative work' are vague and each respondent could interpret it in his or her own way, these responses have to be treated as indicative only.

### Status of Employment, Age and Sector of Employment

Table 6.7 provides time trends in the status of employment of the usually employed in rural and urban areas. Taking principal and secondary activities together, the share of self-employed seems to be going down both in rural and urban areas among males. For females, such a clear trend is not evident, though in rural areas one could see a faint increasing trend.

Table 6.8 shows the trends in age distribution of the usually employed. Other than a welcome, though slow, decline in child (age group 5-14) labour, and a more pronounced downward trend in the employment of the old (60+) there is nothing striking in the trends. What is important to note from the two tables is that self-employment is the single dominant status of employment in rural and urban areas for males and females. Regular wage/salaried employment accounted less than 10 per cent of the usually employed rural males in January-June 2004, with casual labour accounting for the rest. Some might see a rising trend in the share of casual labour in rural areas for males, though it is simplistic to call it as increasing proliferation of labour. However, it is interesting that roughly the same proportion (around 35 per cent) of rural males and females were employed as casual workers. In urban areas, as can be expected, regular wage/salaried employment was close to being as important as self-employment for males. For both males and females, wage/salaried employment is much more important as a source of employment than casual labour in urban areas and there is not much evidence of any significant increasing trend in the share of casual labour in urban areas.

Trends in sectoral or industrial composition of employment for the usually employed are shown in Tables 6.9, 6.10 and 6.11. Although Tables 6.10 and 6.11 have essentially the same data as

## Table 6.7.A

### Per 1000 Distribution of Usually Employed by Status of Employment for Different Rounds

| | All-India | | | | | |
|---|---|---|---|---|---|---|
| Round (Survey Period) | Principal Status | | | All (ps+ss) | | |
| | Self-employed | Regular Wage/Salaried | Casual Labour | Self-employed | Regular Wage/Salaried | Casual Labour |
| (1) | (2) | (3) | (4) | (5) | (6) | (7) |
| | **Rural Males** | | | | | |
| 60(Jan.-June'04) | 564 | 95 | 341 | 572 | 93 | 335 |
| 59(Jan.-Dec.'03) | 573 | 88 | 339 | 578 | 87 | 335 |
| 58(July-Dec.'02) | 563 | 89 | 348 | 569 | 88 | 344 |
| 57(July'01-June'02) | 570 | 83 | 345 | 580 | 81 | 339 |
| 56(July'00-June'01) | 582 | 98 | 320 | 589 | 95 | 316 |
| 55(July'99-June'00)* | 544 | 90 | 366 | 550 | 88 | 362 |
| 54(Jan.-June'98) | 547 | 71 | 382 | 553 | 70 | 377 |
| 53(Jan.-Dec.'97) | 590 | 74 | 336 | 594 | 73 | 333 |
| 52(July'95-June'96) | 585 | 78 | 337 | 590 | 77 | 333 |
| 51(July'94-June'95) | 597 | 69 | 334 | 604 | 68 | 328 |
| 50(July'93-June'94)* | 567 | 87 | 346 | 577 | 85 | 338 |
| 49(Jan.-June'93) | 583 | 81 | 336 | 591 | 79 | 330 |
| 48(Jan.-Dec.'92) | 601 | 85 | 314 | 608 | 83 | 309 |
| 47(July-Dec.'91) | 593 | 91 | 316 | 595 | 92 | 313 |
| 46(July'90-June'91) | 552 | 131 | 317 | 557 | 128 | 315 |
| 45(July'89-June'90) | 591 | 100 | 309 | 597 | 98 | 305 |
| 43(July'87-June'88)* | 575 | 104 | 321 | 586 | 100 | 314 |
| 38(Jan.-Dec.'83)* | 595 | 106 | 299 | 605 | 103 | 292 |

contd. ....

...contd. ...

| Round (Survey Period) | Principal Status | | | All (ps+ss) | | |
|---|---|---|---|---|---|---|
| | Self-employed | Regular Wage/Salaried | Casual Labour | Self-employed | Regular Wage/Salaried | Casual Labour |
| (1) | (2) | (3) | (4) | (5) | (6) | (7) |
| | | | **Rural Females** | | | |
| 60 (Jan.-June'04) | 533 | 51 | 416 | 615 | 38 | 347 |
| 59(Jan.-Dec.'03) | 550 | 43 | 407 | 616 | 33 | 351 |
| 58(July-Dec.'02) | 490 | 46 | 464 | 558 | 36 | 406 |
| 57(July'01-June'02) | 532 | 37 | 430 | 589 | 29 | 382 |
| 56(July'00-June'01) | 532 | 38 | 430 | 593 | 32 | 375 |
| 55(July'99-June'00)* | 500 | 39 | 461 | 573 | 31 | 396 |
| 54(Jan-June'98) | 482 | 31 | 486 | 534 | 25 | 442 |
| 53(Jan-Dec.'97) | 518 | 27 | 455 | 570 | 21 | 409 |
| 52(July'95-June'96) | 507 | 30 | 463 | 564 | 24 | 412 |
| 51(July'94-June'95) | 510 | 30 | 460 | 570 | 22 | 408 |
| 50(July'93-June'94)* | 513 | 34 | 453 | 586 | 27 | 387 |
| 49(Jan.-June'93) | 531 | 29 | 440 | 585 | 23 | 392 |
| 48(Jan.-Dec.'92) | 548 | 36 | 416 | 591 | 32 | 377 |
| 47(July-Dec'91) | 524 | 37 | 439 | 568 | 31 | 401 |
| 46(July'90-June'91) | 545 | 45 | 410 | 586 | 38 | 376 |
| 45(July'89-June'90) | 565 | 33 | 399 | 609 | 28 | 363 |
| 43(July'87-June'88)* | 549 | 49 | 402 | 608 | 37 | 355 |
| 38(Jan.-Dec.'83)* | 541 | 37 | 422 | 619 | 28 | 353 |

*All-India*

*Note:* *: Indicate Quinquennial Rounds.
*Source:* NSS (2005a), Statement 10R.

**Table 6.7.B**

*Per 1000 Distribution of Usually Employed by Status of Employment for Different Rounds*

| Round (Survey Period) | All-India | | | | | | |
|---|---|---|---|---|---|---|---|
| | Principal Status | | | All (ps+ss) | | | |
| | Self-employed | Regular Wage/Salaried | Casual Labour | Self-employed | Regular Wage/Salarie | Casual Labour |
| (1) | (2) | (3) | (4) | (5) | (6) | (7) |
| | **Urban Males** | | | | | | |
| 60(Jan.-June'04) | 437 | 410 | 153 | 441 | 406 | 153 |
| 59(Jan.-Dec.'03) | 425 | 418 | 157 | 429 | 415 | 156 |
| 58(July-Dec.'02) | 440 | 410 | 150 | 443 | 407 | 150 |
| 57(July'01-June'02) | 429 | 417 | 154 | 430 | 415 | 154 |
| 56(July'2000-June'01) | 410 | 415 | 175 | 414 | 411 | 175 |
| 55(July'99-June'2000)* | 412 | 419 | 169 | 415 | 417 | 168 |
| 54(Jan.-June'98) | 422 | 397 | 181 | 425 | 395 | 181 |
| 53(Jan.-Dec.'97) | 397 | 419 | 184 | 400 | 415 | 185 |
| 52(July'95-June'96) | 408 | 427 | 165 | 410 | 425 | 165 |
| 51(July'94-June'95) | 402 | 433 | 165 | 404 | 431 | 165 |
| 50(July'93-June'94)* | 411 | 427 | 162 | 417 | 420 | 163 |
| 49(Jan.-June'93) | 387 | 397 | 216 | 389 | 395 | 216 |
| 48(Jan.-Dec.'92) | 406 | 399 | 195 | 412 | 394 | 193 |
| 47(July-Dec.'91) | 425 | 401 | 174 | 489 | 399 | 172 |
| 46(July'90-June'91) | 404 | 445 | 151 | 407 | 442 | 151 |
| 45(July'89-June'90) | 413 | 421 | 166 | 423 | 413 | 164 |
| 43(July'87-June'88)* | 410 | 444 | 146 | 417 | 437 | 146 |
| 38(Jan.-Dec.'83)* | 402 | 445 | 153 | 409 | 437 | 154 |

*contd. ...*

...contd. ...

| Round (Survey Period) | Principal Status | | | All-India<br>All (ps+ss) | | |
| --- | --- | --- | --- | --- | --- | --- |
| | Self-employed | Regular Wage/Salaried | Casual Labour | Self-employed | Regular Wage/Salaried | Casual Labour |
| (1) | (2) | (3) | (4) | (5) | (6) | (7) |
| | | | **Urban Females** | | | |
| 60(Jan.-June'04) | 367 | 435 | 198 | 446 | 362 | 192 |
| 59(Jan.-Dec.'03) | 373 | 408 | 219 | 454 | 339 | 207 |
| 58(July-Dec.'02) | 405 | 360 | 236 | 459 | 308 | 233 |
| 57(July'01-June'02) | 374 | 371 | 255 | 441 | 298 | 261 |
| 56(July'2000-June'01) | 371 | 372 | 257 | 444 | 315 | 241 |
| 55(July'99-June'2000)* | 384 | 385 | 231 | 453 | 333 | 214 |
| 54(Jan.-June'98) | 330 | 372 | 298 | 384 | 327 | 288 |
| 53(Jan.-Dec.'97) | 333 | 360 | 307 | 397 | 313 | 290 |
| 52(July'95-June'96) | 347 | 380 | 273 | 400 | 332 | 268 |
| 51(July'94-June'95) | 363 | 357 | 280 | 426 | 301 | 273 |
| 50(July'93-June'94)* | 372 | 355 | 273 | 458 | 284 | 258 |
| 49(Jan.-June'93) | 345 | 301 | 354 | 407 | 262 | 331 |
| 48(Jan.-Dec.'92) | 368 | 336 | 296 | 425 | 288 | 287 |
| 47(July-Dec.'91) | 425 | 308 | 267 | 470 | 280 | 250 |
| 46(July'90-June'91) | 439 | 301 | 260 | 490 | 259 | 251 |
| 45(July'89-June'90) | 435 | 331 | 234 | 486 | 292 | 222 |
| 43(July'87-June'88)* | 393 | 342 | 265 | 471 | 275 | 254 |
| 38(Jan.-Dec.'83)* | 373 | 318 | 309 | 458 | 258 | 284 |

*Note:* *: Indicate Quinquennial Rounds.
*Source:* NSS (2005a), Statement 10U.

## Table 6.8.A

*Number of Rural Persons Usually Employed (ps+ss) per 1000 Persons by Broad Age-Groups for Different Rounds*

| Age-group (Years) | Rural (All-India) | | | | | | | |
|---|---|---|---|---|---|---|---|---|
| | Male | | | | Female | | | |
| | 57th | 58th | 59th | 60th | 57th | 58th | 59th | 60th |
| 5-14 | 45 | 47 | 43 | 39 | 53 | 34 | 41 | 38 |
| 15-29 | 774 | 738 | 746 | 747 | 397 | 334 | 377 | 401 |
| 30-59 | 977 | 977 | 974 | 969 | 580 | 538 | 586 | 583 |
| 60+ | 721 | 679 | 690 | 637 | 204 | 222 | 262 | 244 |
| 15-59 | 885 | 867 | 870 | 867 | 494 | 447 | 492 | 500 |
| 5+ | 626 | 614 | 616 | 613 | 355 | 316 | 350 | 355 |

*Sources*: For 57th, 58th, and 59th Rounds: NSS (2005a) National Sample Survey Organisation.
For 60th Round: NSS (2005a).

## Table 6.8.B

*Number of Urban Persons Usually Employed (ps+ss) per 1000 Persons by Broad Age-Groups for Different Rounds*

| Age-group (Years) | Urban (All-India) | | | | | | | |
|---|---|---|---|---|---|---|---|---|
| | Male | | | | Female | | | |
| | 57th | 58th | 59th | 60th | 57th | 58th | 59th | 60th |
| 5-14 | 43 | 31 | 31 | 27 | 35 | 15 | 18 | 14 |
| 15-29 | 637 | 624 | 615 | 628 | 136 | 160 | 154 | 162 |
| 30-59 | 958 | 952 | 954 | 947 | 246 | 249 | 261 | 270 |
| 60+ | 403 | 380 | 374 | 362 | 104 | 92 | 102 | 83 |
| 15-59 | 803 | 794 | 796 | 799 | 195 | 207 | 231 | 223 |
| 5+ | 603 | 589 | 593 | 592 | 152 | 154 | 159 | 149 |

*Source*: Same as for Table 6.8.A.

Table 6.9, the latter includes data from annual as well as quinquennial rounds. However, the sectoral groupings in Table 6.9 are coarser than the ones in Tables 6.10 and 6.11. But it turns out that primary sector in Table 6.9 is the same as agriculture in Tables 6.10 and 6.11. It is evident from all three tables that for rural males the share of employment in primary (agriculture) sector, though it has been

## Table 6.9

*Per 1000 Distribution of Usually Employed by Broad Groups of Industry for Various Rounds*

| Round | Male | | | | | | All-India Female | | | | | |
|---|---|---|---|---|---|---|---|---|---|---|---|---|
| | Primary | | Secondary | | Tertiary | | Primary | | Secondary | | Tertiary | |
| | ps | all | ps | all | ps | all | ps | all | ps | all | ps | all |
| (1) | (2) | (3) | (4) | (5) | (6) | (7) | (8) | (9) | (10) | (11) | (12) | (13) |
| Rural | | | | | | | | | | | | |
| 60 | 654 | 659 | 163 | 160 | 183 | 180 | 820 | 841 | 102 | 94 | 78 | 65 |
| 59 | 704 | 708 | 143 | 141 | 153 | 151 | 841 | 852 | 99 | 95 | 60 | 53 |
| 58 | 685 | 688 | 140 | 138 | 175 | 174 | 834 | 849 | 91 | 87 | 75 | 65 |
| 57 | 672 | 678 | 148 | 145 | 180 | 177 | 819 | 840 | 124 | 109 | 57 | 51 |
| 56 | 688 | 690 | 137 | 136 | 175 | 174 | 812 | 818 | 139 | 133 | 49 | 49 |
| 55* | 712 | 714 | 127 | 126 | 161 | 160 | 841 | 854 | 93 | 89 | 66 | 57 |
| 54 | 755 | 757 | 103 | 102 | 142 | 141 | 876 | 885 | 70 | 66 | 54 | 49 |
| 53 | 757 | 758 | 106 | 106 | 137 | 136 | 875 | 885 | 77 | 72 | 47 | 42 |
| 52 | 746 | 748 | 115 | 114 | 139 | 137 | 854 | 868 | 87 | 80 | 59 | 52 |
| 51 | 752 | 756 | 104 | 103 | 144 | 141 | 862 | 871 | 88 | 83 | 50 | 46 |
| 50* | 739 | 741 | 113 | 112 | 148 | 147 | 847 | 862 | 91 | 83 | 62 | 55 |
| 49 | 749 | 750 | 110 | 109 | 141 | 141 | 862 | 872 | 77 | 74 | 61 | 54 |
| 48 | 753 | 757 | 106 | 104 | 141 | 139 | 858 | 862 | 78 | 78 | 64 | 60 |

*contd. ...*

...contd. ...

All-India

| Round | Male | | | | | | Female | | | | | |
|---|---|---|---|---|---|---|---|---|---|---|---|---|
| | Primary | | Secondary | | Tertiary | | Primary | | Secondary | | Tertiary | |
| | ps | all | ps | all | ps | all | ps | all | ps | all | ps | all |
| 47 | 748 | 749 | 112 | 112 | 140 | 139 | 859 | 863 | 79 | 79 | 62 | 58 |
| 46 | 705 | 710 | 123 | 121 | 172 | 169 | 842 | 849 | 83 | 81 | 75 | 70 |
| 45 | 716 | 717 | 120 | 121 | 164 | 162 | 800 | 814 | 130 | 124 | 70 | 61 |
| 43* | 739 | 745 | 123 | 121 | 138 | 134 | 825 | 847 | 112 | 100 | 63 | 53 |
| 38* | 772 | 775 | 102 | 100 | 123 | 122 | 862 | 875 | 78 | 74 | 57 | 48 |
| **Urban** | | | | | | | | | | | | |
| 60 | 61 | 63 | 348 | 347 | 591 | 590 | 126 | 161 | 289 | 309 | 584 | 530 |
| 59 | 60 | 63 | 338 | 336 | 602 | 601 | 145 | 190 | 299 | 312 | 556 | 497 |
| 58 | 69 | 70 | 338 | 337 | 594 | 593 | 156 | 171 | 298 | 315 | 546 | 513 |
| 57 | 78 | 78 | 322 | 321 | 601 | 600 | 173 | 211 | 309 | 332 | 519 | 457 |
| 56 | 63 | 66 | 359 | 356 | 579 | 578 | 136 | 183 | 342 | 342 | 522 | 475 |
| 55* | 65 | 66 | 329 | 328 | 606 | 606 | 146 | 177 | 293 | 293 | 561 | 529 |
| 54 | 90 | 92 | 324 | 322 | 586 | 586 | 187 | 221 | 292 | 280 | 520 | 499 |
| 53 | 76 | 78 | 343 | 340 | 582 | 581 | 165 | 200 | 328 | 324 | 507 | 476 |
| 52 | 81 | 82 | 335 | 335 | 584 | 583 | 179 | 209 | 310 | 309 | 512 | 482 |
| 51 | 86 | 88 | 330 | 329 | 584 | 583 | 154 | 205 | 354 | 343 | 492 | 452 |
| 50* | 87 | 90 | 331 | 329 | 582 | 581 | 193 | 247 | 299 | 291 | 508 | 462 |

contd. ...

...contd. ...

| Round | All-India | | | | | | | | | | | |
|---|---|---|---|---|---|---|---|---|---|---|---|---|
| | Male | | | | | | Female | | | | | |
| | Primary | | Secondary | | Tertiary | | Primary | | Secondary | | Tertiary | |
| | ps | all | ps | all | ps | all | ps | all | ps | all | ps | all |
| 49 | 101 | 102 | 345 | 344 | 554 | 554 | 232 | 258 | 306 | 306 | 462 | 436 |
| 48 | 104 | 107 | 345 | 343 | 551 | 550 | 195 | 224 | 304 | 308 | 501 | 468 |
| 47 | 95 | 95 | 306 | 307 | 599 | 598 | 217 | 237 | 278 | 282 | 505 | 481 |
| 46 | 91 | 92 | 336 | 336 | 573 | 572 | 223 | 249 | 318 | 316 | 459 | 435 |
| 45 | 95 | 100 | 323 | 319 | 582 | 582 | 214 | 241 | 297 | 303 | 489 | 456 |
| 43* | 85 | 91 | 343 | 340 | 572 | 569 | 218 | 294 | 324 | 317 | 458 | 389 |
| 38* | 97 | 103 | 344 | 342 | 551 | 250 | 255 | 310 | 307 | 306 | 430 | 376 |

*Note:* 1. The broad group of industries *viz.*, primary, secondary and tertiary refers to the group of NIC-98 industry divisions 01-05, 10-45 and 50-99, respectively. Industry group 01-05 actually refers to the agricultural sector.

2. *: Indicate Quinquennial Rounds.

*Source:* NSS (2005a). Statement 11.

## Table 6.10

### Per 1000 Distribution of Usually Employed Persons by Broad Industry Division

| Broad Industry Division | Usually Employed (All-India Rural) | | | |
|---|---|---|---|---|
| | Round | Male | | Female | |
| | | ps | all | ps | all |
| (1) | (2) | (3) | (4) | (5) | (6) |
| | 55 | 712 | 714 | 841 | 854 |
| | 50 | 737 | 741 | 847 | 862 |
| Agriculture | 43 | 739 | 745 | 825 | 847 |
| | 38 | 772 | 775 | 862 | 875 |
| | 32 | 804 | 806 | 868 | 881 |
| | 55 | 6 | 6 | 4 | 3 |
| | 50 | 7 | 7 | 5 | 4 |
| Mining & Quarrying | 43 | 7 | 7 | 5 | 4 |
| | 38 | 6 | 6 | 4 | 3 |
| | 32 | 5 | 5 | 3 | 2 |
| | 55 | 73 | 73 | 77 | 76 |
| | 50 | 70 | 70 | 75 | 70 |
| Manufacturing | 43 | 76 | 74 | 75 | 69 |
| | 38 | 71 | 70 | 65 | 64 |
| | 32 | 65 | 64 | 61 | 59 |
| | 55 | 2 | 2 | - | - |
| | 50 | 3 | 3 | - | - |
| Electricity, Water, etc. | 43 | 3 | 3 | - | - |
| | 38 | 2 | 2 | - | - |
| | 32 | 2 | 2 | - | - |
| | 55 | 45 | 45 | 12 | 11 |
| | 50 | 33 | 32 | 11 | 9 |
| Construction | 43 | 27 | 37 | 32 | 27 |
| | 38 | 23 | 22 | 9 | 7 |
| | 32 | 17 | 17 | 7 | 6 |
| | 55 | 68 | 68 | 23 | 20 |
| | 50 | 55 | 55 | 22 | 21 |
| Trade, Hotel & Restaurant | 43 | 52 | 51 | 24 | 21 |
| | 38 | 44 | 44 | 22 | 19 |
| | 32 | 40 | 40 | 23 | 20 |

*contd. ...*

*...contd. ...*

| Broad Industry Division | Usually Employed (All-India Rural) | | | | |
|---|---|---|---|---|---|
| | Round | Male | | Female | |
| | | ps | all | ps | all |
| (1) | (2) | (3) | (4) | (5) | (6) |
| | 55 | 32 | 32 | 1 | 1 |
| | 50 | 22 | 22 | 1 | 1 |
| Transport, Storage | 43 | 21 | 20 | 1 | 1 |
| & Communications | 38 | 17 | 17 | 1 | 1 |
| | 32 | 13 | 12 | 1 | 1 |
| | 55 | 61 | 61 | 43 | 37 |
| | 50 | 71 | 70 | 40 | 34 |
| Services | 43 | 64 | 62 | 37 | 30 |
| | 38 | 62 | 61 | 34 | 28 |
| | 32 | 54 | 53 | 37 | 30 |
| All | X | 1000 | 1000 | 1000 | 1000 |

*Source:* NSS (2001), Table 6.7.

## Table 6.11

### *Per 1000 Distribution of Usually Employed Persons by Broad Industry Division*

| Broad Industry Division | Usually Employed (All-India Urban) | | | | |
|---|---|---|---|---|---|
| | Round | Male | | Female | |
| | | ps | all | ps | all |
| (1) | (2) | (3) | (4) | (5) | (6) |
| | 55 | 65 | 66 | 146 | 177 |
| | 50 | 87 | 90 | 193 | 247 |
| Agriculture | 43 | 85 | 91 | 218 | 294 |
| | 38 | 97 | 103 | 255 | 310 |
| | 32 | 102 | 106 | 251 | 319 |
| | 55 | 9 | 9 | 4 | 4 |
| | 50 | 13 | 13 | 7 | 6 |

*contd. ...*

*...contd. ...*

| Broad Industry Division | Usually Employed (All-India Urban) | | | | |
|---|---|---|---|---|---|
| | Round | Male | | Female | |
| | | ps | all | ps | all |
| (1) | (2) | (3) | (4) | (5) | (6) |
| Mining & Quarrying | 43 | 13 | 13 | 9 | 8 |
| | 38 | 12 | 12 | 8 | 6 |
| | 32 | 9 | 9 | 6 | 5 |
| | 55 | 225 | 224 | 232 | 240 |
| | 50 | 236 | 235 | 236 | 241 |
| Manufacturing | 43 | 260 | 257 | 269 | 270 |
| | 38 | 270 | 268 | 260 | 267 |
| | 32 | 276 | 276 | 294 | 296 |
| | 55 | 8 | 8 | 2 | 2 |
| | 50 | 12 | 12 | 3 | 3 |
| Electricity, Water, etc. | 43 | 12 | 12 | 3 | 2 |
| | 38 | 11 | 11 | 2 | 2 |
| | 32 | 11 | 11 | 1 | 1 |
| | 55 | 88 | 87 | 55 | 48 |
| | 50 | 70 | 69 | 49 | 41 |
| Construction | 43 | 58 | 58 | 43 | 37 |
| | 38 | 51 | 51 | 37 | 31 |
| | 32 | 42 | 42 | 26 | 22 |
| | 55 | 293 | 294 | 164 | 169 |
| | 50 | 219 | 219 | 107 | 100 |
| Trade, Hotel & Restaurant | 43 | 215 | 215 | 109 | 98 |
| | 38 | 202 | 203 | 99 | 95 |
| | 32 | 216 | 216 | 98 | 87 |
| | 55 | 104 | 104 | 20 | 18 |
| | 50 | 98 | 97 | 15 | 13 |
| Transport, Storage | 43 | 98 | 97 | 12 | 9 |
| & Communications | 38 | 101 | 99 | 17 | 15 |
| | 32 | 98 | 98 | 12 | 10 |
| | 55 | 209 | 210 | 378 | 342 |
| | 50 | 264 | 264 | 388 | 350 |
| Services | 43 | 253 | 252 | 336 | 278 |
| | 38 | 248 | 248 | 314 | 266 |
| | 32 | 245 | 243 | 311 | 260 |
| All | X | 1000 | 1000 | 1000 | 1000 |

*Source:* NSS (2001), Table 6.7.

declining, is still very high. Two-thirds of usually employed (by principal and secondary activity) persons are still working in the primary sector. Dependence on primary sector for employment is even higher 84 per cent for rural females. In urban areas, the share of tertiary sector, which includes services, has been increasing over time and is the single dominant sector of employment for both males and females.

The most striking fact that emerges from Tables 6.9-6.11 is the relative stagnancy of secondary sector (which includes industry in general, and manufacturing in particular) as a source of employment in urban areas both for males and females. What is even more striking is the decline in the share of manufacturing employment in urban areas for both males and females (Table 6.11). Though it is less significant as a source of employment in rural areas, the share of secondary sector (and manufacturing) is slowly increasing, at least for males. The stagnant share of secondary sector employment in urban areas is telling evidence of the failure to industrialise the economy in the last five decades.

*Wages*

Data on wages of agricultural workers and employees of the public sector enterprises are available on a regular basis. Periodic occupational-wage surveys provide data on wages of each occupation. There have been six rounds of the survey starting with the first in 1958-59. EUS collects data on average wage earnings per day received by causal labourers and regular wage/salaried persons during each of seven days of the reference week. The data have been tabulated according to level of education/industry in the case of regular wage/salaried workers and by age/industry group in the case of casual wage labourers.

Obviously, wage income and wage rates are not directly observed for those who are self-employed. During January-June, 2004, the proportion of the usually employed who were engaged in regular wage/salaried employment, as noted in the previous section was less than 10 per cent in rural areas for both males and females and 41 per cent for males and 36 per cent for females in urban areas.

The NCL extensively discussed the issue of wage, its relation if any, to labour productivity, principles of wage determination and review of minimum wage laws, although those were not in its terms of reference (NCL, 2002, Chapter XII, Section III). I would not summarise their findings and recommendations here except to note that the approach of the commission is legalistic, i.e. it emphasises on enforcement of laws and of India's commitments with respect to these matters in its International agreements, rather than undertake a factual evaluation of trends and analytical explanations based on India's labour market conditions. Consistent with my own deliberate focus on descriptions rather than economic analysis, I will note, selectively, some of the available wage data.

First, the Labour Bureau of the Government of India has tabulated the trends in average daily earnings by sex and age over five rounds of the Occupational Wage Surveys. (*http://labourbureau.nic/ in/OWS%20Ne/20*) The data cover 45 manufacturing industries, 5 mining industries, 3 plantation industries and 4 industries in the service sector. However, for the service sector only data from the Sixth Round (2002–on) are available. Unfortunately, some of the six rounds except the first, which covered 1958-59, extended over five years or longer. It is hard to tell whether the surveys covered all establishments and their workers in each industry. This being the case, it is hard to interpret the round-wise averages. Also, to convert daily earnings, at current prices to real earnings, an appropriate price index is needed. The consumer price index for industrial workers is the only one that is potentially useful. However, the base of this series was changed from 1960 to 1982 and since then, it has not been rebased. Table 6.12 reports average nominal earnings per day of adult men and women for some major industries. It is no surprise that nominal earnings have been rising over time, for example, roughly doubling between the fourth and fifth rounds. The price index for industrial workers, rose 2.25 times between 1988 (the mid-point of Round IV) and 1998 (mid-point of Round V). Thus, roughly speaking, real earnings stayed constant over the two rounds. Comparing male and female earnings, it is no surprise that males earned more, and except in tea plantations, males dominated the work force. In tea plantations, not only male-female earnings differences were much less and the overall earnings were closer to female earnings suggesting female dominance (besides the significance of child labour) in this sector.

## Table 6.12

### *Average Daily Earnings (Rupees)*

| Industry | Round | Men | Women | Overall |
|---|---|---|---|---|
| Sugar | I (1958-1959) | 2.28 | 2.26 | 2.28 |
| | II (1963-1965) | 3.23 | 2.20 | 3.17 |
| | III (1974-1978) | 11.87 | 9.25 | 11.86 |
| | IV (1985-1992) | 54.39 | - | 54.39 |
| | V (1993-2002) | 128.63 | 130.41 | 128.63 |
| Cotton Textiles | I (1958-1959) | 4.03 | 2.86 | 3.94 |
| | II (1963-1965) | 6.06 | 4.76 | 5.69 |
| | III (1974-1978) | 14.58 | 11.63 | 11.99 |
| | IV (1985-1992) | 42.78 | 29.74 | 42.22 |
| | V (1993-2002) | 78.12 | 73.24 | 77.77 |
| Coal Mines | I (1958-1959) | 3.51 | 3.05 | 3.46 |
| | II (1963-1965) | 4.73 | 3.70 | 4.60 |
| | III (1974-1978) | 16.36 | 13.34 | 14.82 |
| | IV (1985-1992) | 68.02 | 54.77 | 67.34 |
| | V (1993-2002) | 139.00 | 120.38 | 138.02 |
| Tea Plantations | I (1958-1959) | 1.76 | 1.65 | 1.66 |
| | II (1963-1965) | 2.35 | 2.15 | 2.15 |
| | III (1974-1978) | 4.26 | 3.31 | 3.60 |
| | IV (1985-1992) | 16.43 | 16.54 | 15.86 |
| | V (1993-2002) | 29.06 | 28.44 | 28.08 |
| Electricity Generation | VI (2002-cont) | 309.83 | 238.83 | 308.89 |
| Railways | VI (2002-cont) | 266.82 | 190.15 | 264.29 |

*Source*: Labour Bureau Government of India, "Statistics: Occupational Wage Surveys". *http://labourbureau.nic.in/OWS%20New%20Table.htm* Accessed Feb 22, 2006.

Turning to EUS data, I did not tabulate the information from all quinquennial and annual rounds. Table 6.13 gives the data for 1999-2000 (a quinquennial round) and first half of 2004 (part of an annual round). Interestingly, average wages seem to have increased more for casual workers (male and female) in rural areas than for their urban counterparts. Moreover, earnings of regular wage/salaried workers seem to have risen less than those of casual workers and, in fact, the earnings of rural female workers fell. Again, without a deeper analysis one cannot conclude much from these from a policy perspective. The rich EUS time series data on characteristics of workers and their household and their earnings await rigorous

## Table 6.13

### Average Daily Wage Earnings (Rupees)

| | Casual Workers (Age 15-59) | | | | Regular Wage/Salaried (Age 15-59) | | | |
|---|---|---|---|---|---|---|---|---|
| | Male | | Female | | Male | | Female | |
| | Rural | Urban | Rural | Urban | Rural | Urban | Rural | Urban |
| Jan-June 2004 | 56.53 | 75.51 | 36.15 | 44.28 | 141.56 | 195.77 | 91.60 | 163.13 |
| 1999-2000 | 45.48 | 63.25 | 29.39 | 38.22 | 127.32 | 169.71 | 114.01 | 140.26 |
| Per cent Increase | 24 | 19 | 23 | 16 | 11 | 15 | -20 | 16 |

*Source:* NSS (2000, 2005a).

analysis. Let me note one such analysis by Dutta (2004) of the data of just three years, 1983, 1993 and 1999. She examines the wage determination process for different types of adult male workers–those with regular wage or salaried jobs and those with casual or contractual jobs. Her main finding is that the returns to education and experience are significantly different for regular and casual workers consistent with the notion of dual primary and secondary labour markets. Casual workers face at best flat returns to education while the returns to education for regular workers are positive and rising in education levels. I am sure scholars could do many more such analyses.

### Summary and Conclusions

It is unfortunate that available data do not allow a thorough documentation of trends in total employment since 1950, the year India embarked on its planned development path with the establishment of the Planning Commission which formulated the first of five-year plans. The Approach Paper of the Eleventh Plan has been circulated for public discussion (Planning Commission, 2006). Systematic surveys of employment and unemployment (EUS) by NSS began only in the early seventies. Because of their different methods and coverage, NSS surveys have underestimated total population and its components (rural-workers, male-female, age groups, etc) as compared to corresponding figures from projections of decennial census. The extent of underestimation seems to be rising over time. The official estimates of work force, labour force and unemployment are obtained by multiplying their estimated ratios to total population from the EUS by the census-based projections of the relevant population. Three such NSS ratios are available, two of which (usual status and current weekly status) are person rates and the third (current daily status) is a person-day rate. Official projections, seem to treat the third as if it is a person rate. Moreover, official projections of employment growth, etc., are based on estimates of employment elasticity of GDP growth. Such an elasticity has no analytical foundation. In sum, not only reliable estimates of employment are unavailable, but projections of employment growth are being made without making even a rudimentary attempt at estimating growth in demand and supply of labour. This is indeed a sorry state of affairs. I have confined myself in this paper to a description of the data (deemed more reliable) on the structure of employment and changes in it over time based on EUS, the only source of comprehensive data on employment. Other sources of data on particular components of employment, such as the organized private and public sectors are also used in such a description where appropriate. The description leads to some rather unsettling findings.

First, during six decades since independence, with the state playing a dominate role in the economy, and a conscious attempt at industrialisation, the industrial structure of employment in the economy has changed extremely slowly, although the structure of value added (GDP) has changed much more. Primary activity (mostly agriculture) is still the dominant source of employment (around 66 per cent in the first half of 2004 as compared to 78 per cent in 1977-1978) for rural males, the largest single group among usually employed persons. Second, is the failure of the industrialisation strategy that emphasised investment in capital intensive, heavy industry on the one hand and promoted small-scale industry (SSI) through reservation of many products for production by SSI only on the other. This failure is seen from the stagnation since 1977-78 in the share of the secondary sector as a source of employment for rural males, and an alarming fall in the share of manufacturing both in rural and urban areas. The only redeeming feature is a slow rising trend in the small share of both in rural areas. As is well known, transformation of a less developed economy into a developed one consists in shifting work force from employment in lower productivity primary activities to higher productivity secondary and tertiary sectors. Viewed from this perspective, Indian development strategy has failed miserably.

It is true that since the development strategy of the three decades of 1950-1980 was modified in a limited way in mid eighties, and systemically and more extensively after the reforms initiated in 1991, economic growth, (growth of real GDP) accelerated, primarily driven by the service sector. What this has meant, given the modest change in the structure of employment, is that the productivity gap between the large share of workers in primary activity and those in secondary and tertiary activities have grown. This also has the implication that the welcome reduction in poverty that has occurred since the early eighties would have been higher had the employment structure shifted more towards, rather than away from, secondary activities including manufacturing. Given my deliberate focus on description rather than causal analysis, I will not comment on the policy implications of this failure except to point out first, that the focus of many of our policies towards agriculture and farmers seem oriented towards keeping poor and marginal farmers in agriculture rather than shifting them to higher productivity activities. Second, the potential for making such a shift exists and there are already some signs of it taking place. What I am referring to is the potential for greater outsourcing to India of manufacturing as has happened in services and to the signs that the auto component sector is leading the way. China has been a great beneficiary of outsourcing of manufacturing. In my view, a far greater interpretation of Indian with the world economy is needed for realising this potential. Establishing Special Economic Zones as imitation of China is not enough. Third, given the slow change in employment structure in the context of faster output growth, and its implications for the poor as noted earlier, it is understandable that an expanded Employment Guarantee programme is being implemented. N.S.S. Narayana, Kirit Parikh and I (1998) long ago analysed the growth-enhancing and poverty reducing potential of a well-designed (i.e. to create productive assets) and well-executed (i.e. involving no leakage to the non-poor) rural work program. I very much hope that the current program would indeed be well-designed and well-executed. But, it is important to note (Srinivasan, 2005) that even if it is, it can only be a palliative and not one that will eradicate poverty, once and for all within a recognisable time horizon. The latter has been the vision of our founding fathers and mothers. Realising that vision requires, in my mind, though I will not provide here an analytical justification for it, not only a deepening, widening and acceleration of economic reforms, but also a rethinking of our agricultural policies ranging from price supports, input subsidies, credit and foreign trade.

Let me conclude with an appeal to researchers in India and elsewhere to analyse the rich data available in the quinquennial and annual rounds of EUS from the perspective of understanding the determinants of labour supply, including occupational choice decisions of household and of labour demand decisions of producers including former employees. Fortunately, NSS has made household level data available. Building up a foundation that is based on a sound analysis of variations across states and over time is obviously essential. Crude aggregate projections based on elasticity estimates without any economic foundation and worse still, policy choices based on them, cannot possibly substitute for a sound foundation.

# References

Deshpande, Sudha, Guy Standing and Lalit Deshpande (1998). *Labor Market Flexibility in a Third World Metropolis*, Vedams eBooks, New Delhi .

Dutta, Puja Vasudeva (2004). "The Structure of Wages in India, 1983-1999," *Working Paper* 25, Poverty Research Unit, Department of Economics, University of Sussex.

GoI (2006). "Provisional Results of Economic Census 2005: All India Report," Government of India, Ministry of Statistics and Programme Implementation, Central Statistical Organisation, New Delhi. *http://www.mospi.gov.in*

———. (2001). "Population Projection," Chapter 4, in *Provision Population Totals*, Census of India 2001, Series 1, India, Paper 1 of 2001, Registrar General and Census Commissioner of India, New Delhi.

———. (1981). *Instructions to Enumerators for Filling up the Individual Slips*, Registral General and Census Commission of India, New Delhi.

Labour Bureau. *Statistics: Occupational Wage Surveys*, Government of India. *http://labourbureau.nic.in/OWS%20New%20Table.htm*, Accessed 2/22/2006

Mahalanobis, P.C. (1969). "The Asian Drama: An Indian View", *Sankhya: The Indian Journal of Statistics*, Series B (31), Parts 3&4.

———. (1961). "Talks on Planning", *Indian Statistical Series* No. 14, Statistical Publishing Society, Calcutta.

MoF (2006). *Economic Survey, 2005-06*, Ministry of Finance, New Delhi.

———. (2004). *Economic Survey 2003-04*, Ministry of Finance, New Delhi.

NAD (2004). *Report of the Working Group on Work Force Estimates for Compilation of National Accounts Statistics with Base Year 1978-2000*, National Accounts Division, Central Statistical Organisation, New Delhi.

Nagaraj, R. (2000). "Organised Manufacturing Employment", *Economic and Political Weekly*, Vol. 35(38), pp.3445-448.

———. (2004). "Fall in Organised Manufacturing Employment: A Brief Note" *Economic and Political Weekly*, 39(30), pp.3387-90.

Narayana, N.S.S., Kirit S. Parikh and T.N. Srinivasan (1988). "Rural Works Programs in India: Costs and Benefits," *Journal of Development Economics* 29(2), pp.131-56.

NCL (2002). *Report of the National Commission on Labour*, Ministry of Labour, New Delhi.

NSS (2005a). *Employment and Unemployment Situation in India*, January-June 2004, Report No. 506 (60/10/1), National Sample Survey Organisation, New Delhi.

———. (2005b). *Household Consumer Expenditure and Employment-Unemployment*, Report No. 490 (59/1.0/1), National Sample Survey Organisation, New Delhi.

———. (2001). *Employment and Unemployment in India*, Parts I and II, Report No. 458 (55/10/2), National Sample Survey Organisation, New Delhi.

———. (2000). *Employment and Unemployment in India*, 1998-2000: Key Results, Report No. 455 (55/10/1), National Sample Survey Organisation, New Delhi.

Planning Commission (2006). *Towards Faster and More Inclusive Growth: An Approach to the 11th Five Year Plan*, Planning Commision, New Delhi.

———. (2005). *Mid-term Appraisal of the 10th Five Year Plan (2002-2007)*, Planning Commision, New Delhi.

———. (2002). *Report of the Special Group on Targeting Ten Million Employment Opportunities Per Year*, Planning Commision, New Delhi.

———. (2001). *Report of the Task Force on Employment Opportunities*, Planning Commision, New Delhi.

Roy, Sudipta Dutta (2004). "Employment Dynamics in Indian Industry: Adjustment Lags and the Impact of Job Security Regulations," *Journal of Development Economics*, Vol. 73, pp.233-256.

Srinivasan, T.N. (2005). "Guaranteeing Employment: a Palliative?" *The Hindu*, Chennai.

———. (2000). *Eight Lectures on India's Economic Reforms*, Oxford University Press, New Delhi.

Sundaram K. and Suresh Tendulkar (2005). "Trends in Labour and Employment in India 1983-2003: Some Fresh Results", Delhi School of Economics, New Delhi. (*mimeo*).

World Bank (1998). *India: 1998 Macro-Economic Update*, Washington DC.

## Appendix 6.1

### Chapter 2

### Concepts and Definitions

2.0 The concepts and definitions of some important terms used in the survey and which are relevant to this report *viz.*, those used to generate the tables and various estimates on employment-unemployment are explained in the following paragraphs.

2.1 *Household:* A group of persons who normally lived together and took food from a common kitchen constituted a household. The adverb 'normally' means that temporary visitors were excluded but temporary stay-aways were included. Thus, a child residing in a hostel for studies was excluded from the household of his/her parents, but a resident employee or a resident domestic servant or paying guest (but not just a tenant in the house) was included in the employer's/host's household. 'Living together' was given more importance than 'sharing food from a common kitchen' in drawing the boundaries of a household in case the two criteria were in conflict. However, in the special case of a person taking food with his family but sleeping elsewhere (say, in a shop or a different house) due to space shortage, the household formed by such a person's family members was taken to include the person also. Each inmate of a hotel, mess, boarding-lodging house, hostel etc,, was considered to be a single-member household except that a family living in a hotel (say) was considered one household only. The same principle was applicable for the residential staff of such establishments.

2.2 *Economic activity.* Any activity resulting in production of goods and services that add value to national product was considered as an economic activity. Such activities included production of all goods and services for market (market activities), i.e. production for pay or profit, and, the production of primary commodities for own consumption and own account production of fixed assets, among the non-market activities.

2.2.1 The entire spectrum of human activity falls into two categories—economic and non-economic activities. The economic activities have two pints—market activities and non-market activities.

Market activities are those that involve remuneration to those who perform it i.e., activity performed for pay or profit. These are essentially production of goods and services for the market including those of government services, etc. Non-market activities are the production for own consumption of primary products including own account processing of primary products and own account production of fixed assets.

2.2.2 The full spectrum of economic activities as defined in the UN system of National Accounts (1968) was not covered in the definition adopted for the NSS 55th Round survey of Employment and Unemployment. The former included activities like own account processing of primary products amony other things. In the NSS surveys, activities relating to the production of primary goods for own consumption, was restricted to the agriculture sector only and did not include the activities in mining and quarrying sector. The coverage of economic activities was, however, the same as in the 50th Round.

The term 'economic activity', therefore, included:

(i)    all the market activities performed for pay or profit which result in production of goods and services for exchange.

(ii)   of the non market activities,

(a)    all the activities relating to the agricultural sector (industry Divisions 01 to 05 of NIC 1998) which result in production (including gathering of uncultivated crops, forestry, collection of firewood, hunting, fishing etc) of agricultural produce for own consumption, and

(b)    the activities relating to the own-account production of fixed assets. Own account production of fixed assets include construction of own houses, roads, wells etc., and of machinery, tools etc. for household enterprise and also construction of any private or community facilities free of charge. A person may be engaged in own account construction either in the capacity of it labourer or a supervisor.

As per the practise followed in earlier rounds, certain activities like prostitution, begging, smuggling etc., which though fetched earnings, were not considered as economic activities.

*2.3 Activity status:* It is the activity situation in which a person was found during a reference period with regard to the person's participation in economic and non-economic activities. According to this, a person could be in one or a combination of the following three broad activity statuses during a reference period:

(i) working or being engaged in economic activity (work) as defined above.

(ii) being not engaged in economic activity (work) but either making tangible efforts to seek 'work' or being available for 'work' if the 'work' is available, and

(iii) being not engaged in any economic activity (work) and also not available for 'work'.

Broad activity' statuses mentioned in (i) and (ii) above are associated with 'being in labour force' and the last with 'not being in the labour force'. Within the labour force broad activity status (i) and (ii) were associated with 'employment' and 'unemployment', respectively.

*2.3.1 Categories of activity status:* Identification of each individual into a unique situation could pose a problem when more than one of the three broad activity statuses listed above were concurrently obtained for a person. In such an eventuality, the identification uniquely under any one of the three broad activity statuses was done by adopting 'either the major time or priority criterion.' The former was used for classification of persons according to the 'usual activity status' approach and the latter for classification of persons according to the 'current activity status' approach. Each of the three broad activity statuses was further sub-divided into several detailed activity categories. If a person categorised as engaged in economic activity by adopting one of the two criteria mentioned above was found to be pursuing more than one economic activity during the reference period, the appropriate detailed activity status code related to that activity in which relatively more time had been spent. A similar procedure was adopted for assigning detailed activity code for persons categorised as engaged in non-economic activity and pursuing more than one non-economic activity. The detailed activity categories under each of the three broad activity statuses used in the survey (along with the codes assigned to them as indicated in brackets) are stated below:

(i) situation of working or being engaged in economic activities (employed):

  (a) worked in household enterprise (self-employed) as own account worker (11);

  (b) worked in household enterprise (self-employed) as employer (12):

  (e) worked as helper in household enterprises (unpaid family worker) (21);

  (d) worked as regular salaried/wage employee (31);

  (e) worked as, casual wage labour (i) in public works (41), (ii) in other types of work (51);

  (f) had work in household enterprise but did not work due to: (i) sickness (61), (ii) other reasons (62); and

  (g) had regular salaried/wage employment but did not work due to: (i) sickness (71), (ii) other reasons (72);

(ii) situation of being not engaged in work but seeking or available for work (unemployed):

  (a) sought work (81); and

  (b) did not seek but was available for work (82);

(iii) situation, of being not available for work (not in labour force):

  (a) attended educational institutions (91);

  (b) attended domestic duties only (92);

  (c) attended domestic duties and was also engaged in free collection of goods (vegetables, roots, firewood, cattle-feed, etc.) sewing, tailoring, weaving, etc. for household use (93);

  (d) rentiers, pensioners, remittance recipients, etc. (94);

  (e) not able to work due to disability (95);

(f)   beggars, prostitutes (96):

(g)   others (97) and

(h)   did not work due to sickness (for casual workers only) (98).

*2.4 Workers (or employed);* Persons who were engaged in any economic activity or who, despite their attachment to economic activity, abstained from work for reason of illness, injury or other physical disability, bad weather, festivals, social or religious functions or other contingencies necessitating temporary absence from work, constituted workers. Unpaid helpers who assisted in the operation of an economic activity in the household farm or non-farm activities were also considered as workers. All the workers were assigned one of the detailed activity statuses under the broad activity category 'working' or 'being engaged in economic activity' (or employed).

*2.5 Seeking or available for work (or unemployed):* Persons, who owing to lack of work, had not worked but either sought work through employment exchanges, intermediaries, friends or relatives or by making applications to prospective employers or expressed their willingness or availability for work under the prevailing conditions of work and remuneration, were considered as those who were, seeking or available for work' (or unemployed).

*2.6 Labour force:* Persons, who, were either 'working' (or employed) or 'seeking or available for work' (or unemployed.) constituted the labour force. Persons who were neither 'working' nor 'seeking or available for work' for various reasons during the reference period were considered as 'out of labour force'. The persons under this latter category are students, those engaged in domestic duties, rentiers, pensioners, recipients of remittances, those living on alms, infirm or disabled persons, too young or too old persons, prostitutes, smugglers, etc., and casual labourers not working due to sickness.

*2.7 Self-employed:* Persons who operated their own farm or non-farm enterprises or were engaged independently in a profession or trade on own-account or with one or a few partners were deemed to be self-employed in household enterprises. The essential feature of the self-employed is that they have 'autonomy' (i.e., how, where and when to produce) and 'economic independence' (i.e., market, scale of operation and money) for carrying out their operation. The fee or remuneration received by them comprised two parts—share of their labour and profit of the enterprise. In other words, their remuneration was determined wholly or mainly by sales; or profits of the goods or services which were produced.

2.7.1 *Categories of self-employed persons:* Self-employed persons were categorised as follows:

    (i)   *own-account workers:* those self-employed persons who operated their enterprises on their own acoount or with one or a few partners and who, during the reference period, by and large, ran their enterprise without hiring any labour. They could however, have had unpaid helpers to assist them in the activity of the enterprise;

    (ii)  *employers:* those self-employed persons who worked on their own account or with one or a few partners and, who, by and large, ran their enterprise by hiring labour; and

    (iii) *helpers in household enterprise:* those self-employed persons (mostly family members) who were engaged in their household enterprises, working full or part time and did not receive any regular salary or wages in return for the work performed. They did not run the household enterprise on their own but assisted the related person living in the same household in running the household enterprise.

2.8 *Regular salaried/wage employee:* These were persons who worked in others, farm or non-farm enterprises (both household and non-household) and, in return, received salary or wages on a regular basis (i.e., not on the basis of daily or periodic renewal of work contract). This category included not only persons getting time wage but also persons receiving piece wage or salary and paid apprentices, both full time and part-time.

2.9 *Casual wage labour:* A person who was casually engaged in others' farm or non-farm enterprises (both household and non-household) and, in return, received wages according to the terms of the daily or periodic work contract, was a casual wage labour.

2.10 *Different approaches followed to determine activity status:* The persons surveyed were classified into various activity categories on the basis of the activities pursued by them during certain specified reference periods. There were three reference periods for this survey. These are: (i) one year (ii) one week and (iii) each day of the reference week. Based on these three periods, three different measures of activity status are arrived at. These are termed respectively as usual status, current weekly status and the current daily status. The procedure adopted to arrive at these three measures is given below.

2.10.1 *Usual activity status:* The usual activity status relates to the activity status of a person during the reference period of 365 days preceding the date of survey. The activity status on which a person spent relatively longer time (i.e. major time criterion) during the 365 days preceding the date of survey is considered as the 'principal usual activity status' of the person. To decide the principal usual activity of a person, he/she was first categorised as belonging to the labour force or not during the reference period 'on the basis of major time criterion.' Persons thus adjudged as not belonging to the labour force were assigned the broad activity status 'neither working nor available for work'. For persons belonging to the labour force, the broad activity status of either 'working' or 'not working but seeking and/or available for work' was ascertained based on the same criterion *viz.*, relatively longer time spent in accordance with either of the two broad statuses within the labour force during the 365 days preceding the date of survey. Within the broad activity status so determined, the detailed activity status of a person pursuing more than one such activity was determined once again on the basis of the relatively longer time spent on such activities. In terms of activity codes (stated earlier in para 1.3.1), codes 11-51 were applicable for persons classified as workers, while code 81 was assigned to people either seeking or available for work (unemployed persons) and codes 91-97 for those who were out of labour force.

2.10.2 *Subsidiary economic activity status:* A person whose principal usual status was determined on the basis of the major time criterion could have pursued some economic activity 'for a relatively shorter time' (minor time) during the reference period of 365 days preceding the date of survey. The status in which such economic activity was pursued was the subsidiary economic activity status of that person. Thus, activity status codes 11-51 only were applicable for persons reporting some subsidiary economic activity. It may be noted that engagement in work in subsidiary capacity could arise out of the following two situations, *viz.*

(i)   a person could be engaged for a relatively longer period during the last 365 days in one economic/non-economic activity and for a relatively shorter period in another economic activity, and

(ii)  a person could be pursuing one economic activity/non-economic activity almost throughout the year in the principal usual activity status and simultaneously pursue another economic activity for a relatively shorter period in a subsidiary capacity.

2.10.3 *Number of subsidiary economic activities pursued during last 365 days:* For persons reporting some subsidiary activity, the number of subsidiary activities pursued by him/her during last 365 days was ascertained and recorded. However, details of a maximum of two such subsidiary economic activities were recorded. The activities having different work status was considered as different activities. Activities within the same work status but with different industry and/or occupation were also considered as different activities. If the person was engaged in two or more subsidiary economic activities, the details of the subsidiary economic activity pursued for the maximum time period among all the subsidiary economic activities, or in other words, the major subsidiary economic activity was deemed as 'subsidiary status number I' and the next major one as 'subsidiary status number II' were recorded.

2.10.4 *Current weekly activity status:* The current weekly activity status of a person is the activity status obtaining for a person during a reference period of 7 days preceding the date of survey. It is decided 'on the basis of a certain priority cum major time criterion.'

2.10.4.1 According to ('the priority criterion', the status of 'working' gets priority over the status of 'not working but seeking or available for work' which, in turn, gets priority over the status of 'neither working nor available for work'. A person was considered working (or employed) if he/she, while pursuing any economic activity, had worked for at least one hour on at least one day during the 7 days preceding the date of survey: A person was considered 'seeking or available for work (or unemployed)' if during the reference week, no economic activity was pursued by the person but he/she made efforts to get work or had been available for work any time during the reference week though not actively seeking work in the belief that no work was available. A person who had neither worked nor was available for work any time during the reference week was considered as engaged in non-economic activities (or not in labour force).

2.10.4.2 After deciding the 'broad current weekly activity status' of a person on the 'basis of 'priority' criterion', the 'detailed current activity status' was then decided 'on the basis of 'major time' criterion if that person pursued multiple economic activities.' The current weekly activity status of a person could be any one of the detailed activity status (ref. para 1.3.1) and could have codes 11 to 98. Of these codes, 11 to 72 pertained to workers, 81 to 82 for unemployed and 91 to 98 for persons out of labour force. It may be noted that these are the same as the usual status codes (stated in para 1.10.1 before) except that codes 61, 62, 71, 72, 82 and 98 are not applicable for usual status and code 81 for usual status is used to indicate both the situations of seeking and being available for work.

2.10.5 *Current daily activity status:* The activity pattern of the population, particularly in the unorganised sector, is such that during a week, and sometimes, even during a day, a person could pursue more than one activity. Moreover, many people could even undertake both economic and non-economic activities on the same day of a reference week. The current daily activity status for a person was determined on the basis of his/her activity status on each day of the reference week 'using a priority-cum-major time criterion' (day-to-day labour time disposition). Time disposition was recorded for every member of a sample household. This involved recording of different activities pursued by the members along with the time intensity in quantitative terms for each day of the reference week. The different activities were identified and recorded in terms of 'activity status' and 'industry' codes for persons in urban areas and 'activity status', 'industry' and 'operation' codes for persons in rural areas. The terms 'industry' and 'operation' are explained later. The following points were considered for assigning the time intensity and determining the current daily status of a person:

i)    Each day of the reference week was looked upon as comprising either two 'half days' or a 'full' day for assigning the activity status.

ii)    A person was considered 'working' (employed) for the entire day if he/she had worked for four hours or more during the day.

iii)    If a person was engaged in more than one of the economic activities for 4 hours or more on a day, he/she was assigned two out of the various economic activities on which he/she devoted relatively longer time on the reference day (for each of those two activities, the intensity was 0.5).

iv)    If the person had worked for 1 hour or more but less than 4 hours he/she was considered 'working' (employed) for half day and 'seeking or available for work' (unemployed) or 'neither seeking nor available for work' (not in labour force) for the other half of the day depending on whether he was seeking/available for work or not.

v)    If a person was not engaged in any 'work' even for 1 hour on a day but was seeking/available for work even for 4 hours or more, he was considered 'unemployed' for the entire day. But, if he was 'seeking/available for work' for more than 1 hour and less than four hours only, he was considered 'unemployed' for half day and 'not in labour force' for the other half of the day.

vi)    A person who neither had any 'work' to do nor was available for 'work' even for half a day was considered 'not in labour force' for the entire day and was assigned one or two of the detailed non-economic activity statuses depending upon the activities pursued during the reference day.

The description (and codes used) of current daily activity statuses are the same as those of current weekly activity status.

*2.11 Industry-occupation:* The description of the industry-occupation was relevant to the type of economic activity pursued by the person, NIC-1998 was followed for classifying industries and NCO-1968 was followed for classifying occupations. In case two or more industry-occupation combinations corresponding to the status code were reported by a person, the principal industry-occupation was taken as the one in which 'relatively more time' was spent during the reference period by the person. It may be noted that under Division 95 of NIC 1998, on "Private households with employed persons", six additional codes have been introduced for recording five digit entries for industry codes in the survey *viz.*, housemaid/servant (95001), cook (95002), gardener (95003), gatekeeper/*chowkidar*/watchman (95004), governess/baby-sitter (95005) and for 'others' (95009).

*2.12 Operation:* This was the type of work performed by a person during a reference period. It could be manual or non-manual and could pertain to activities in agricultural or non-agricultural sector. Operation was combined with activity status and industry corresponding to the work performed. Information regarding the type of operation was collected 'only for rural areas' and related to 'current status only.' The different types of operations came under four categories: Ploughing, sowing, transplanting, weeding, harvesting and other cultivation activities fell under the category 'manual work in cultivation.' Against the category 'manual work in other agricultural activities' were the following types: forestry, plantation, animal husbandry, fisheries and other agricultural activities. 'Manual work in non-agricultural activities' constituted the third category. The last category *viz.*, 'non-manual work' comprised two broad types: (i) in 'cultivation' and (ii) in 'other than cultivation". Under (iv), the type could be either activities in 'cultivation' or in 'other than cultivation.' In the last two cases, the sector in which the work was performed is indicated by the industry. It may be noted that for 'regular salaried wage employees' on leave or on holiday, the 'operation' related to their respective function in the work or job from which he/she was temporarily off, Similarly, for persons categorised as 'self-employed' but not working on a particular day in spite of having work on that day, the operation related to the work that he/she would have done if he/she had not enjoyed leisure on that day.

*2.13 Cultivation:* All activities relating to production of crops and related ancillary activities are considered as cultivation. Growing of trees, plants or crops as plantation or orchards (such as rubber, cashew, coconut, pepper, coffee, tea etc.) are not considered as cultivation activities for the purpose of this survey. In general, the activities covered under NIC 1998 sub-classes 01111-01112, 01113, 01115, 01119, 01121, 01122 and 01135 (excepting plantation of pepper and cardamom) are to be considered as cultivation (equivalent to the activities under industry Groups 000 to 008 of NIC 1987).

*2.14 Manual work:* A job essentially involving physical labour was considered as manual work, However, jobs essentially involving physical labour but also requiring a certain level of general, professional, scientific or technical education were not termed as 'manual work'. On the other hand, jobs not involving much of physical labour and at the same time not requiring much educational (general, scientific, technical or otherwise) background were treated as 'manual work'. Thus, engineers, doctors, dentists, midwives, etc., were not considered manual workers even though their jobs involved same amount of physical labour, But, peons, *chowkidars*, watchman, etc., were considered manual workers even though their work might not involve much physical labour. Manual work was defined as work pursued in one or more of the following occupational groups of the National Classification of Occupations (NCO 1968):

Division 5: Service workers:

Group 52: Cooks, Waiters, Bartenders and Related workers (domestic and institutional).

Group 53: Maid and Other housekeeping service workers (not elsewhere classified).

Group 54: Building caretakers, Sweepers, Cleaners and Related workers.

Group 55: Launders, Dry cleaners and Pressers.

Group 56: Hair dressers, Barbers, Beauticians and Related workers.

Family 570: Fire fighters

Family 574: Watchmen, Gate-keepers.

Family 579: Protective Service Workers not elsewhere classified.

Division 6: Farmers, Fishermen, Hunters, Loggers and related workers:

Group 63: Agricultural labourers

Group 64: Plantation labourers and related workers

Group 65: other farm workers

Group 66: Forestry workers

Group 67: Hunters and related workers

Group 68: Fishermen and related workers.

Division 7-8-9: Production and related workers, Transport equipment operators and labourers:

All groups excluding group 85 (electrical fitters and related workers) and group 86 (broadcasting station and sound equipment operators and cinema projectionists).

*2.15 Rural Labour:* Manual labour working in agricultural and /or non-agricultural occupations 'in return for wages' paid either in cash or in kind (excluding exchange Inbour) and 'living in rural areas', was taken as rural labour.

*2.16 Agricultural labour:* A person was considered as engaged as agricultural labour, if he/she followed one or more of the following agricultural occupations in the capacity of a wage paid manual labour, whether paid in cash or kind or both:

(i) Farming.

(ii) Dairy farming.

(iii) Production of any horticultural commodity.

(iv) Raising of livestock, bees or poultry.

(v) Any practise performed on a farm as incidental to or in conjunction with farm operations (including forestry and timbering) and the preparation for market and delivery to storage or to market or to carriage for transportation to market of farm produce.

Working in Fisheries was 'excluded' from agricultural labour. Further, 'carriage for transportation' refers 'only to the first stage of the transport' from farm to the first place of disposal.

*2.17 Wage paid-manual labour:* A person who did manual work in return for wages in cash or kind or partly in cash and partly in kind (excluding exchange labour) was a wage paid manual labour. Salaries are also to be counted as wages. A person who was self-employed in manual work was 'not treated' as a wage paid manual labour,

*2.18 Skill:* Any marketable expertise, however acquired, irrespective of whether marketed or not, whether the intention is to market it or not was considered as skill. Thus, a person holding a certificate or diploma on an appropriate subject was considered to possess the specified skill along with the persons who have acquired the said skill without receiving any such certificate or even without attending any institution. When a person has acquired skill in more than one trade, the skill in which he/she is more (most) proficient is considered as his/her skill.

*2.19 Nominal work:* Work done by a person for 1 to 2 hours in a day of the 7 days reference week is said to be a day with nominal work for the person. In the day-to-day labour time disposition of the reference week, such a day's work was. considered as 'half-days' work.

*2.20 Earnings:* Earnings referred to the wage/salary income (and not total earnings) receivable for the wage/salaried work done during the reference week by the wage/salaried employees and casual labourers. The wage/salary receivable may be in cash or kind or partly in cash and partly in kind.

   i)   The wages in kind were evaluated at the current retail price.

   ii)  Bonus and perquisites evaluated at retail prices and duly apportioned for the reference week were also included in earnings.

   iii) Amount receivable as 'over-time' for the additional work done beyond normal working time was also included.

# 7

## Protecting the Poor against Risk through Anti-poverty Programmes

*International Experience*

### K. SUBBARAO

The experience of India in the 1990s shows that even impressive growth has not generated enough employment opportunities and livelihoods. Moreover, the poor in India now face not only the age-old vulnerabilities such as exposure to health shocks but also new vulnerabilities in a globalising world such as sudden loss of employment both in organised and in unorganised sectors. Not surprisingly, growth with equity and Common Minimum Programme are now important strategic thrusts of the Government of India. New programmes and initiatives, such as the National Rural Employment Guarantee Scheme and social security for unorganised workers are now on cards, and there has been much debate in India in recent years on the role and effectiveness of safety net programmes. In this context, it is important to learn from the experience of other countries for better implementation of ongoing and planned safety net programmes. This is what I propose to do. I will begin with a brief historical perspective, and provide an overview of the conceptual relationship between risk, poverty and vulnerability. I will then illustrate some recent experiments in providing social assistance transfers under widely varying country circumstances: low-income countries facing periodic weather shocks (Bangladesh), middle-income and low-income countries subjected to macroeconomic crisis (Korea, Indonesia, Argentina), countries protecting the indigent from the shock of transition from socialism to a market economy (Uzbekistan), a low-income country struggling to deal with elderly poverty (Nepal), and health security (India), and a country coming to grips with shocks associated with globalisation (China). I conclude by drawing some general lessons from this diverse country and programme experience.

The concern for the poor and the debate on the role of the State and the design of safety net programmes are centuries old. Across the developed and the developing world, then as now, poor households experience sudden downturns in their income/welfare position due to adverse and unpredictable shocks. Some of these are covariate in nature, such as floods, hurricanes, droughts and other natural disasters, or sudden swings in terms of trade or other macro-economic variables that affect whole communities and vast regions. Some shocks are idiosyncratic and household-specific, such as loss of a breadwinner (widowhood or orphanhood) or unemployment or long-term illness or old age. These risks are present in all countries. Individuals in developed countries have financial instruments and options to insure themselves against such sudden downturns in income. In most of the developing world, however, the risks faced by the poor are often uninsured; some are even not insurable due to lack of marketable instruments for insurance. As a result, poor households in developing countries are particularly vulnerable to such shocks, both covariate and idiosyncratic, affecting adversely their consumption and investment decisions and contributing to 'poverty trap' situations and to the persistence of chronic poverty.

The primary objective of publicly funded social protection programmes is to reduce the economic vulnerability of low-income households and to help them cope with economic downturns, and thus, prevent the emergence of poverty traps. The instruments of social protection in the developing countries comprise, (a) social insurance policies which aim to meet the risks of illness, disability, unemployment, and old age, and (b) social assistance programmes (often called 'safety net' or 'transfer' or 'anti-poverty' programmes) whose aim is to provide assistance (either in cash or in kind) to vulnerable households, to enable them to maintain a critical minimum consumption level, and also help them participate in the growth process. Some programmes, such as public workfare, perform an insurance function, a safety net (transfer) function and also contribute to economic growth via development of critical infrastructure.

Recent research has pointed out three major shortcomings in the design and actual implementation of safety net programmes across the developing world. First, several programmes failed to reach the poorest and the most vulnerable (Subbarao *et al.* 1997). In fact, in a quarter of the world's programmes surveyed by Coady, Grosh and Hoddinott (2002), the incidence has been found to be regressive. Second, in many countries, transfer programmes have not been cost-effective (Subbarao, *et al.* 1997; Radhakrishna and Subbarao, 1997). Third, in several countries, multiple programmes exist often with the same objective and attempting to reach the same vulnerable group, while leaving out many vulnerable households from the coverage of any programme. Thus, in Malawi, Smith and Subbarao (2002), found that 14 programmes were launched by various donors, including three different types of public works programmes, and yet some of the poorest groups were excluded from any of the programmes. Likewise in India and Bangladesh, multiple programmes exist with the same objective and attempting to reach the same vulnerable group.

In an attempt to overcome these deficiencies, several countries have, experimented with newly designed programmes or reformed their existing programmes towards greater efficiency, reducing both exclusion errors (i.e., excluding the entry of eligible households into the programme) and inclusion errors (i.e., including non-eligible households into the programme). Several developments during the 1990s triggered the renewed emphasis on new and innovative safety net programmes. During the 1990s, different countries were impacted by different types of shocks. The macroeconomic and financial crises in East Asia and Latin America, a series of covariate weather shocks (severe floods and droughts–the El Nino effects) including recently even in the United States, the shock of transition from socialism to a market economy, and the impact of moves towards globalisation—have all lent an added urgency to put in place newly designed innovative safety net programmes or reform and adjust the existing ones to cushion poor households from severe, crisis-induced shortfalls in consumption.

Poverty at any point in time is estimated with reference to a critical minimum consumption basket (food and non-food) necessary for survival, the poverty line. Cross-section survey information is used to estimate the number of households falling below the poverty line. A part of the head count poverty, thus estimated contains some poor people who were hit by an adverse shock and fell into poverty temporarily because they were unable to cope with the downside risk (the transient poor) and another segment of poor who happened to be always poor for structural reasons (the chronically poor). Exposure to risk is at the core of transitions between the two groups. However, because of data limitations, it is difficult to empirically capture these poverty transitions.[1]

Both the chronically poor and the transient poor are vulnerable to shocks. The risks faced by the chronically poor and the transient poor, differ across countries and across regions and age groups within a country. A recent study by Dercon provides a typology of risks and the nature of vulnerability generated by exposure to such risks for a typical low-income country, Ethiopia (Appendix A-7.2). In Ethiopia, 78 per cent of rural population reported harvest failure as their biggest risk, followed by policy-induced risks (such as resettlement, taxation), illness and death in the family, and livestock-related problems. A recent panel study of rural households in Orissa (van Dillen, 2004) reached similar conclusions: most households reported exposure to weather shocks and health shocks (malaria) as their prime source of vulnerability.

In responding to risky situations, households have been adopting both *ex ante* risk management strategies as well as *ex post* risk-coping strategies. Informal insurance mechanisms and community savings schemes (such as funeral societies in Africa), and labour-sharing practices in East Africa are an integral part of the households' '*ex ante*' efforts to manage risk. Evidence suggests that there could be serious constraints on the effectiveness of such informal arrangements especially during a major covariate shock, such as drought (Dercon, 2002). Once hit by a shock, in the absence of both formal and informal '*ex ante*' arrangements, households adopt '*ex post*' informal coping strategies available to them. Some of the coping strategies might lead to further impoverishment, e.g., ICRISAT panel

---

1. Unfortunately, panel data are required to disentangle transient from chronic poverty. There are not many countries with such panel data sets. In Appendix A-7.1, the available information on transitions in-and-out of poverty for different countries is presented.

survey data had shown that asset-poor households in India's arid zone often grow safer traditional varieties rather than riskier but high-yielding new varieties (Morduch, 1990). Moreover, in some situations, poor households are exacerbated by risk compounding or bunching of risks: conflict, drought, health shocks (malaria, AIDS). In such circumstances, coping strategies adopted by the household could inflict long-term damage to itself, such as pulling children out of school or selling productive assets.

Vulnerability to shocks, thus, is an intrinsic aspect of well-being. In evaluating one's well-being, one cannot limit oneself to the person's actual welfare status today, but must also account for his/her prospects of being well in the future—and being well today does not imply or guarantee being well tomorrow.

Understanding vulnerability is important from an instrumental perspective as well. In the absence of effective public intervention programmes, repeated exposure to shocks/risks may permanently damage poor people's future welfare as households try to seek current stability for adopting *ex ante* risk-mitigating or *ex post* coping strategies that potentially lock them into 'poverty traps'.

Clearly, the chronically poor are always vulnerable and in need of programmes that raise their mean consumption levels. For the transient poor, programmes are needed that reduce the variance around the mean so they do not slip into poverty with the onset of a shock. Safety net programmes (also called poverty-alleviation programmes) thus, need to consist of programmes and policies that raise the mean consumption of poor households, as well as reduce the variance around the mean (i.e., smooth consumption over time). An implicit rationale is also to achieve some equity with redistribution, to the extent these programmes reach the poorest groups and are financed out of general tax revenues in countries with a progressive tax structure.

In many countries, a variety of transfer programmes have been launched to support and expand opportunities for vulnerable groups: the elderly, able-bodied unemployed, disabled, widows, orphans and vulnerable children, etc. Typically, the needs, institutional capabilities and important sources of risk vary across countries; so do programmes. I now discuss recent experiments in the design of safety net programmes in select countries. The country selection is governed entirely by the innovativeness of a new programme launched and/or an existing programme reformed during the 1990s in response to old and some new and emerging risks.

## Linking Food Security with Human Development: Bangladesh and Mexico

Bangladesh is known for its efforts to identify specific high-risk vulnerable groups, and for its innovativeness in tailoring programmes to address the risks of such groups largely using food as the mode of transfer, and for achieving significant pro-poor targeting outcomes. Over the past two decades, a wide variety of food transfer programmes have been implemented: Food for Work (FFW), Food for Education (FFE), Vulnerable Group Development Programme (VGD), Vulnerable Group Feeding (VGF), Test Relief (TR) and Gratuitous Relief (GR). During 1999-00, over 1.7 million metric tonnes of food was allocated to these programmes. While in the early years (1980s) these programmes were run on donated food, now most of these programmes are run without donor support. Studies have shown that targeting in all food-based programmes has substantially improved over time.

Of these programmes, the Food for Education programme has received much recognition for pioneering a new approach to transfer assistance, i.e., making the in-kind (food) transfer conditional upon the recipient (poor) household taking the responsibility for guaranteeing children's schooling. The programme now covers all 460 *thanas* (districts). At the district-level, a two-stage targeting approach is adopted: first, in each *thana*, a committee of local representatives recommend one or more unions (a lower level administrative unit somewhat similar to 'block' in India) to be eligible for the programme on considerations of low literacy rate, and economic backwardness. Based on these recommendations, about 1250 unions (out of approximately 4500 unions) have been covered by the programme. Within each union, all government and non-government schools are eligible for the programme. Second, at the school level, no more than 40 per cent of all students enrolled may be included in the programme. The government has defined the criteria for eligibility to include female-headed families, low-income families (fishermen, potters, day labourers, etc.) and households nearly landless (owning less 0.5 acres). In addition, in order to be eligible for FFE, the household should not be included in other programmes (VGD, RMP, or any other targeted food transfer programmes).

Evaluations have shown, that enrolment in participating schools have increased by 35 per cent per school over a two-year period; enrolment of girls jumped by 44 per cent; and the programme has been significantly pro-poor (Ahmed and Billah, 1994). The incremental impact may have been reduced over the years, but poor households, and children of these households, continue to benefit. A study (BIDS, 1997) found that only 12 per cent of participants were non-poor. A further evaluation of targeting performance by Galasso and Ravallion (2000), has shown that the pro-poor outcomes were largely due to pro-poor targeting within villages, and geographic targeting was less pro-poor. Moreover, research has also confirmed that the programme reduced child labour appreciably—a significant accomplishment of the programme.

FFE programme is now monetised: instead of food, cash is being given as a transfer. While no evaluation has been done after it has been monetised, cash seems to offer improved welfare benefits to the poor who could now identify for themselves their pressing needs; and savings to the government in terms of reduced handling costs of grains and reduced risk of agricultural disincentives.

Two other programmes deserve a special mention. The VGD programme is aimed at disadvantaged women who could work, and VGF is aimed at disadvantaged men and women who cannot work. Under VGD, disadvantaged women receive 30 kilos of wheat per month, but must undergo training (for income-generating small-scale ventures) for 18 months, and must comply with cash savings of 25 taka per month. At the village level, both VGD and VGF reached some of the poorest vulnerable groups (del Ninno and Dorosh, 2002); moreover, the transfer was found to be important for the survival of this vulnerable group.

## Mexico's *Progresa* Experiment

Mexico was hit by a series of macroeconomic crisis and severe recession during 1994-95, and a mild recession in 1998. As in

Bangladesh, the basic elements of a safety net programme package existed in Mexico prior to the crisis. Until 1996, Mexico operated 19 different safety net programmes implemented by 10 different agencies.[2] Of the total resources channelled, urban areas received 77 per cent. Close to 60 per cent were generalised (universal) subsidies. Nearly 60 per cent of rural poor never received any of the benefits of these programmes. In October 1997, Mexico launched a series of reforms designed to eliminate universal subsidies and consolidate all programmes into one integrated intervention originally known as PROGRESA, now called Oportunidades.[3] It is a federally designed and administered conditional cash-transfer programme, and it targets poor households in marginal rural communities. It provides two types of cash transfers: an unique amount per family, regardless of its composition, conditioned on the regular attendance of the entire family to the health clinic; and transfers for scholarships and school supplies, differentiated by school year and sex, conditioned on regular school attendance. It is a conditional cash-transfer programme (CCT), and is aimed at redressing current poverty, and short-circuiting future poverty by enlisting all school-age children into school. Children between the ages 6-17 years must meet an 85 per cent attendance requirement; households with children between 6-24 months also received nutritional supplements. Cash transfers are paid to mothers. Transfer levels varied by the nature of conditions (health clinic visits, school attendance, etc.) but the maximum a single household could receive was set at $ 75 per month. The average transfer received was around $ 40 per month, equivalent to about one-fifth of household's monthly total expenditure.

Oportunidades approach to targeting is sophisticated. It combines geographic targeting with a proxy means test applied at

---

2. The situation appears to be very similar in India. A recent paper by Radhakrishna and Ray (2003), provides an inventory of safety net programmes. The authors note five different types of public works programmes and five different types of social assistance programmes operated by central funds, and numerous other programs operated by various state governments and NGOs, each with a different administrative and implementation structure.

3. Programmes similar to Mexico's PROGRESA are now in operation in Brazil, Columbia, Honduras, Jamaica, and Nicaragua. For a brief overview of experiments with conditional transfer programmes in the Latin America Region, see Coady (2002). For a rigorous evaluation of Mexico's Progresa, see Skoufias (2001). The discussion on Progress draws from Skoufias and McClafferty (2001) and Coady (2001).

the local level. At the first stage, poorest communities are selected using information on community characteristics (demography, housing, infrastructure, education characteristics, etc.) from national census and a 'marginality index' (community score) is constructed. This is used to identify marginalised communities. At the second stage, socioeconomic data of each household in the locality is collected, and using a proxy-means score, households classified as 'poor and vulnerable' are selected for entry into the programme. By 2000, 2.6 million households, equivalent to 40 per cent of rural households and 10 per cent of all households in Mexico have been enrolled into the programme. The annual programme budget is about 0.2 per cent of GDP.

Unlike programmes elsewhere in the world, Oportunidades has been subjected to rigorous evaluation (Skoufias and McClafferty, 2001). Analysis of targeting efficiency has shown that 58 per cent of programme benefits go to households in the bottom 20 per cent of the income distribution. Administrative costs accounted for less than 10 per cent of total programme costs.[4] Evaluation results have shown substantial decrease in the incidence of sickness among young children, significant improvements in child's height and weight, and a dramatic reduction in anaemia among children, and a significant improvement in the health status of adults. Secondary school enrolments went up (attributable to the programme) by 7-9 percentage points for girls, and 4-6 percentage points for boys.

Since Mexico's innovative Oportunidades, CCTs have become very popular in many countries. Brazil has launched a similar programme called Bolsa Familia, whereby very poor families receive about $ 41 a month transfer and in return all beneficiary families have to get their children vaccinated, health monitored, and sent to school. Of the 11 million ultra poor families in the country, the programme now covers 7.5 million households, and is expanding to cover all poor households. A fairly sophisticated yet transparent targeting procedure has been put in place that begins with every beneficiary household first registering at the local village office for programme benefits. Prospective beneficiary must list all family assets including income, housing condition, number of children, assets, etc. These are

---

4. This contrasts with India's public distribution system which costs Rs. 5 to Rs. 6 to transfer Re. 1 transfer to poor households (Radhakrishna and Subbarao, 1997).

then assessed by a committee comprising local officials, NGOs, federal officials with significant and transparent oversight by interested outsiders. Impressive results have ensued: prior to the programme, only 19 per cent of schools reported children of poor households attending the school; now 79 per cent do so; drop-out rates significantly dropped to 5 per cent for boys and 8 per cent for girls, and vaccinations and health check-ups have expanded. In fact, the poor have now begun to demand better government services.

CCTs popularity is now spreading from Latin America to Africa. Kenya, Nigeria, Swaziland and South Africa, are now piloting the programme in districts with the lowest school enrolment rates. There is more to be done for coordinating federal, state and local officials in order to run the programme efficiently, but a beginning has been made to think afresh and float new and well-designed programmes to redress current and future poverty.

## Safety Net Responses to Financial Crisis: Indonesia, Korea and Argentina

I now turn to two of those countries that have been hit by macro-economic and financial crises during the mid-1990s. A variety of programmes have been launched, and the budget for safety net programmes has been enhanced.[5] I review the experience of a low-income country (Indonesia) and a middle-income country (Korea), both caught unawares by the macroeconomic/financial crisis in 1997.

Following the crisis, in Indonesia per capita GDP fell by 13 per cent, unemployment rose, and inflation (especially, the price of staple food) skyrocketed. In Indonesia, the crisis has reversed years of progress in human development and poverty reduction.

Responding to the crisis, Indonesia expanded its outreach of safety net programmes which included, (a) sales of subsidised rice, (b) work creation programmes, (c) scholarships to students and block grants to schools, (d) targeted health cards, and (e) community block grants. The budget for these programmes is released to the regions by the Centre. Owing to lack of readily available information on the severity of the crisis in each region, the budget was released

---

5. Appendix A-7.3, provides an overview of programmes and budget allocations for selected countries hit by the crisis.

according to administrative criteria (rather than severity of the crisis). Within each region, households were classified into four categories depending upon some index of 'vulnerability'. A household was placed in the lowest welfare category, if the household could not practice religious faith, its members could not eat two meals a day, could not have different sets of clothing for school and work, and if the household could not seek modern medical assistance for sick children, and if the largest floor area of the house was made of earth (mud). A slightly less rigorous criteria was adopted for the second poorest category. Access to different programmes depended upon which category a household fell. An elaborate targeting criteria was drawn for each determining eligibility for each programme, though in principle it combined geographic and household targeting. It is worth stressing that reliance was placed on non-income measures of poverty and vulnerability since incomes are hard to assess, especially during a crisis and particularly, for informal sector activities. Access to subsidised rice was granted to the bottom two categories. Scholarships were granted to children of the bottom two welfare criteria, and school-level grants depended upon a score of administrative criteria. The decisions had to be approved by local committees. Health card enabled all members of the household to obtain free health services. Subsidised rice accounted for the bulk of the budget.

Indonesia's experience is evaluated by Pritchett (2002). Three findings are worth stressing. First, for all programmes generally, the incidence was only weakly correlated to consumption expenditures. While the poor benefited, several non-poor households also accessed most of the programmes, notwithstanding the complicated programme-specific targeting criteria. Second, the actual implementation was not according to 'intended' rhetoric; communities decided that access to certain merit goods was regarded as a concern independent of poverty. As a result, the incidence of programmes across different expenditure groups was similar. Pritchett's findings, underscore the point, while communities equipped with good information on both the level and intensity of shocks to households are better placed to target assistance to the needy, the discretion enjoyed by communities could either lead to better targeting, elite capture (Bardhan and Mookherjee, 2002) or simply spreading of benefits more evenly across all expenditure groups.

Korea's experience stands in sharp contrast to Indonesia's. Prior to the crisis, Korea relied almost exclusively on rapid economic growth and informal family support; public expenditure on safety net programmes was minimal. The expectation was that the informal family-based safety net was strong, and so the country did not require welfare programmes of the scale that existed in OECD countries. The crisis induced a 'paradigm shift' inasmuch as the Government of Korea quickly moved towards instituting a strong, publicly-funded, and well-designed safety net (Subbarao, 1997).

Prior to the crisis, Korea's formal unemployment insurance programme was limited to workers employed in enterprises hiring 30 or more workers. Virtually, all workers in informal sectors and small enterprises were excluded from unemployment insurance. The crisis hit these informal workers hard. The government immediately expanded the programme of unemployment insurance to workers employed in enterprises hiring five or more workers. As a result, beneficiaries of unemployment insurance compensation increased ten-fold, from around 18,000 in January 1998 to 174,000 in March 1999. However, most of the jobless did not benefit immediately. To respond to those jobless who did not benefit from the expanded insurance programme, the government launched a low-wage public workfare programme in May 1998, initially enrolling 76,000 workers. In less than six months, after its inception, the programme was providing short-term employment to 437,000 workers. Korea showed exemplary attention to the design of the public workfare programme. The programme wage was set at a level slightly lower than the market wage for unskilled labour to induce self-selection. A shelf of projects was drawn, and labour coefficients for each activity estimated, and local authorities were consulted in the choice of activities that were needed most by communities. The crisis did not prevent the country from paying close attention to detail in order to achieve the highest possible productivity from public works—a notable example of good practice in public works (Subbarao, 2003).

Under Korea's regular (pre-crisis) Livelihood Protection Programme, benefits were provided for home care and institutional care recipients (livelihood aid, self-support aid, education aid, maternity aid, burial aid, and medical aid), and self-support care (job training, self-support grants and occasional medical aid) for needy individuals. The selection criteria for entitlement of the regular programme consisted of a means-test that combined both income and asset value. Only individuals with an income level no higher than W 210,000 per person, and a household property of less than W 29 million, are entitled for livelihood protection. Out of these, only those who cannot support themselves and those with chronic illness are eligible for home care.

Following the crisis, the government has introduced a 'new' special livelihood protection programme for the self-support recipients and allocated a budget of W 39.8 billion in FY 98; this was increased to W 234 billion for FY 99. In addition, home care benefit was extended on a temporary basis to an additional 78,000 persons in 1998, and 190,000 persons in 1999; the budget was correspondingly increased by 67 billion and 128 billion for 1998 and 1999. Overall, an additional 311,000 persons were brought into the fold of Livelihood Protection Programme in 1998 and 570,000 persons in 1999. The regular and the new special programmes were integrated in October 2000, into a National Basic Livelihood Security System. Close to 2 million persons (or 4.4 per cent of the population) now have access to this programme (Lee, 2001). The budget allocation for welfare measures comprising all of the above programmes increased from negligible levels in 1997 to 1.1 per cent of GDP by 1999 and to 3.2 per cent of GDP in 2000—a level that clearly signalled a paradigm shift towards publicly-funded redistributive safety net programme package.

Like Korea, Argentina too experienced severe macroeconomic crisis during the mid-1990s that led to massive unemployment. The government considered it imperative to launch a temporary public workfare programme called Trabajar. The programme was launched nationwide, to be implemented by local authorities. Right from the beginning, very clear and transparent guidelines were issued by the central government, leaving details (beneficiary selection) to local authorities. Central funds were distributed to municipalities following transparent and objective criteria, according to the distribution of the poor unemployed. Committed staff were enlisted to the programme who did an excellent job of monitoring the program so problems could be identified quickly and dealt with. Proven programme evaluation and supervision procedures were adapted up front. The main targeting mechanism was low-wage rate, supplemented by a sub-project selection process that geographically targeted poor areas to receive public works projects. In 2000, as market wage fell, programme wage was further lowered from 200 pesos to 160 pesos which was below the minimum wage. Payment to workers was called 'economic assistance' rather than a 'wage'. To ensure quality of assets created, skilled workers (foremen) were also hired at a higher wage. Low wage plus geographical targeting enabled self-selection of the poor into the programme. Evaluation results had shown that 80 per cent of wage benefits went to households in the bottom 20 per cent of income distribution.

## Dealing with the Shock of Transition from Socialism to a Market Economy: Uzbekistan's *Mahalla* System of Social Assistance

Prior to the transition to a market economy, Uzbekistan, like most former Soviet Union countries, operated extensive publicly-funded social assistance and social insurance programmes. The transition to the market economy was quickly accompanied by severe shocks, including rapidly falling output and employment and the end of all subsidies and transfers, including especially food subsidies. In response to rapidly declining living standards, the government implemented two main social assistance programmes: a means-tested child allowance, and a low-income cash-assistance programme.[6] Both programmes are administered by *Mahallas*, traditional local committees operating in the village. *Mahallas* existed even during pre-Soviet days in Uzbek and Tajik cultures.

Approximately 15 per cent of households received the child allowance benefit, and the coverage is clearly higher for poorer households (Rashid and Mehra, 2002). Twenty-six per cent of the poorest households received the benefit relative to only six per cent

---

6. Social protection system in Uzbekistan is extensive for its level of income, reflecting its socialist heritage. It included pay as you go pension system, active and passive unemployment programmes, and means-tested poverty benefits, *viz.*, child allowance and low income cash benefits. This section is concerned only with this latter poverty benefits administered by *Mahalla* committees.

of the richest group. One of the reasons for relatively successful pro-poor targeting of this programme is the fact that the poor are overrepresented among households with many children. However, some of the poorest households did not receive the benefit; some did not even apply for the benefit, notwithstanding widespread knowledge about the programme. While several reasons have been given by non-recipients, respondents from the poorest quintile (30 per cent) felt that they would be unjustly treated by the *Mahalla* committee if they applied.

Taking advantage of the time-honoured community organisation at the local level, the government also began to channel cash assistance to vulnerable groups through *Mahallas* whose local knowledge forms the basis for targeting. Typically, households apply to the *Mahalla* committee stating their current economic condition and seek support. Representatives of *Mahalla* committee then visit the household to determine the status (employment, income, assets, household size, etc.) and eligibility for assistance. The Ministry of Labour does provide some broad guidelines (indicators) to identify eligible households, but *Mahallas* committees, while taking into account these guidelines, enjoy considerable discretion in the selection of beneficiaries. Cash assistance is provided for three months but it can be renewed. The quantum of assistance is modest, one third of the total cash income received in the month prior to the award.

Rigorous evaluations, based on household data sets, have confirmed the programme is well-targeted (Rashid and Mehra, 2002). Though targeting outcomes appear to be lower than what was achieved by the child allowance programme, low income households were nonetheless found to be seven or eight times more likely to be in the programme than high-income households (Coudouel, Marnie and Micklewright, 1998). Several unique features of the programme contributed to its success in reaching the poorest: (a) the use of a variety of indicators of vulnerability in addition to cash income; (b) highly decentralised local-level administration; (c) a combination of broad guidelines and community discretion; and (d) wide dissemination of information regarding the programme. However, the wide discretion given to *Mahalla* committees has also proven to be its chief disadvantage, inasmuch as the entry of richest groups into the programme reflected some degree of 'discretionary favoritism' exercised by the committees. In addition, the varying competence of local-level administration resulted in horizontal inequity in the distribution of benefits: some very poor households in certain locations could not gain access to the programme, whereas some relatively less poor households gained access in some locations. Limited fiscal resources at the community level, or the need for 'connections', difficulty of the application process and the potential for stigma in the event of home visit–all these factors may have contributed to some very poor households opting not to approach the *Mahalla* committee. Notwithstanding these limitations, evidence does suggest to Uzbekistan's remarkable success in channelling assistance to indigent families who fell in between the cracks in the newly emerging market economy.

## Addressing Risks of Globalisation: China

Chinese governments have always been committed to constructing a social safety net to guarantee basic living for urban and rural poor. Since the 1990s, however, several quick changes have occurred in urban areas following globalisation and gradual integration of the urban manufacturing economy with the global economy. Short-term unemployment, as firms contract and expand in response to external forces, has become a serious problem. In addition, access to medical and other basic facilities has also come under stress. In response, the government has established 'urban *dibao* system' which provided a basic social safety net for the unemployed. By the end of 2004, the urban *dibao* system covered 22 million nationwide, of which 4.6 million are laid-off workers, 1.4 million are employees, 0.7 million are retirees, and 4.2 are unemployed, and 10 million are employees with special difficulties. Financing of benefits under the scheme were shared between the central government (60 per cent) and local finance (40 per cent). Temporary unemployed workers were among the major beneficiaries of the programme.

There is now an active drive towards establishment of urban and rural medical assistance system. Urban medical assistance programme began in 2005, and rural medical assistance programme is being finalised.

The goal of the government is to establish a "National Dibao System" that covers both urban and rural areas. Rural system is now entering the implementation stage. What is interesting about China's program is that before announcing the programme, a lot of attention is being paid to detail: procedures regarding financing and implementation procedures are being worked out, and a state-of-the-art management network is being created. China's experience stands in sharp contrast to countries where schemes are announced and laws are passed, leaving details to be worked out later, hoping that everything will be all right!

## Providing Income Security to the Elderly: Nepal

Unlike natural and economic shocks, ageing is predictable. Nevertheless it is a shock, particularly for the elderly who are poor. Because the poor have lower life expectancies than the rich, ageing and poverty could be inversely related. However, those poor who do survive to old age, are less likely to have savings or access to social insurance.

With 63 ethnic groups in a population of 23 million, Nepal is one of the least developed countries in the world. Responding to concerns of destitution and high levels of poverty and malnutrition among the elderly, the Government of Nepal launched an universal flat pension programme (of Rs. 100 per month) to all elderly above 75 years of age in 1994. The pension is paid four times a year. Two additional social security measures were added in 1997: Helpless Widows Allowance for widows over 60 years, and a pension for the disabled. Considering Nepal's per capita income is among the lowest in the world, the three social security measures adopted by the government reflected a remarkable concern for the poorest segments of Nepalese society.

A survey of a sample of villages by S.I. Rajan (2004), has shown that the government has been remarkably successful in reaching the elderly. Close to 90 per cent of eligible beneficiaries were covered by the programme. Village surveys have also shown that the government is maintaining records with great care, including those who have become eligible and removing those who are deceased. Expectation of life at the age of 75 is estimated to be about 7 years for males and 7.2 years for females. Fifty-seven per cent of recipients of the pension were women. Most elderly lived in extended families; only 3 per cent lived alone. An interesting finding of village surveys is that the virtual absence of corruption or bribes, and the high cooperative attitude of government officials administering the programme. Within the family, the majority of recipients reported 'better treatment', including improved health care, following the pension programme.

## Health Security to Women in Informal Sectors: India[7]

Work is fundamental to every self-employed woman, which is contingent upon her being healthy. A woman's health (and thus, her ability to work and earn a livelihood) can be interrupted by widowhood, accident, long-term illness, fire, and communal riots. SEWA's (Self-Employed Women's Association) experience in providing health security to self-employed women is one of the most remarkable examples of self-sustaining social security in a low-income country.

SEWA's approach comprised of both health education and curative care. In 1992, SEWA initiated an integrated insurance scheme in collaboration with national insurance companies, and its experience suggests that insurance for the poor is a workable and financially viable proposition.

The insurance scheme operates as follows. Every woman saves Rs. 1000 and this is placed in a fixed deposit. The annual interest accrued goes towards the premium, which ensures that they are covered annually without a break. Those who opt for the programme obtain maternity benefits of Rs. 300 per childbirth. Since 1997, occupation-related health conditions and gynecological problems are also covered as 'risks' and thus, eligible for insurance payments. Those women who are past their child-bearing age are eligible to get financial support under the insurance cover for dentures and hearing aids. Some women have saved an extra Rs. 650 and placed a total of Rs. 1650 to cover their husbands as well under the medical insurance programme. Many SEWA members's health was affected during the communal riots of 2002. Several claims related to riots were accepted by the insurance company. The programme is self-sustaining, and has

---

7. This section is based on SEWA (2002). *Annual Report.*

been functioning without incurring any losses ever since its inception. SEWA has shown that risk pooling among poor women is possible and financially feasible.[8]

## Summary

In much of the developing world, poor households encounter a variety of risks. Lacking instruments to protect themselves against shocks, the poor resort to informal coping strategies that often lock them into poverty trap situations. While labour-demanding economic growth is essential for raising the mean incomes of poor households, cost-effective and fiscally sustainable programmes to cushion households from fluctuations around the mean are also critical for consumption-smoothing. The 1990s, witnessed a spate of innovative approaches—some small-scale and some nationwide—that are aimed at combining 'protective' and 'productive' functions of safety net interventions. In this chapter, I surveyed some recent experiments implemented in diverse country environments. This overview yields these conclusions:

- Safety net programmes have a role to play even in very low incomes where almost everyone (and the state) is poor. Programme choice and attention to programme design can go a long way to ensure sustainability of interventions.

- Several low income as well as some middle income countries are coming to grips with the common problem of multiplicity of programmes, ineffective targeting and substantial leakage of benefits, and high administrative costs. Different countries have adopted different approaches—some experimented with new and innovative programmes while others have experimented consolidating existing programmes but with innovative approaches to targeting.

- Countries as diverse as Bangladesh and Mexico, have opted for innovative programmes that offer both protection from

---

8. This experiment is similar to Kerala's experiment with insurance for maternity benefits for landless women. Every woman subscribes a given amount every week. In return, the woman gets her average wages for three months during pregnancy and childbirth. Close to 80 per cent of landless women workers have joined the programme. Unlike the SEWA programme, Kerala scheme does involve a state subsidy.

downturns, and also, be productive by ensuring longer-term goals such as promoting school enrolments or health outcomes. In both low and middle-income countries, recent experience with conditional cash/near cash transfer programmes seem to offer a promising approach to manage income transfer programmes.

- As for minimising targeting errors, community-led identification procedures for targeting assistance, often coupled with proxy means-tests, seem to work much better than administrative targeting based on income-based means tests, especially when some broad guidelines are provided while at the same time, leaving some discretion to communities in the selection of households for assistance.

- Finally, recent experiments have also shown that it is possible to provide *ex ante* insurance against health (and weather shocks)[9] by creatively pooling the risk even among very-low-income households. Likewise, some of the extremely vulnerable individuals, such as the elderly and widows can be protected from severe consumption shortfalls by careful design of programmes and innovative approaches to targeting.

- Finally, by far the worst approach is to 'announce' ambitious programmes and hope that someday somebody will think about finding resources and an implementation strategy: such an approach is a recipe for frustration. We have now a rich array of experience from across the developing and developed world to avoid errors in the choice, design and implementation of safety net programmes.

---

9. Insurance against weather shocks is not discussed in this chapter. For discussion of a case for weather-index-based crop insurance for a low-income agrarian economy, see Christaensen and Subbarao (2003).

# References

APEC (2001). *Social Safety Net in Response to Crisis: Lessons and Guidelines from Asia and Latin America*, Paper submitted to APEC Finance Ministers, February.

Ahmed, Akhtar and K. Billah (1994). *Food for Education Program in Bangladesh: An Early Assessment*, International Food Policy Research Institute, Washington DC.

Bardhan, Pranab and Dilip Mookherjee (2002). "Decentralizing Anti-Poverty Program Delivery in Developing Countries", Institute of International Studies, University of California, Berkeley, CA.

Baulch, B. and J. Hoddinott (2000). "Economic Mobility and Poverty Dynamics in Developing Countries", *Journal of Development Studies*, Vol. 36(6), pp.1-24.

BIDS (1997). *The Development Impact of Food for Education Program in Bangladesh.*

Christaensen, L. and K. Subbarao (2003). "Towards an Understanding of Vulnerability in Rural Kenya", *Africa Human Development*, World Bank.

Coady, D. (2001). "An Evaluation of the Distributional Power of PROGRESA's Cash Transfers in Mexico", *FCND Discussion Paper* No. 117, International Food Policy Research Institute, Washington DC.

Coady, D., M. Grosh and J. Hoddinott (2002). "The Targeting of Transfers in Developing Countries: Review of Experience and Lessons", *Social Safety Net Primer Series*, World Bank, Washington DC.

Coudouel, A., S. Marnie and J. Micklewright (1998). "Targeting Social Assistance in a Transition Economy: The Mahallas in Uzbekistan", *Innocenti Occasional Papers: Economic and Social Policy Series* No. 63.

del Ninno, Carlo and P. Dorosh (2002). "In-kind Transfers and Household Food Consumption: Implications for Targeted Food Programs in Bangladesh", *FCND Discussion Papers* 134, IFPRI, Washington DC.

Dercon, Stefan (2002). "Income Risk, Coping Strategies and Safety Nets", *World Bank Research Observer*, Vol. 17(2), pp.141-166.

Galasso, E. and M. Ravallion (2000). "Distributional Outcomes of a Decentralized Welfare Program", *Policy Research Working Paper* No. 2316, World Bank, April.

Lee, H. (2001). *Labor Market Policies and Programs for Pro-Poor Growth in Republic of Korea*, Asia and Pacific Forum on Poverty.

Morduch, J. (1990). *Risk, Production and Saving: Theory and Evidence from Indian Households*, Unpublished Manuscript, Harvard University.

Pritchett, Lant (2002). *Targeted Programs in an Economic Crisis: Empirical Findings from Indonesia's Experience*, Kennedy School of Government, Harvard University.

Radhakrishna, R. and S. Ray (2003). *South Asia Poverty Alleviation Programme: Poverty-Inventory Study for India*, Indira Gandhi Institute of Development Studies, Mumbai, India.

Radhakrishna, R. and K. Subbarao (1997). "India's Public Distribution System: A National and International Perspective", *World Bank Discussion Paper* 380, The World Bank, Washington DC.

Rajan, S.I. (2004). *Old Age Allowance Program in Nepal*, Centre for Development Studies, Trivandrum, India.

Rashid, M. and K. Mehra (2002). *Social Protection in Uzbekistan*, World Bank.

Self-Employed Women's Association (SEWA) (2002). *Annual Report 2002*, Ahmedabad, India.

Skoufias, E. (2001). *PROGRESA and its Impacts on the Human Capital and Welfare of Households in Rural Mexico: A Synthesis of the Results of an Evaluation by IFPRI*, International Food Policy Research Institute, Washington DC.

Skoufias, E. and B. McClafferty (2001). *Is Progress Working? Summary of the Results of an Evaluation by IFPF,* IFPRI Washington DC.

Smith, W. James and K. Subbarao (2002). "What Role for Safety Net Transfers in Very Low Income Countries", *S P Discussion Paper* 301, World Bank Institute, World Bank, Washington DC.

Subbarao, K., A. Bonnerjee, J. Braithwaite, S. Carvalho, C. Graham and A. Thompson (1997). *Safety Net Programs and Poverty Reduction: Lessons from Cross-Country Experience*, Washington DC, World Bank.

Subbarao, K. (1997). "Public Works as an Anti-Poverty Program: An Overview of Cross-Country Experience", *American Journal of Agricultural Economics*, Vol. 79, May, pp.678-683.

————. (2003). "Systemic Shocks and Social Protection: Role and Effectiveness of Public Workfare Programs", *Human Development Discussion Paper*, World Bank.

van Dillen, Susan (2004). *Poverty and Vulnerability in Orissa: A Panel Study, mimeo.*

# Appendix A-7.1

## Chronically Poor, Transient Poor, and the Non-poor in Selected Countries

| Countries | Years | Percentage of Households Who are | | |
|---|---|---|---|---|
| | | Always Poor | Sometimes Poor | Never Poor |
| China | 1985-1990 | 6.2 | 47.8 | 46.0 |
| Côte d'Ivoire | 1987-1988 | 25.0 | 22.0 | 53.0 |
| Ethiopia | 1994-1997 | 24.8 | 30.1 | 45.1 |
| India | 1976/76-83/84 | 21.9 | 65.9 | 12.4 |
| Indonesia | 1997-1998 | 8.6 | 19.8 | 71.6 |
| Pakistan | 1986-1991 | 3.0 | 55.3 | 41.7 |
| Russia | 1992-1993 | 12.6 | 30.2 | 57.2 |
| South Africa | 1993-1998 | 22.7 | 31.5 | 45.8 |
| Vietnam | 1992/93-97/98 | 28.7 | 32.1 | 39.2 |
| Zimbabwe | 1992/93-1995/96 | 10.6 | 59.6 | 29.8 |

*Source*: Baulch and Hoddinott (2000).

# Appendix A-7.2

## Assessed Risk in Ethiopia by Rural Population during the Past 20 Years

| Type of Risky Event | Percentage of Household Reportedly Effected by Type of Event | Mode Year of Most Recent Severe Event |
|---|---|---|
| Harvest failure (due to drought, flooding, etc.) | 78 | 1984 |
| Policy problems (resettlement, taxation, etc.) | 42 | 1985 |
| Labour problems (illness or death, divorce, etc.) | 40 | 1993 |
| Oxen problem (disease,, theft, distress sale, etc.) | 39 | 1993 |
| Other livestock (as above) | 35 | 1984 |
| Land problem (land reform, transfer to family member) | 17 | 1989 |
| Asset losses (Fire, theft, villagisation, etc.) | 16 | 1885 |
| War | 07 | 1989 |
| Crime/banditry | 03 | 1986 |

*Source:* Dercon, 2002.

# Appendix A-7.3

## Social Safety Net Characteristics of Case Study Countries

| | | Indonesia | Korea | Thailand | Chile | Mexico | Peru |
|---|---|---|---|---|---|---|---|
| GNP per capita1/ | | $ 580 | $ 8,940 | $ 1,960 | $ 4,740 | $ 4,400 | $ 2,390 |
| Poverty 2/ | | 18 | 19 | 13 | 23 | 30 | 37 |
| Social spending 3/ (per cent of GDP) | Social security and welfare spending | 0.9 | 1.9 | 0.8 | 7.3 | 2.9 | 6.8 |
| Social assistance programmes | Cash transfers | ✓ | ✓ | ✓ | ✓ | ✓ | |
| | Public works | ✓ | ✓ | ✓ | ✓ | ✓ | ✓ |
| | In-kind transfers | ✓ | | ✓ | | ✓ | ✓ |
| | Unemployment assistance | | ✓ | ✓ | ✓ | ✓ | |
| | Wage subsidies | | ✓ | | ✓ | ✓ | |
| | Food subsidies | ✓ | | | | ✓ | ✓ |
| | Energy subsidies | ✓ | | | | ✓ | ✓ |
| | Housing subsidies | | ✓ | ✓ | ✓ | ✓ | |
| | Conditional transfers | | | | | ✓ | |
| | Fee waivers | ✓ | ✓ | ✓ | | ✓ | |
| | Food and nutrition | ✓ | ✓ | ✓ | ✓ | ✓ | ✓ |
| | Microfinance | ✓ | | ✓ | ✓ | ✓ | ✓ |
| Social insurance | Retirement pension | ✓ | ✓ | ✓ | ✓ | ✓ | ✓ |
| | Unemployment Insurance | | ✓ | | ✓4/ | ✓ | |
| | Health insurance | ✓ | ✓ | | | ✓ | ✓ |
| | Disability Insurance/benefits | ✓ | ✓ | ✓ | ✓ | ✓ | |
| Largest budget category | | Fuel subsidies | Public works | Public works | Pension | Conditional transfers | Public works |

# 8

# Lumbering Elephant or Running Tiger?

## Independent India, Half A Century Later

### DEEPAK NAYYAR

The object of this chapter is to assess the performance of the economy since Independence, with reference to the colonial past during the first half of the 20th century. In doing so, it seeks to focus on economic growth. In particular, it endeavours to establish turning points in economic performance, or structural breaks in economic growth, and explores the underlying factors. It does not even attempt to consider the implications of this economic growth for the well-being of people in India. That would require another essay.

The structure of the discussion is as follows. Section I outlines the dramatic changes in perceptions about the story of economic development in India, in retrospect and prospect, to set the stage before the play begins. Section II examines the turning points in India's economic performance during the 20th century by situating it in historical perspective, to provide a comparison with the colonial era. Section III provides an assessment of economic growth in India since Independence, with reference to the past and compared with the performance of other countries, to suggest that it was respectable to begin with and impressive thereafter. Section IV draws together some conclusions.

## Changing Perceptions in Retrospect and Prospect

The second half of the 20th century witnessed remarkable swings of the pendulum in perceptions about economic development in

This paper is a shorter version of the author's Kingsley Martin Lecture at the University of Cambridge on 7th November 2005. It has been published in *Economic and Political Weekly*, Vol. XLI, No. 15, 15-21 April 2006, pp.1451-1458. For the complete essay, see "India's Unfinished Journey: Transforming Growth into Development", *Modern Asian Studies*, Vol. 40, No. 3, pp.797-832, July 2006. The author would like to thank Amit Bhaduri and Romila Thapar for helpful suggestions.

Independent India. In the early 1950s, India was a path-setter, if not a role model. And the optimism extended beyond those who had a dream about India.[1] For some, its mixed economy was an answer to the challenge posed by communism in China. For others, its strategy represented a non-capitalist path to development. For yet others, who recognised the problems of industrial capitalism, India was on the road to their ideal of a social democracy and a welfare state. Just 25 years later, in the mid-1970s, perceptions were almost the polar opposite. India became an exemplar of everything gone wrong.[2] For some, the slow growth and the persistent poverty in the economy represented failure. For others, the inefficient industrialisation was a disaster. For yet others, the political democracy was unaffordable if not inviable. Another 25 years later, in the early 2000s, there was a dramatic change in perceptions once again. The same India came to be seen as a star performer, if not a role model.[3] For some, rapid economic growth turned the lumbering elephant into a running tiger. For others, the impressive economic performance combined with strong institutions which have matured over time in a political democracy mean that India may be the next Asian giant competing with, if not displacing, China.[4] For yet others, India's economy is the latest poster child to demonstrate the virtues of markets and openness.

These are, of course, caricatures of perceptions. Even so, these do reflect the popular mood at each of the junctures in time. It would be natural to ask: what has changed? In part, the process of development has changed realities in India over five decades. But, in part, changes in thinking about development have shaped perceptions over time. And it needs to be said that perceptions have changed more than realities.

The present juncture, strongly influenced by the dominant ideology of our times, has not only shaped thinking about the future but has also reshaped thinking about the past. In caricature form, the orthodox story about the economy of Independent India, half a

---

1. For a discussion on perceptions about India in the early 1950s, see Nayyar (1998).

2. This strongly critical view of India is articulated by Lal (1998).

3. Such optimism about India is more characteristic of international business and captured attention in the media following the study on BRICs by Goldman Sachs (Wilson and Purushothaman, 2003). But it is beginning to find mention in the academic literature on the subject.

4. See, for example, Khanna and Huang (2003).

century later, runs as follows. The era of planned development, which began life in 1950, was characterised by misguided, possibly counterproductive, economic policies. The strategy of industrialisation, which protected domestic industries from foreign competition and led to excessive state intervention, in the market, was responsible for high costs and low growth in the economy. The prime culprits were inward-looking policies, particularly in the sphere of trade, which stifled competition, and extraordinarily cumbersome licensing with controls on domestic economic activity that suffocated entrepreneurship and initiative in the private sector.[5] Some blame the first Prime Minister, Jawaharlal Nehru, who was strongly influenced by the colonial past and the socialist present, in this error of judgment. Others lay the blame at the door of post-colonial elites who were followers of Fabian socialists in Britain. And a few blame the political process in which mobilising the poor through rhetoric was seen as more important than resolving their problems through growth.[6] In this worldview, which almost ignores the significant achievements of that era, more than four decades were simply wasted. For them, the economic liberalisation in the early 1990s, which reduced the role of the state to rely more on the market, dismantled controls to rely more on prices, cut back on the public sector to rely more on the private sector and increased the degree of openness of the economy at a rapid pace, represented a new dawn. It is almost as if the economy began life in 1991. And the ideologues are convinced that the economic reforms of the early 1990s unleashed economic growth and led to the superb economic performance that is now much admired.[7]

This worldview is also beginning to shape thinking about the future. It has led to many aspirations for India 2025. The incorrigible optimists hope for a developed India that has caught up with industrial societies. Political leaders aspire for recognition as a nuclear power in the P-5 club, membership of the Security Council in the United Nations, and a seat at the dinner table with the G-8.

---

5. Bhagwati and Desai (1970) developed this view in their elaborate critique of the industrialisation experience in India.

6. These perceptions, which border on rhetoric, are summed up nicely by DeLong (2003).

7. India's impressive economic performance is attributed to the economic reforms of the early 1990s by several economists. See, in particular, Ahluwalia (2002), Srinivasan and Tendulkar (2003), and Panagariya (2004).

Their ultimate aspiration is India as a superpower in the world. The corporate elite hope for dynamic entrepreneurship, technological capabilities, and wealth creation. Their ultimate aspiration is India as a lead player in the global market with its own transnational firms. The pink pages of our newspapers and the electronic media have similar, even if somewhat more nuanced, hopes for India two decades hence. Such beliefs about India in the World stem primarily from aspirations about the economy in 2025, that it would become the third largest economy in the world in terms of national income at purchasing power parity; that it would become a middle-income country in terms of per capita income; and that poverty would be banished from the republic. And if China is the world's factory, India would be the world's office.

In my view, this belief system about the story of economic development in independent India is open to serious question for two reasons. First, it represents a misreading, if not a misinterpretation of the past. Second, it rests on oversimplified thinking about the future.

## The Long Twentieth Century

In seeking to establish turning points in the performance of the economy, or structural breaks in the pace of economic growth, most studies focus on the period since 1950. This is not quite appropriate. Indeed, any meaningful assessment of economic performance in Independent India must situate it in a long-term historical perspective to provide at least some comparison with the colonial era. Therefore, it would be logical to consider the performance of the economy before and after independence during the 20<sup>th</sup> century.

In this historical perspective, available evidence shows that the turning point came in the early 1950s. The trends in national income and per capita income, at constant prices, during the period from 1900-01 to 1946-47 are outlined in Figure 8.1. It reveals that during the first half of the 20<sup>th</sup> century, there was a near stagnation in per capita income while the growth in national income was minimal. The trends in GDP and GDP per capita, at constant prices, during the period 1950-51 to 2004-05 are outlined in Figure 8.2. The contrast is clear. There was a steady growth in both GDP and GDP per capita during the second half of the 20<sup>th</sup> century. This is confirmed by Table

## Figure 8.1

### A. Trends in National Income—India: 1900-01 to 1946-47 (in Rupees million at 1938-39 prices)

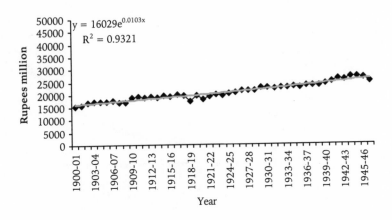

### B. Trends in Per Capita Income—India: 1900-01 to 1946-47 (in Rupees at 1938-39 prices)

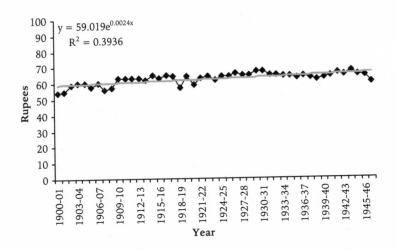

*Source*: Sivasubramonian (2000).

## Figure 8.2

### A. Trends in GDP—India: 1950-51 to 2004-05
### (at factor cost in Rupees million at 1993-94 prices)

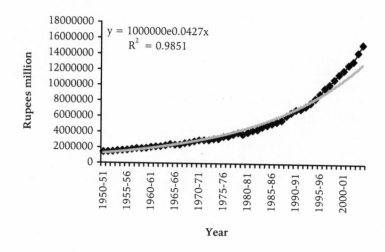

### B. Trends in GDP Per Capita—India: 1950-51 to 2004-05
### (at factor cost in Rupees at 1993-94 prices)

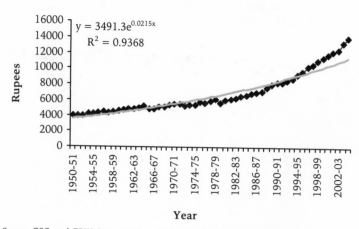

*Source*: CSO and EPW Research Foundation, *National Accounts Statistics of India.*

8.1 which sets out average annual rates of growth in national income and per capita income during each of the two periods. There are two sets of growth rates for the period 1900-01 to 1946-47 based on two different estimates of national income. The Sivasubramonian estimates suggest that, in real terms, the growth in national income was 1 per cent per annum whereas the growth in per capita income was 0.2 per cent per annum. The Maddison estimates suggest that the growth in national income was 0.8 per cent per annum whereas the growth in per capita income was almost negligible at 0.04 per cent per annum. The growth rates for the period from 1950-51 to 2004-2005 provide a sharp contrast. In real terms, the growth in GDP was 4.2 per cent per annum while the growth in per capita income was 2.1 per cent per annum. The step-up in sectoral growth rates was just as substantial. The magnitude of the increase over the entire period is also revealing. Between 1900-01 and 1946-47, at constant 1938-39

**Table 8.1**

*Rates of Economic Growth in India during the 20ᵗʰ Century*
*(per cent per annum)*

| A. 1900-01 to 1946-47 | | |
|---|---|---|
| | *Sivasubramonian Estimates* | *Maddison Estimates* |
| Primary Sector | 0.4 | 0.8 |
| Secondary Sector | 1.7 | 1.1 |
| Tertiary Sector | 1.7 | 0.8 |
| National Income | 1.0 | 0.8 |
| Per Capita Income | 0.2 | 0.04 |
| B. 1950-51 to 2004-05 | | |
| Primary Sector | 2.5 | |
| Secondary Sector | 5.3 | |
| Tertiary Sector | 5.4 | |
| GDP Total | 4.2 | |
| GDP Per Capita | 2.1 | |

*Note:* The average annual rates of growth, sectoral and aggregate, for the period 1950-51 to 2004-05, have been calculated by fitting a semi-log linear regression equation Ln Y=a + bt and estimating the values of b.

*Sources:* For 1900-01 to 1946-47, Sivasubramonian (2000) and Maddison (1985). For 1950-51 to 2004-05, CSO and EPW Research Foundation, *National Accounts Statistics of India.*

prices, national income for the undivided India increased from
Rs. 15.4 billion to Rs. 24.9 billion by 60 per cent, whereas per capita
income increased from Rs. 54 to Rs. 60 by a mere 11 per cent.[8]
Between 1950-51 and 2004-05, at constant 1993-94 prices, GDP
increased by 1000 per cent, while GDP per capita increased by 250
per cent.[9] For those who are not persuaded by the trends in graphs,
the step-up in growth rates, or the proportionate increases in income,
there is conclusive evidence provided by statistical analysis. There is
a complete time series for national income aggregates, GDP at
constant 1948-49 prices, for the entire period 1900-01 to 1999-2000.
Econometric analysis based on this data set shows that the most
important structural break, which is statistically the most significant,
for the growth rate in national income is 1951-52.[10]

Interestingly enough, even if we focus on the performance of the
economy in India since Independence, it is clear that the turning
point in economic growth is *circa* 1980, more than a decade before
economic liberalisation began in 1991.

Figure 8.3 outlines the trends in GDP and GDP per capita, at
constant prices, in India during the period from 1950-51 to 2004-05.
In doing so, it makes a distinction between two sub-periods 1950-51
to 1979-80 and 1980-81 to 2004-05. The break in the trend is clearly
discernible in 1980-81 with a marked acceleration in economic
growth thereafter. This is also borne out by Figure 8.4, which
outlines trends in GDP and GDP per capita, at constant prices, during
the period from 1980-81 to 2004-05. In doing so, it makes a
distinction between two sub-periods: 1980-81 to 1990-91 and 1991-92

---

8. Cf. Sivasubramonian (2000: 369-371).

9. Between 1950-51 and 2004-05, GDP at factor cost in 1993-94 prices increased
   from Rs. 1405 billion to Rs. 15294 billion while GDP per capita increased from
   Rs. 3913 to Rs. 14018.

10. See Hatekar and Dongre (2005). The authors situate the debate on structural
    breaks in India's economic growth in a longer term perspective by considering
    the period from 1900-1901 to 1999-2000. This exercise is based on the
    Sivasubramonian estimates of national income at 1948-49 prices. It needs to
    be said that the time-series before 1947, which relates to undivided India, is
    not strictly comparable with that after 1947, which relates to partitioned India.
    In addition, there are also some definitional differences in national income
    accounts for India before and after independence. Even so, the statistical
    analysis carried out by Hatekar and Dongre is based on plausible assumptions
    which minimise the problems of comparability and provide the basis for robust
    conclusions.

## Figure 8.3

### A. Two Phases of Economic Growth in India: 1950-51 to 1979-80 and 1980-81 to 2004-05

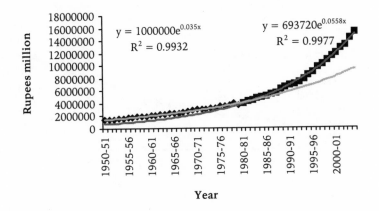

### B. GDP Per Capita (at factor cost in Rupees at 1993-94 prices)

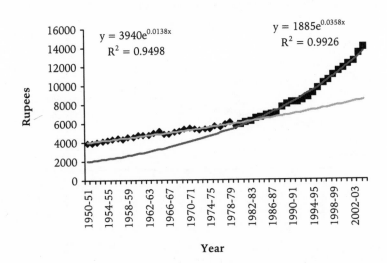

*Source*: CSO and EPW Research Foundation, *National Accounts Statistics of India*.

## Figure 8.4

*A. Trends in India's GDP: 1980-81 to 1990-91 and 1991-92 to
2004-05 (at factor cost in Rupees million at 1993-94 prices)*

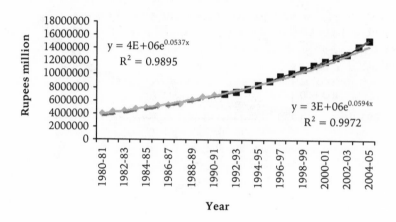

*B. Trends in India's GDP Per Capita: 1980-81 to 1990-91 and
1991-92 to 2004-05 (at factor cost in Rupees at 1993-94 prices)*

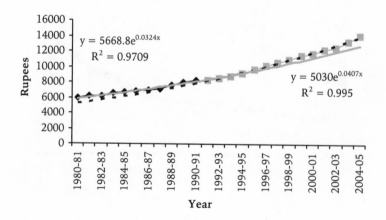

*Source:* CSO, *National Accounts Statistics of India.*

to 2004-05. The picture that emerges is clear enough. Almost the same trend continues, without any break, throughout the period. The evidence presented in Table 8.2, on average annual rates of growth in GDP and GDP per capita, for each of these sub-periods, provides further confirmation. During the period from 1950-51 to 1979-80, growth in GDP was 3.5 per cent per annum while growth in GDP per capita was 1.4 per cent per annum. During the period from 1980-81 to 2004-05, growth in GDP was 5.6 per cent per annum while growth in GDP per capita was 3.6 per cent per annum. The sharp step-up in growth rates, not only aggregate but also sectoral, suggests that 1980-1981 was the turning point. This conclusion is reinforced by a comparison of growth rates, aggregate and sectoral, during the sub-periods 1980-81 to 1990-91 and 1991-92 to 2004-05. The growth rates were almost the same. In fact, during the period from 1991-92 to 2004-05, growth in the primary sector and the secondary sector was somewhat slower while growth in the tertiary sector was somewhat faster in comparison with the period from 1980-81 to 1990-91. Growth in GDP was 5.9 per cent per annum as compared with 5.4 per cent per annum, while growth in GDP per capita was 4.1 per cent per annum as compared with 3.2 per cent per annum. There was some acceleration in the rate of growth of GDP per capita which was largely attributable to the slowdown in population growth. For those not persuaded by trends in graphs or comparison of growth rates, statistical analysis should be conclusive. And there is now some literature on this subject.[11] Econometric analysis of time series data on GDP and GDP per capita for the period from the early 1950s to the early 2000s establishes that the structural break in economic growth since Independence, which is statistically the most significant, occurs around 1980.[12]

There are two conclusions that emerge from the available evidence and the preceding discussion. First, if we consider the 20th century in its entirety, the turning point in economic performance, or the structural break in economic growth, is 1951-52. Second, if we

---

11. Indeed, there are several papers that seek to establish structural breaks in economic growth in India since Independence: DeLong (2003), Wallack (2003), Rodrik and Subramanian (2004), Sinha and Tejani (2004) and Virmani (2004).

12. See Wallack (2003) and Rodrik and Subramanian (2004). See also DeLong (2003) and Sinha and Tejani (2004).

## Table 8.2

*Sectoral and Aggregate Economic Growth in India since Independence (Per cent Per Annum)*

| Sector/ Period | 1950-51 to 1979-80 | 1980-81 to 2004-05 | 1980-81 to 1990-91 | 1991-92 to 2004-05 |
|---|---|---|---|---|
| Primary Sector | 2.2 | 2.9 | 3.1 | 2.5 |
| Secondary Sector | 5.3 | 6.1 | 6.7 | 6.0 |
| Tertiary Sector | 4.5 | 7.1 | 6.6 | 7.8 |
| GDP Total | 3.5 | 5.6 | 5.4 | 5.9 |
| GDP Per Capita | 1.4 | 3. 6 | 3.2 | 4.1 |

Notes: (a) This table is based on data for GDP at factor cost and at 1993-94 prices.

(b) The primary sector includes agriculture, forestry and fishing. The secondary sector includes: mining and quarrying; manufacturing; electricity, gas and water; and construction. The tertiary sector includes: trade, hotels and restaurants; transport, storage and communication; financing, insurance, real estate and business services; and community, social and personal services.

(c) The average annual rates of growth, sectoral and aggregate, for each of the selected periods, have been calculated by fitting a semi-log linear regression equation LnY=a+bt and estimating the values of b.

*Source:* CSO and EPW Research Foundation, *National Accounts Statistics of India.*

consider India since Independence, during the second half of the 20th century, the turning point in economic performance, or structural break in economic growth, is 1980-81. In either case, 1991-92 is not a turning point. Therefore, it is simply not possible to attribute India's growth performance to economic liberalisation even on a *post hoc ergo propter hoc* basis. It is also clear that the turning point in the early 1950s was much more significant than the structural break during the early 1980s. This proposition is validated by econometric analysis.[13] It is also worth noting that the proportionate change in growth rates, both aggregate and sectoral, was much larger *circa* 1950 than it was *circa* 1980.

It needs to be stressed that this turning point in the early 1950s was not just statistical, nor was it simply about growth rates. It was far more significant for the polity and economy of independent India in a substantive sense.

---

13. Cf. Hatekar and Dongre (2005).

The conception and the birth of political democracy in independent India was unique in its wider historical context.[14] For democracy did not follow but preceded capitalist industrialisation and development. What is more, democracy came to India neither as a response to an absolutist state nor as the realisation of an individualist conception of society. In each of these attributes, it provided a sharp contrast with the experience elsewhere, particularly Europe. In fact, it was not even an obvious outcome of the nationalist movement. The struggle for independence was much more about autonomous space for the nation than about freedom for the individual. Indeed, the Gandhian notion of a just state was premised on the idea that the collective interest must take precedence over individual interests. Yet, the Constitution adopted by Independent India created a democratic republic and pledged to secure justice, liberty, equality and fraternity for all its citizens. Universal adult franchise was provided at one stroke. The republicanism of the Western world was perhaps the role model. This was, in a sense, India invented. A liberal democracy was constructed by an enlightened elite in accordance with its conception of a modern nation state. It was democracy from above provided to the people. And not democracy from below claimed by the people. This is perhaps an oversimplified view. The reality was obviously more complex. For the nationalist movement meant a dialectical relationship between the provision from above and the claim from below. In this construct, the state was the essential mediator. It had to perform a critical role in reconciling the conflict between market economy and political economy as also mediating between economic development and social needs.

In this milieu, the strategy of economic development was shaped by the colonial past and the nationalist present. For one, there was a conscious attempt to limit the degree of openness and of integration with the world economy, in pursuit of a more autonomous path to development. For another, the state was assigned a strategic role in development because the market, by itself, was not perceived as sufficient to meet the aspirations of a latecomer to industrialisation. Both represented points of departure from the colonial era which was characterised by open economies and unregulated markets. But this approach also represented a consensus

---

14. For a more detailed discussion, see Nayyar (1998).

in thinking about the most appropriate strategy for industrialisation. It was, in fact, the development consensus of the times. The objectives were clear enough: to catch up with the industrialised world and to improve the living conditions of the people.

It should be obvious that the economic liberalisation which began in the early 1990s did not match the significance of the changes in the realm of politics and the sphere of economics in the early 1950s. In fact, the changes that were introduced in the early 1990s were concerned with economic policies and did not even touch upon the political domain. In the wider context of the economy, the changes were significant.[15] And it is worth highlighting three dimensions of the change. First, economic growth combined with economic efficiency became the explicit objective. The earlier concern about preventing a concentration of economic power or attempting a redistribution of wealth, never more than rhetoric, was explicitly abandoned. The objective of bringing about a reduction in poverty and inequality was not set aside but such concerns about equity were subsumed in the pursuit of growth on the premise that it is both necessary and sufficient for an improvement in the living conditions of people. Second, there was a conscious decision to substantively reduce the role of the state in the process of economic development and rely far more on the market. The government no longer sought to guide the allocation of scarce investible resources, whether directly through industrial licensing or indirectly through intervention in the financial sector, and left this role to the market. Third, the degree of openness of the economy was increased significantly and at a rapid pace. The object was not simply to enforce a cost-discipline on the supply side through international competition, but also to narrow the difference between domestic and world prices. Foreign capital and foreign technology were expected to perform a strategic role in the process of integration with the world economy. These changes in policies did represent a radical departure from the past. But these were changes in economic policies. In contrast, the regime change during the early 1950s was wide-ranging and far-reaching. It was in part about policies but only in part. It was about establishing institutions, not only economic but also social and political. It was

---

15. This issue is discussed, at some length, in Nayyar (1996). See also Bhaduri and Nayyar (1996).

about creating the initial conditions for development in a country that was a latecomer to industrialisation. It was about the pursuit of national development objectives in a long-term perspective.

## Two Phases of Growth

Growth matters because it is cumulative. If GDP growth, in real terms, is 3.5 per cent per annum income doubles over 20 years, if it is 5 per cent per annum income doubles over 14 years, if it is 7 per cent per annum income doubles over 10 years, and if it is 10 per cent per annum income doubles over 7 years. Of course, the complexity of economic growth cannot be reduced to a simple arithmetic of compound growth rates, for there is nothing automatic about growth. In retrospect, however, the cumulative impact of growth on output is a fact.

There are two discernible phases of economic growth in India since Independence: 1950 to 1980 and 1980 to 2005. It is worth providing an assessment of economic performance during these periods. An assessment of performance, in terms of economic growth, should address two questions. First, how does this performance compare with performance in the past? Second, how does this performance compare with the performance of other countries?

It is clear that the pace of economic growth during the period from 1950 to 1980 constituted a radical departure from the colonial past. For the period 1900 to 1947, there are two sets of growth rates based on alternative estimates of national income. If the economy had continued to grow at the rate based on the Sivasubramonian estimates, national income would have doubled in 70 years whereas per capita income would have doubled in 350 years. If the economy had continued to grow at the lower rate, based on the Maddison estimates, national income would have doubled in 87.5 years whereas per capita income would have doubled in 1750 years. The reality in independent India turned out to be different. The growth rates achieved during the period from 1950 to 1980 meant that GDP doubled in 20 years while GDP per capita would have doubled in 50 years. In fact, between 1950 and 1980, GDP multiplied by 2.86 while GDP per capita multiplied by 1.5.[16] The latter was not as modest

---

16. Between 1950-51 and 1980-81, GDP at factor cost in 1993-94 prices increased from Rs. 1405 billion to Rs. 4011 billion while GDP per capita increased from Rs. 3913 to Rs. 5908.

as it seems because, during this phase, the rate of population growth was more than 2 per cent per annum.

Obviously, this growth was impressive with reference to the near-stagnation during the colonial era. It was also much better than the performance of the now industrialised countries at comparable stages of their development.[17] However, this growth was not enough to meet the needs of a country where the initial level of income was so low. For this reason, perhaps, it was described as the 'Hindu rate of growth' by Raj Krishna. This phrase, which became larger than life with the passage of time, meant different things to different people. For some, it meant a performance that was disappointing but not bad. For others, it meant an acceptance of the performance in a spirit of contentment without an effort to change. Interestingly enough, the phrase which was used to describe a reality was used by a few to deride the same reality. But this was not warranted.

It has been shown that, during this period, India's performance in terms of economic growth was about the same as in most countries in the world.[18] It was certainly not as good as East Asia. But it was definitely not as bad as Africa. It was average. In fact, the actual rate of growth of output per worker in India was very close to the average across the world. What is more, the rate of growth predicted for India, based on its initial output per worker, its share of investment in GDP and its population growth rate, was also very close to the world's average.[19] Is it possible to reconcile this conclusion with the view that India did badly in this era? There are two possible explanations: either that inefficiencies of the regime in India were paralleled by similar shortcomings in most countries of the world, or that without its misguided policies India would have experienced a miracle in growth.[20] Neither of these explanations is plausible. It

---

17. See Bairoch (1993) and Maddison (1995). See also Chang (2002).

18. For a lucid analysis of, with evidence on, this proposition, see DeLong (2003).

19. This is established by DeLong (2003).

20. These two possible explanations are suggested by DeLong (2003), who also puts forward a third explanation which is somewhat more plausible. It suggests that if there was a failure of economic policies it was in large part offset by the success at mobilising resources which raised levels of saving and investment in the economy. In other words, even if resource-allocation or resource-utilisation constrained growth, resource-mobilisation fostered growth. This macroeconomic perspective, somewhat different from the orthodox view, is developed elsewhere by the author (Nayyar, 1994 and 1997).

would seem that the story that depicts an average India is much more plausible than the caricature which portrays a failed India.

It is clear that there was a sharp acceleration in the rate of growth *circa* 1980. It went almost unnoticed but for a few of us. And India grew almost by stealth. It came into the limelight in the early 2000s. Some analysts, as also many casual observers, attributed this performance to economic liberalisation which began in the early 1990s.[21] However, discerning scholars recognised the reality that the structural break, which was a second turning point in the economic performance of independent India, occurred around 1980.[22]

In comparison with the preceding 30 years, there was a distinct step-up in rates of growth for GDP and GDP per capita. The growth rates achieved on an average, during the period from 1980 to 2005, meant that GDP doubled in 12.5 years where GDP per capita doubled in 20 years. In fact, between 1980-81 and 2004-05, GDP multiplied by 3.81 while GDP per capita multiplied by 2.37.[23] This growth was impressive, not only in comparison with the past in India but also in comparison with the performance of most countries in the world. Indeed, in terms of growth, India performed much better than the industrialised countries which experienced a slowdown in growth, the transition economies which did badly, and much of the developing world. And it was only East Asia, particularly China, which performed better.

There is an emerging literature on the subject which seeks to analyse this rapid economic growth in India that has been sustained for 25 years. Interestingly enough, the search for explanations is competitive. And some hypotheses are driven by an ideological worldview. It would be impossible to provide an exhaustive analysis. It would also mean too much of a digression. Nevertheless, some explanations deserve mention.

---

21. See, for example, Ahluwalia (2002) and Srinivasan and Tendulkar (2003).

22. See, in particular, DeLong (2003) and Rodrik and Subramanian (2004), who highlighted the fact that the structural break in economic growth in India since Independence occurred around 1980 and not in 1991.

23. Between 1980-81 and 2004-05, GDP at factor cost in 1993-94 prices increased from Rs. 4011 billion to Rs. 15294 billion while GDP per capita increased from Rs. 5908 to Rs. 14018.

The earliest explanation suggested that the expansion of aggregate demand, mostly through a rapid increase in public expenditure on investment and consumption, was the major factor underlying rapid economic growth during the 1980s.[24] This is widely accepted. Even so, orthodoxy argues that this growth supported by the expansionary macroeconomic policies was not sustainable and culminated in the crisis of 1991.[25] But this view is not quite correct. In so far as the increase in fiscal deficits did not translate into a corresponding increase in current account deficits, the increase in aggregate demand would, in the presence of excess capacity and unemployment, have led to an increase in output. Such an increase in capacity utilisation would also have raised the productivity of investment which is reflected in significant productivity growth during the 1980s.[26] And even if the macroeconomic crisis of 1991 was induced in large part by the fiscal imbalances, the expansion in aggregate demand does provide a plausible expansion for the rapid growth during the 1980s.

The most fashionable explanation, advocated by orthodoxy, is that the rapid economic growth in India is largely attributable to economic reforms. There is, however, a fly in the ointment. The turning point in growth was 1980, whereas economic liberalisation began in 1991. Confronted with this reality, orthodoxy relies on two explanations. First, it argues that the economic growth of the 1980s was not sustainable.[27] But there was growth. Second, it argues that the growth could have been unleashed by the mild doses of industrial deregulation and trade liberalisation.[28] But this process started only in the mid-1980s. Therefore, such hypotheses which seek to explain the step-up in economic growth entirely in terms of economic reforms are simply not plausible.

---

24. See Nayyar (1994) and Joshi and Little (1994).

25. Cf. Ahluwalia (2002), Srinivasan and Tendulkar (2003), and Panagariya (2004).

26. Rodrik and Subramanian (2004) develop this argument to question the orthodox view, but conclude that the increase in capacity utilisation was not enough to explain the actual productivity increase in the period since 1980.

27. See Ahluwalia (2002) and Srinivasan and Tendulkar (2003).

28. See Panagariya (2004). Joshi and Little (1994), on the other hand, believe that these changes were more than trivial but were piecemeal and limited. Hence they do not attribute rapid growth to this mild dose of reforms. It is also worth noting that Rodrik and Subramanian (2004) do not accept this as a possible explanation for the step-up in growth during the 1980s.

There is yet another explanation.[29] It argues that there was an attitudinal change on the part of government in the early 1980s, which signalled a shift in favour of the private sector although this was not quite reflected in actual policy changes. The limited policy changes that were introduced were pro-business rather than pro-competition or pro-market so that the benefit accrued to existing players rather than new entrants. Even these small changes elicited a large productivity response because India was far away from its production possibility frontier. And existing manufacturing capacities established earlier performed a critical role in shaping responses. This explanation is both interesting and perceptive, although it is somewhat far-fetched. And there are some obvious questions that arise. Why did the change in attitudes alone spur growth starting 1980 even though the mild policy changes were introduced in the mid-1980s? Why did the economic liberalisation of the early 1990s not produce a similar response in terms of productivity increase and output growth because, even in 1991, India was somewhere inside its production possibility frontier?

In my judgment, the search for a single explanation which seeks to exclude, or to deny, competing explanations is futile. There is, perhaps, the bit of truth in every nook. Hence, a convincing explanation must recognise that the acceleration in economic growth, *circa* 1980, was attributable to several factors. First, expansionary macroeconomic policies which led to an increase in aggregate demand did stimulate an increase in the rate of growth of output.[30] Second, beginning in the late 1970s, there was a significant increase in the investment-GDP ratio which was sustained through the 1980s.[31] Unless there was a decline in the productivity of investment, which was not the case, this would also have contributed to the step-up in economic growth during the 1980s. Third, starting in the

---

29. This is the main hypothesis put forward by Rodrik and Subramanian (2004), who argue that none of the other explanations are plausible or convincing.

30. In fact, this proposition is accepted by Ahluwalia (2002, p.67), as also Srinivasan and Tendulkar (2003, p.9), even if they argue that the growth was not sustainable.

31. Gross capital formation as a proportion of GDP at current prices rose from 18.7 per cent in 1980-81 to 24.1 per cent in 1990-91. Adjusted for errors and omissions, this proportion rose from 20.3 per cent in 1980-81 to 26.3 per cent in 1990-91. See *National Accounts Statistics of India: 1950-51 to 2002-03*, EPW Research Foundation, Mumbai, 2004.

late 1970s, there was also a significant increase in public investment which was sustained through the 1980s.[32] Obviously, this contributed to the increase in aggregate demand. However, in so far as such public investment created new infrastructure or improved existing infrastructure, it could have stimulated growth in output by alleviating supply constraints. Fourth, trade liberalisation beginning in the late 1970s, combined with some deregulation in industrial policies introduced in the early 1980s, also probably contributed to productivity increase and economic growth.[33] In particular, liberalisation of the regime for the import of capital goods and broad-banding which reduced industrial licensing, could have played a contributory role.

It is also misleading, perhaps, to search for explanations which focus on observed changes *circa* 1980 that might explain the turning point in economic growth. In so far as outcomes are shaped by initial conditions, the cumulative impact of economic policies or public actions over the preceding 30 years possibly played an important role in the turnaround.[34] Institutional capacities were created. The social institutions and the legal framework for a market economy were put in place. A system of higher education was developed. Entrepreneurial talents and managerial capabilities were fostered.

---

32. Gross capital formation in the public sector as a proportion of GDP at current prices rose from an average level of 7.7 per cent during the period 1971-72 to 1975-76, to 9.1 per cent during 1976-77 to 1980-81 and 10.3 per cent during 1981-82 to 1985-86. This average level was 9.8 per cent during 1986-87 to 1990-1991. See *National Accounts Statistics of India*: 1950-51 to 2002-03, EPW Research Foundation, Mumbai, 2004. If the effects of public investment, particularly in infrastructure, are lagged, by say 5 years, the surge in public investment does provide an important part of the explanation for economic growth in India during the 1980s. Statistical analysis by Rodrik and Subramanian (2004) confirms this proposition, who argue that the contribution of public investment to economic growth would have been small if there were no time lags in its effects.

33. The Rodrik and Subramanian (2004) hypothesis, which is an interesting variation around this theme, could, perhaps, constitute a part of the explanation. The problem is their claim that it is the only possible explanation. Similarly, the Panagariya (2004) conclusion could provide a part of the explanation but his claim in terms of cause and effect is exaggerated. The difficulty is that the step-up in economic growth occurred about 5 years before the much cited economic reforms of the mid-1980s. But there were some earlier piecemeal changes in trade policies and industrial policies, such as the liberalisation in the regime for the import of capital goods, which could also have contributed to growth, in conjunction with the other factors outlined in this paragraph. In fact, Sinha and Tejani (2004) suggest that imported capital goods probably contributed to increases in the productivity of labour, hence economic growth, during the 1980s.

34. For a discussion, see Nayyar (2004).

Science and technology was accorded a priority. The capital goods sector was established. Much of this did not exist in colonial India. But it was in place by 1980 and probably provided the essential foundations. In other words, the second turning point in the economic performance of independent India may not have been possible starting from scratch.

This wonderful story about economic growth in India is not quite a fairy tale. And everybody does not live happily hereafter. Both phases of economic growth had something in common. It is essential to recognise that economic growth in independent India, respectable in the first phase and impressive in the second phase, was not transformed into development, for it did not bring about an improvement in the well-being of people. Independent India did make significant progress during the second half of the 20th century, particularly in comparison with the colonial past. But poverty and deprivation persist, for at least one-fourth, possibly one-third, of India's one billion people. In fact, there are more poor people in India now than the total population at the time of Independence. And, in terms of social development, India has miles to go.

## Conclusion

The story of economic development in independent India is often distorted by beliefs in fashion or caricatures of perceptions which shape conventional wisdom. I have argued that this is misleading, not only in analysing the past but also in contemplating the future. If we consider India during the 20th century as a whole, the turning point in economic growth was *circa* 1951. If we consider India since Independence, the turning point in economic growth was *circa* 1980. And it is clear that the turning point in the early 1950s was much more significant than the structural break in the early 1980s. In any case, 1991 was not a watershed. Thus, it is not possible to attribute the turnaround in India's growth performance to economic liberalisation. Economic growth in India was respectable during the period 1950-1980. It was a radical departure from the colonial past. And it was no worse than the growth performance of most countries during that period. But it was simply not enough in relation to India's needs. Economic growth in India was impressive during the period 1980-2005. Indeed, it was much better than in most countries. But even this was not enough. The moral of the story is clear. Caricature perceptions about the economic growth in India since Independence are not correct. In the first phase, from 1950 to 1980, India was not the lumbering elephant that it is often made out to be. In the second phase, from 1980 to 2005, India was not quite the running tiger that some believe it has become.

The real failure, throughout the second half of the 20th century, was India's inability to transform its growth into development, which would have brought about an improvement in the living conditions of people, the ordinary people. India's unfinished journey in development would not be complete so long as poverty, deprivation and exclusion persist. The destination, then, is clear. India must provide all its citizens with the capabilities, opportunities and rights they need to exercise their own choice for a decent life.[35] In the pursuit of this objective, economic growth is essential. But it cannot be sufficient. What is more, it is neither feasible nor desirable to separate economic growth from distributional outcomes because they are inextricably linked with each other. This link is provided by employment creation. Jobless growth is not sustainable either in economics or in politics. The creation of employment would only reinforce economic growth through a virtuous circle of cumulative causation.

---

35. For a detailed discussion on the issues set out in this paragraph, see Deepak Nayyar (2006). "India's Unfinished Journey: Transforming Growth into Development", *Modern Asian Studies*, Vol. 40(3), July, pp.797-832.

# References

Ahluwalia, Montek S. (2002). "Economic Reforms in India since 1991: Has Gradualism Worked?", *Journal of Economic Perspectives*, Vol. 16(7), pp.67-88.

Bairoch, Paul (1993). *Economics and World History: Myths and Paradoxes*, University of Chicago Press, Chicago.

Bhaduri, Amit and Deepak Nayyar (1996). *The Intelligent Person's Guide to Liberalization*, Penguin Books, New Delhi.

Bhagwati, Jagdish and Padma Desai (1970). *India: Planning for Industrialization*, Oxford University Press, London.

Chang, Ha-Joon (2002). *Kicking Away the Ladder: Development Strategy in Historical Perspective*, Anthem Press, London.

DeLong, J. Bradford (2003). "India since Independence: An Analytic Growth Narrative", in Dani Rodrik (ed.), *In Search of Prosperity: Analytic Narratives on Economic Growth*, Princeton University Press, New Jersey.

EPW Research Foundation (2004). *National Accounts Statistics of India, 1950-51 to 2002-03, Linked Series with 1993-94 as the Base Year*, Economic and Political Weekly Research Foundation, Mumbai.

Hatekar, Neeraj and Amrish Dongre (2005). "Structural Breaks in India's Growth", *Economic and Political Weekly*, Vol. 40(14), pp.1432-1435.

Joshi, Vijay and I.M.D. Little (1994). *India: Macroeconomics and Political Economy, 1964-1991*, World Bank and Oxford University Press, Washington DC and New Delhi.

Khanna, Tarun and Yasheng Huang (2003). "Can India Overtake China?", *Foreign Policy*, Issue 137, July-August, pp.74-81.

Lal, Deepak (1998). *Unfinished Business: India in the World Economy*, Oxford University Press, New York.

Maddison, Angus (1985). "Alternative Estimates of the Real Product of India: 1900-1946", *Indian Economic and Social History Review*, Vol.22(2), pp.201-210.

———. (1995). *Monitoring the World Economy: 1820-1992*, OECD Development Centre, Paris.

Nayyar, Deepak (ed.) (1994) *Industrial Growth and Stagnation: The Debate in India*, Oxford University Press, Bombay.

———. (1996). *Economic Liberalization in India: Analytics, Experience and Lessons: R.C. Dutt Lectures on Political Economy*, Orient Longman, Calcutta.

———. (1997). "Themes in Trade and Industrialization", in Deepak Nayyar (ed.), *Trade and Industrialization*, Oxford University Press, Delhi.

———. (1998). "Economic Development and Political Democracy: Interaction of Economics and Politics in Independent India", *Economic and Political Weekly*, Vol. 33(49), pp.3121-3131.

———. (2004). "Economic Reforms in India: Understanding the Process and Learning from Experience", *International Journal of Development Issues*, Vol. 3(2), pp.31-55.

Panagariya, Arvind (2004). "Growth and Reforms during 1980s and 1990s", *Economic and Political Weekly*, Vol. 39(25), pp.2581-2594.

Rodrik, Dani and Arvind Subramanian (2004). "From Hindu Growth to Productivity Surge: The Mystery of the Indian Growth Transition", *IMF Working Paper* WP/04/77, International Monetary Fund, Washington DC.

Sinha, Ajit and Shirin Tejani (2004). "Trend Breaks in India's GDP Growth Rate", *Economic and Political Weekly*, Vol. 39(52), pp.5634-5639.

Sivasubramonian, S. (2000). *The National Income of India during the Twentieth Century*, Oxford University Press, Delhi.

Srinivasan, T.N. and Suresh Tendulkar (2003). *Reintegrating India with the World Economy*, Institute for International Economics, Washington DC.

Virmani, Arvind (2004). "India's Economic Growth: From Socialist Rate of Growth to Bharatiya Rate of Growth", *ICRIER Working Paper* No. 122, Indian Council for Research on International Economic Relations, New Delhi.

Wallack, Jessica S. (2003). "Structural Breaks in Indian Macroeconomic Data", *Economic and Political Weekly*, Vol. 38(41), pp.4312-4315.

Wilson, D. and Purushothaman R. (2003). "Dreaming with BRICs: The Path to 2050", *Global Economics Paper* No. 99, Goldman Sachs.

# 9

# A Stronger Social Dimension for Globalisation

GERRY RODGERS

## What is the Social Dimension of Globalisation?

The preamble to the ILO's constitution includes the following phrase: "Whereas also the failure of any nation to adopt humane conditions of labour is an obstacle in the way of other nations which desire to improve the conditions in their own countries."

In 1919, after the First World War had marked the end of the phase of—largely colonial—globalisation of the 19th and early 20th centuries, it was apparent to the founders of the ILO that the increasing interdependence among countries extended to social goals, expressed as humane conditions of labour.

At one level this is obvious. When national policies must increasingly adapt to global economic forces, and economic and social policies are intertwined, then interdependence in economic policies must imply interdependence in social policies too. The argument for a social clause in international trade, making trade dependent on respect for certain social minima, is built on this foundation.

But the debate on the social clause over the last decade or two has made it clear that the connection is not simple. Progress has been made in defining a set of fundamental enabling principles and rights at work which can be seen as the social floor of the global economy. The ILO's 1998 Declaration on Fundamental Principles and Rights at Work proclaims the universal validity of rights to freedom of association, freedom from child labour, forced labour and discrimination. But beyond this level there are strong disagreements. Attempts to make a wider range of social standards a precondition for access to global markets are viewed with deep suspicion by countries where standards are lower, on the argument that social progress depends on economic progress, and cannot be imposed by external fiat. Nor can it be reduced to a single model. While some goals are shared, there is also a wide range of national social priorities, responding to the history, culture and political environment of the countries concerned, rather than a uniform vision of social progress.

Alongside this debate over the social floor for globalisation, there is an equally intense debate over the social impact of globalisation. The word social covers a lot of ground. Education and health are social, as are political rights and collective organisation. The social dimension of globalisation includes issues of social inclusion and exclusion, inequality and discrimination, culture and identity, rights and responsibilities. These are the everyday concerns of people and the priorities of the societies in which they live. Globalisation affects them by opening new spaces, but also by restricting options. State autonomy to pursue social goals may be restricted by the need to attract international investors, or by the effects of social regulation on production costs. Whole communities may suddenly find that shifts in the global economy take away their sources of livelihood, while the expansion of market forces can devalue the assets and identities of particular ethnic groups and undermine stable communities built around traditional production methods. But globalisation also supports thriving communities built around new markets and technology, and provides enormous new economic opportunities to those with the capabilities and resources to take advantage of them.

Within this complex interaction between globalisation and social goals, work and employment play a central role. Work is where the social and economic aspirations come together in peoples' lives. Work is about production and income. But it is also about identity and social integration. Many of the social impacts of globalisation come through geographical and skill shifts in the demand for labour, through changes in the organisation of work and production, through the effects of changing product markets on returns to labour, through the security and protection of workers. In other words, work and employment, and the conditions under which they are performed, are one of the principal means by which the effects of globalisation, both positive and negative, reach people. The social dimension of globalisation is, to a large extent, concerned directly or indirectly with work and employment, along with all that goes with employment in terms of its content and value, rights at work, protection and representation.

## The Impact of Globalisation on Work and Employment

The dynamics of international integration generate vast differences between countries in opportunities and in the ability to take advantage of those opportunities. Some countries have succeeded in making globalisation a force for development. Higher rates of economic growth and poverty reduction in East Asia, notably in China, and to a lesser extent in South Asia and a few countries in other parts of the world, cannot only be attributed to globalisation, for many other factors were involved, but successful exploitation of global economic opportunities clearly played an important role. Meanwhile, in other parts of the world, notably but not exclusively in Africa, growth has been low and poverty increasing. Latin America has shuttled between these extremes, with periods of growth interspersed with periods of stagnation and growing poverty, and diverse national experiences. It is hard to generalise from these patterns, for national and regional structures, institutions, capabilities and policies have a major effect. But as in all walks of life the new opportunities are disproportionately captured by those with the capabilities, the resources and the power to do so. Globalisation may well be a positive sum game, but that does not mean that all benefit.

The impact of globalisation on work and employment illustrates this well. Successful integration in the global economy can lead to increased employment and rising wages. This was the experience of several East and Southeast Asian countries, at least until the financial crisis of the late 1990s. Chile, Ireland and a number of other small, open economies have likewise experienced periods of sustained employment creation associated with growing international integration. At the same time, there are a number of ways in which different aspects of globalisation have adverse effects on the labour market.

First, the increased economic and financial volatility noted above, associated with the liberalisation of international financial markets, has led to more frequent economic crises, with significant consequences for unemployment.[1] In many countries a ratchet effect can be observed, in which unemployment does not fall to pre-crisis levels in the recovery (Figure 9.1). Thus in Latin America, open unemployment rose through the 1980s and 1990s to reach historic highs of around 10 per cent for the continent as a whole in 2003.[2]

## Figure 9.1

*Unemployment Hysteresis*

**Pre- and Post-crisis Unemployment in Selected Latin American and Asian Countries (in per cent)**

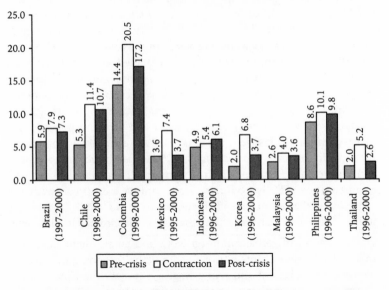

*Source*: World Commission on the Social Dimension of Globalization, *A Fair Globalization: Creating Opportunities For All* (Geneva, ILO, 2004), Figure 14.

Second, increased competitive pressures in global markets are widely believed to result in erosion of labour protection or the informalisation of employment relationships. There are frequent

---

1. An argument developed in some depth by Joseph Stiglitz. See for instance his book *Globalization and its Discontents* (London, Allan Lane, 2002).

2. See ILO (2003). *Panorama Laboral 2003: América Latina y El Caribe*, ILO, Lima.

reports of restrictions on trade union rights or other exemptions from labour laws in export processing zones, for example.[3] Workers who are essentially organised at the national level find their bargaining power weakened in the face of mobile enterprises.

Third, increased international tax competition results in lower rates of taxation of high personal incomes[4] and of corporate profits (Figure 9.2), and the liberalisation of trade reduces government revenues from tariffs—all of which is likely to reduce the resources available for government social expenditure, and to put pressure on public sector employment.

### Figure 9.2

*OECD and EU Corporate Tax Rates*

Average Company Tax Rates in the EU and OECD, 1996-2003 (in per cent)

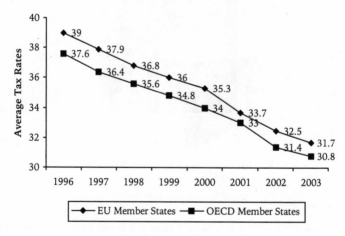

*Source:* World Commission on the Social Dimension of Globalization: *A Fair Globalization: Creating Opportunities For All* (Geneva, ILO, 2004), Figure 12.

Fourth, globalisation leads to increased restructuring of production, involving relocation and outsourcing, substantial job loss

---

3. For instance, see ILO (2002). *Employment and Social Policy Committee*, "Employment and Social Policy in Respect of Export Processing Zones (EPZs)", GB.285/ESP/5, Geneva, November.

4. Torres, Raymond (2001). *Towards a Socially Sustainable World Economy: An Analysis of the Social Pillars of Globalization*, ILO, Geneva.

in some countries and labour market instability. While the adverse impact in industrialised countries is given most coverage by the global media, developing countries are not always beneficiaries. For instance, changes in the rules of the international trading system for textiles and garments are likely to lead to a substantial job losses in Bangladesh and some other low-income countries, to China's advantage (Figures 9.3, 9.4).

### Figure 9.3

*Clothing Exports: Shares of US Market in 2004*

**Major Clothing Exporter's Share of the US Market in 2004**

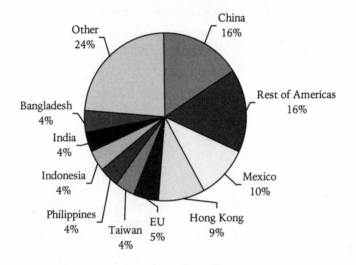

*Source: Financial Times*, July 19, 2004, p.11 (from Gary Gereffi, ILO Social Policy Lectures, Jamaica, 2005).

Fifth, and most obviously the capability of countries to take advantage of global market opportunities is highly polarised. In many countries there is little opportunity for employment creation through participation in global markets. On the contrary, liberalisation tends to undermine some existing employment because of import competition and the pressures for productivity growth.

## Figure 9.4

*Clothing Exports, Forecast US Market Shares Post MFA*

How US Market Shares May Rank After Elimination of MFA Quatas

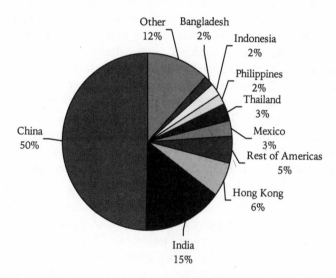

Source: *Financial Times*, July 19, 2004, p.11 (From Gary Gereffi, ILO Social Policy Lectures, Jamaica, 2005).

Low productivity national industries in low-income countries may collapse when exposed to international competition, enterprises close and jobs are lost. On the other hand, some countries have been able to take advantage of a reservoir of natural resources, skills or entrepreneurial capabilities to generate substantial employment growth—the software industry in India is a good skill-based example.

All this implies that globalisation can and often does increase decent work deficits. This is not an inevitable outcome. There are examples of countries which have successfully used the space for national policy and taken advantage of global opportunities. But there is a tendency to polarisation rather than convergence, and the simultaneous creation of groups of both winners and losers.

## The World Commission and its Impact

These were among the key issues addressed by the World Commission on the Social Dimension of Globalisation.[5] Its report was widely welcomed when it was released in early 2004. There were positive responses from many governments, from parliamentarians and trade union organisations, from business, from national economic and social councils and other non-governmental organisations. At the United Nations, the General Assembly adopted a resolution which called for countries and multilateral organisations to consider the report. The Secretary General of the UN, the President of the World Bank and the heads of other multilateral organisations all welcomed the report. There was strong support for its recommendations from the European Commission and the African Union, and from Heads of State and Government around the World.

An initiative of the International Labour Organization, the World Commission was an independent group of eminent people chaired by two Heads of State in office, the Presidents of Tanzania and Finland. It was a deliberately not like-minded group, "broadly representative", as they themselves put it, "of the diverse and contending actors and interests that exist in the real world...we came from countries in different parts of the world and at all stages of development. Our affiliations were equally diverse: government, politics, parliaments, business and multinational corporations, organized labour, academia and civil society."

Their report analysed the different perspectives on globalisation and summarised the evidence on its impact. But most of the report focused on the ways in which the inequities and imbalances of globalisation could be overcome, in particular through improved governance at all levels. Arguing that concerted action was needed on a broad front the Commission made 57 recommendations, addressed to a diversity of actors. They ranged from the need to strengthen the capabilities of the state to promote employment and social protection, and to ensure that countries had the policy space to promote their own goals, to a stronger foundation of freedom of

---

5. World Commission on the Social Dimension of Globalization (2004). *A Fair Globalization: Creating Opportunities For All*, ILO, Geneva.

association and expression and the rule of law, fair rules for international markets in goods, capital and labour and more accountable international institutions. In particular, the World Commission argued that decent work should become a global goal, and coherent policies should be built around that goal.

Why did the message of the Commission and its analysis have such a powerful impact? After all, there have been many reports on globalisation. There is surely no simple answer, just as there is no simple solution to the problems of globalisation. But there were a number of key elements which seemed to fit together.

First, the diversity and balance of the Commission's membership helped to build a consensus to which others could adhere. There was a search for common ground with dialogue between, say civil society and international business, which is often difficult to achieve. As a result, the analysis was balanced, critical without being shrill, recognising the positives as well as the negatives. The recommendations were realistic and responded to the diverse goals and needs of a range of actors.

Second, the Commission clearly met an urgent need. The tensions over globalisation had not been resolved by the competing forums around the world, and there was a growing fatigue with unproductive conflict and a sense that the time was right to find reasonable answers.

Third, the Commission built its argument on the idea that the potential of globalisation for good was being seriously underutilised, and focussed its attention on the reforms that were needed if this was to change—an idea with widespread appeal.

Fourth, the Commission called for a focus on people, their aspirations and insecurities. That led it to insist on the need for greater voice for people in the path of globalisation, better institutions for representation and dialogue, and a particular focus on work, which for the majority of people is a source of both income and social integration. Decent work was a compelling goal.

Finally, the Commission insisted that globalisation had to be fair, and this too struck a widespread chord. Fairness implied both fair rules, and greater solidarity and sharing—globalisation could not be built on the principle of winner takes all.

## The Space to Make Decent Work a Global Goal

The World Commission, then, in searching for the instruments which could lead to a stronger social dimension of globalisation, turned naturally to work and employment as the crucial domain for action. The issue was in part a question of the overall level of employment. Globalisation without jobs was clearly not going to lead to a fair and balanced distribution of its benefits. But it was equally obvious, once a broader concept of the social dimension was acknowledged, that the issue was not only a question of the quantity of jobs. Globalisation had to create productive jobs, which generated adequate incomes and security, and supported social integration. Rights of workers and enterprises had to be respected, and the voices of both had to be heard. Institutions and policies had to be in place to provide protection and ensure decent working conditions. In other words, the global goal was decent work.

But it was clear that in the current path of globalisation, these are not central policy goals. The global economy is driven by competitive forces, in which employment is a cost. Because innovation is concentrated in high income, high labour cost countries, there is a bias in technological progress towards labour saving investment, spread throughout the global economy through global production chains. Mainstream macroeconomic policy prescriptions aim to resolve imbalances through deflationary policies in deficit countries, rather than expansionary policies in surplus countries. Shifts in global markets lead to the destruction of employment in one location and its creation in another, but there are no global instruments to promote compensation of the losers by the winners. Within countries there are mechanisms (of variable effectiveness) for sharing, solidarity and protection but these have no real counterparts at the global level. In general, this can be summed up as a lack of coherence between economic and social policies at the global level. It can be seen, for instance, in the failure of the poverty reduction strategies promoted by the Bretton Woods Institutions to pay enough attention to employment, even though this is the primary route out of poverty.

The World Commission argued that it was both necessary and possible to make decent work a global goal. It made recommendations in a number of areas:

- Embedding employment goals in policy formulation. The Commission argued that international trade, finance and other economic policies need to be more effectively integrated with employment goals. Increasingly, countries cannot achieve employment goals alone, for arguments similar to those in the preamble of the ILO's constitution, but there is little effective international coordination of employment policy. Higher priority should be given to counter-cyclical macroeconomic policy and to maintaining adequate levels of demand in the global economy—in other words, there should be a global growth strategy. Trade negotiations too should take into account the employment impact of changing trade regimes. This was one of the key areas for policy coherence among international organisations, which should, "deal with international economic and labour policies in a more integrated and consistent way."

- Decent work in global production chains. The goals of employment and decent work need more attention in the rapidly growing global production systems. The problems of employment quality are often found not in multinational firms or even their immediate suppliers, but further down the subcontracting chain where controls are weak. The Commission called for stronger efforts to raise labour standards at the base of these production chains, and argued that social dialogue among organisations of workers and employers was an important means to this end. There are in fact, encouraging signs of a growth of global agreements between global unions and multinational firms around respect for basic rights at work and other key issues.

  These global value chains are of critical importance for the incorporation of decent work goals in development. The global economy is concentrated at the top and fragmented at the bottom: Thus, the real opportunities to move up in value chains are concentrated in a small number of developing economies.

- Strengthening national policies for decent work. In line with the basic argument that a stronger social dimension requires action at all levels, from the local to the global, the

Commission placed a great deal of emphasis on local and national policies for decent work. It argued, first of all that it was important to preserve the national space for policies to achieve national goals, and that the rules of the global economy needed to take that into account. Within that framework, it highlighted the range of possible national policies to promote employment creation and social protection, noting in particular the importance of a free and independent labour movement and organisations of the poor, policies to support enterprise growth, commitment to a 'high road of business-labour collaboration' as well as the need for better governance of the informal economy. It called for a focus on local action, both in order to respect and protect local communities, and also because action at that level can more easily respond to the specific needs and aspirations of the communities concerned.

• The Commission was concerned to find the right balance between the creation of opportunities on the one hand, and the need to deal with vulnerability on the other. It argued, for instance in favour of a rights-based multilateral framework for the cross-border movement of people which could encompass both opportunity and protection. It also argued for more work on the design of a socioeconomic floor, which could provide greater economic security and a more effective instrument for poverty reduction.

The obstacles to such policies, the Commission argued, lay mainly in the spheres of political will and governance. It argued that the process of globalisation had run ahead of the development of economic and social institutions necessary for its smooth and equitable functioning. The deficiencies included asymmetrical effects of the rules of the global economy as between rich and poor countries, and a serious democratic deficit in the setting of those rules. In many countries the rule of law and the representation of key interests were weak, and the capabilities of the state and other actors needed to be reinforced in order to manage economic growth and social progress in the interests of all. And at the global level, the multilateral system was not sufficiently accountable to people and there was considerable imbalance in the voice and power of the actors concerned. These were general concerns, but they explained the failure to develop adequate policies to promote employment and decent work.

## Improving the Governance of the Global Economy

What, then, might be the key governance issues which need to be addressed to make decent work a global goal? The Commission explored two aspects of this question. The first concerned the key actors: their goals and capabilities, their behaviour, their accountability. The second concerned the instruments through which better governance could be achieved.

### The Role of Different Social Actors

The State: At the national level, the Commission argued for an effective and democratically accountable state that can support high economic growth through appropriate macroeconomic policies, provide public goods and social protection, raise capabilities of people and enterprises and deal with vulnerability. Contrary to the prevailing fashion to downsize the state, it argued that there is a great deal that the state can do to promote decent work, and that this is a widespread political demand in the democratic process. The State should, for instance, provide and enforce fair rules of the game across the economy, and in particular protect the rights of both workers and enterprises in the informal and rural economies—a key issue for decent work. A range of specific policies can aim to both maximise the rate of growth of new jobs that yield incomes above the poverty line, and raise the productivity and incomes of those in informal employment.

The responsibilities of the state do not, however, end at the national level. There is a clear responsibility to build global policies in ways which take into account the interests of others, rather than to pursue narrow national interests. There are, in practice, many difficulties in achieving coordinated action on social policies between States. They include problems of monitoring and enforcement, democratic deficits in the reaching of agreements and the obvious tendency for the agenda to reflect power relations as much as real needs. But the interdependence between states implies that the gains from coordination are large. Too little effort of international coordination addresses the social goals of countries, and employment and decent work in particular.

Key private actors: By its nature, many aspects of the global economy lie beyond state regulation or—because of weak international coordination—respond poorly to national policies. This makes it all the more important to consider the role of other actors.

- The enterprise: Given the limits to public action and regulation in the global economy, voluntary enterprise behaviour will inevitably play an important role in achieving social objectives, as it does within national boundaries. Deep rooted differences in corporate culture make it difficult to establish a common global model, but there are diverse ways in which decent work and other social goals are embedded in corporate behaviour—through various approaches to corporate social responsibility, many of which embrace rights at work and working conditions; through the synergy between social and economic goals, since many aspects of decent work contribute to the stability and sustainability of the global economy, and often directly raise productivity at the enterprise level; and through the development of new institutional forms for private economic activity in the 'social economy'. The latter in particular may help to reinforce the capacity for local action in the face of globalisation.

- Organised labour: Globalisation and informalisation have clearly affected the capability of the trade union movement to promote national social agendas. But in recent years there has been a growth in cross-border trade union organisation, and attempts in some sectors to engage in regional or global social dialogue over wages and working conditions. The global trade union federations actively pursue the social agenda around major negotiating forums such as the World Trade Organization, and pursue a dialogue with the Bretton Woods Institutions. In some sectors, such as the maritime sector, there has been definite progress towards global agreements. There is resistance to this movement, but the development of cross-border social dialogue between representative organisations of workers and employers may well grow in importance.

- Civil society is an increasingly visible actor, or rather multiplicity of actors, since this term embraces a wide variety of citizen actions, organisations and advocacy. Organisations of civil society are a powerful source of ideas and debate, and effective mobilisers of minority groups and specific interests at both national and international levels. Within the framework of the market economy, non-governmental organisations have led the movement to take social criteria into account in consumer and investor choice. Socially responsible investing is now big business. Consumers too are widely willing to pay a premium for goods that are certified free of child labour or based on the payment of a living wage. Major civil society organisations are active in monitoring how far governments, enterprises and other organisations live up to their commitments, and so make important contributions to ensuring accountability.

The multilateral system: Perhaps the most obvious actors, when we speak of globalisation, are the organisations of the multilateral system. Different parts of the UN system have responsibility for major fields of global social action—human rights, international labour standards, education, environment, development more generally—which need to be embedded more deeply in the process of globalisation. Two key issues here concern coherence and accountability.

The mechanisms for the governance of the global economy are concentrated in the international economic and financial institutions—the IMF, the World Bank and the WTO—where financial and economic commitments generally take precedence over social ones. This is part of a broader problem, in that there is a tendency for the economic and social institutions of the multilateral system to operate independently of one another, so that the negotiations over international trade, for instance, do not explicitly take employment and other social goals into account. This lack of coherence is not only a problem of the institutions themselves, but often reflects different perspectives in the national ministries that are responsible for the governance of these institutions. A more effective role for the multilateral system in pursing social goals clearly requires greater coherence across its different fields of action. The World Commission Report points to these problems, calling for specific initiatives to promote greater coherence and greater accountability through, for example, parliamentary oversight. It argues that because of the central role of employment in both economic and social goals, more attention should be paid, in global economic management, to ways to promote employment.

## Policy Instruments to Achieve a Fair Globalisation

The World Commission Report insisted on the responsibility of these different actors in the social dimension of globalisation. But this responsibility can only be exercised if the instruments of governance are adequate to the task. The goal of policy coherence requires agreed policy frameworks and institutions within which the actors can work, and the mechanisms by which they can affect economic and social outcomes. The World Commission highlighted a number of key domains where reflection is needed on how to make the existing instruments more effective, or develop new ones:

- The Commission highlighted the weakness or unfairness of multilateral frameworks in certain key areas with a major impact on social goals. It notably pointed to the imbalance between the strong international regime for trade, compared with the weaker regimes for capital flows, financial markets and international migration. The development of new multilateral instruments in these areas is exceptionally difficult because of the strong interests involved, but would be of great importance for a wide range of social goals.

- Mechanisms for macroeconomic coordination at the international level are notably weak, and—as noted above—more work is required on the design of the instruments for coordination which can more effectively incorporate employment objectives.

- The role of international labour standards is sometimes questioned by neoclassical economists, but they retain a considerable degree of legitimacy. Longstanding voluntary methods of application of these standards in the ILO have proved their worth, but there is a case to explore additional means for their effective enforcement, especially as concerns the key enabling standards. There is also a need for a broader reflection on the role of legal instruments of different types in this domain—both 'soft' and 'hard'—which might expand the possibilities for action. Instruments such as the Declaration on Fundamental Principles and Rights at Work may provide a model that can be emulated in other domains.

- Better mechanisms and institutions to support the initiatives of the key economic actors, enterprises and workers, are also likely to increase their effectiveness. That includes both the frameworks for corporate social responsibility and the mechanisms for social dialogue at the international level. These are issues on which research is required to explore the demands and interests of the actors concerned, and the real effectiveness of different existing and prospective instruments for the promotion of decent work.

- More generally, the policy instruments for social protection and solidarity at the global level are exceptionally weak, and there is a need for frameworks which can provide resources and redistribution towards this goal.

In important ways, the regional space provides an important first step towards these goals. Attempts at building a common set of social standards, better macroeconomic coordination and a degree of redistribution through social or restructuring funds are clearly much easier to launch at the regional level, and the European Union offers the best example both of what can be achieved and of the difficulties of rapid progress. Outside Europe there is a clear global trend towards stronger regional frameworks, with growing attention to the incorporation of social goals. This process is most evident in the Americas, where the experience of Mercosur and more recently at continental level has demonstrated a widespread commitment to building decent work goals into a regional agenda. But there is progress in Africa, and more slowly in Asia, as well. These are the testing grounds for future global policies.

In all of these fields, the experience of the World Commission itself in dialogue and consensus building provides a model for progress. The engagement of a wide range of actors in the construction of these frameworks and instruments is an essential condition for their viability, whether at regional or at global level. That is the logic behind the idea of a Globalisation Policy Forum, still under discussion in the ILO, which could bring together a wide range of networks of important social actors around the global goal of decent work.

## Conclusion

A fair globalisation is possible, indeed it is essential for global stability. And while a range of different actions are needed, the key lies in stronger and more systematic policies and institutions for decent work. A focus on work illustrates a more general principle: a fairer globalisation needs to be built on a better integration of economic and social policies. The challenge is finding the policies, rules and mechanisms by which economic and social goals can be coordinated in the global economy, whether through social legislation or through other means, in the common interest. That is a long-term agenda. But there is growing recognition that it is an essential task if the process of globalisation is to respond to the expectations and aspirations of the people.

# Some Recent Issues in Agriculture

# 10

# From the Green Revolution to the Gene Revolution

## How will the Poor Fare?

### PRABHU PINGALI and TERRI RANEY

## Introduction

The past four decades have seen two waves of agricultural technology development and diffusion to developing countries. The first wave was initiated by the Green Revolution in which improved germplasm was made available to developing countries as a public good through an explicit strategy for technology development and diffusion. The second wave was generated by the Gene Revolution in which a global and largely private agricultural research system is creating improved agricultural technologies that are flowing to developing countries primarily through market transactions. Asymmetries between developed and developing countries in research capacity, market institutions and the commercial viability of technologies raise doubts regarding the potential of the Gene Revolution to generate benefits for poor farmers in poor countries.

The Green Revolution was responsible for an extraordinary period of growth in food crop productivity in the developing world over the last 40 years. Productivity growth has been significant for rice in Asia, wheat in irrigated and favourable production environments worldwide and maize in Mesoamerica and selected parts of Africa and Asia. A combination of high rates of investment in crop research, infrastructure and market development, and appropriate policy support fuelled this land productivity. These elements of a Green Revolution strategy improved productivity growth despite increasing land scarcity and high land values (Pingali and Heisey, 2001).

The transformation of global food production systems defied conventional wisdom that agricultural technology does not travel well because it is either agro-climatically specific, as in the case of biological technology, or sensitive to relative factor prices, as with mechanical technology (Byerlee and Traxler, 2002). The Green Revolution strategy for food crop productivity growth was explicitly based on the premise that, given appropriate institutional mechanisms, technology spillovers across political and agro-climatic boundaries can be captured. Hence, the Consultative Group on International Agricultural Research (CGIAR) was established specifically to generate spillovers particularly for nations that are unable to capture all the benefits of their research investments. What happens to the spillover benefits from agricultural research and development in an increasingly global integration of food supply systems?

Over the past decade the locus of agricultural research and development has shifted dramatically from the public to the private multinational sector. Three interrelated forces are transforming the system for supplying improved agricultural technologies to the world's farmers. The first is the strengthened and evolving environment for protecting intellectual property in plant innovations. The second is the rapid pace of discovery and growth in importance of molecular biology and genetic engineering. Finally, agricultural input and output trade is becoming more open in nearly all countries. These developments have created a powerful new set of incentives for private research investment, altering the structure of the public/private agricultural research endeavour, particularly with respect to crop improvement (Pingali and Traxler, 2002).

Developing countries are facing increasing transactions costs in access to and use of technologies generated by the multinational sector. Existing international networks for sharing technologies across countries and thereby maximising spillover benefits are becoming increasingly threatened. The urgent need today is for a system of technology flows which preserves the incentives for private sector innovation while at the same time meeting the needs of poor farmers in the developing world.

## Green Revolution R&D: Access and Impact

The major breakthroughs in yield potential that kick started the Green Revolution in the late 1960s came from conventional plant breeding approaches. Crossing plants with different genetic backgrounds and selecting from among the progeny individual plants with desirable characteristics, repeated over several cycles/generations, led to plants/varieties with improved characteristics such as higher yields, improved disease resistance, improved nutritional quality, etc. The yield potential for the major cereals has continued to rise at a steady rate after the initial dramatic shifts in the 1960s for rice and wheat. For example, yield potential in irrigated wheat has been rising at the rate of 1 per cent per year over the past three decades, an increase of around 100 kilograms per hectare per year (Pingali and Rajaram, 1999).

Prior to 1960, there was no formal system in place that provided plant breeders access to germplasm available beyond their borders. Since then, the international public sector (the CGIAR) has been the predominant source of supply of improved germplasm developed from conventional breeding approaches, especially for self-pollinating crops such as rice and wheat and for open pollinated maize. CGIAR managed networks of international nurseries for sharing crop improvement results evolved in the 1970s and 1980s, when financial resources were expanding and plant IPR laws were weak or non-existent.

The international flow of germplasm has had a large impact on the speed and the cost of NARs' crop development programmes, thereby generating enormous efficiency gains (see Evenson and Gollin, 2003, for a global assessment of gains from the international exchange of major food crop varieties and breeding lines). Traxler and Pingali (1999), have argued that the existence of a free and uninhibited system of germplasm exchange that attracts the best of international materials allows countries to make strategic decisions on the extent to which they need to invest in plant breeding capacity. Small countries behaving rationally choose to ride free on the international system rather than invest in large crop breeding infrastructure of their own (Maredia, Byerlee and Eicher, 1994).

Evenson and Gollin (2003), report that even in the 1990s, the CGIAR content of modern varieties was high for most food crops; 36

per cent of all varietal releases were based on CGIAR crosses. In addition, 26 per cent of all modern varieties had a CGIAR-crossed parent or other ancestor. Evenson and Gollin (2003) suggest that germplasm contributions from international centres helped national programmes to stave off the 'diminishing returns' to breeding that might have been expected to set in had the national programmes been forced to work only with the pool of genetic resources that they had available at the beginning of the period.

### Impacts of Food Crop Improvement Technology

Substantial empirical evidence exists on the production, productivity, income, and human welfare impacts of modern agricultural science and the international flow of modern varieties of food crops. Evenson and Gollin (2003) provided detailed information for all the major food crops on the extent of adoption and impact of modern variety use, they also show the crucial role played by the international germplasm networks in enabling developing countries to capture the spillover benefits of investments in crop improvement made outside their borders. The adoption of modern varieties during the first 20 years of the Green Revolution—aggregated across all crops—reached 9 per cent in 1970 and rose to 29 per cent in 1980. By the 1990, adoption of Modern Varieties (MVs) had reached 46 per cent, and by 1998, 63 per cent. Moreover, in many areas and in many crops, first generation MVs have been replaced by second and third generation MVs (Evenson and Gollin, 2003).

Much of the increase in agricultural output, over the past 40 years, has come from an increase in yields per hectare rather than an expansion of area under cultivation. For instance, FAO data indicate that for all developing countries, wheat yields rose by 208 per cent from 1960 to 2000; rice yields rose 109 per cent; maize yields rose 157 per cent; potato yields rose 78 per cent; and cassava yields rose 36 per cent (FAOSTAT). Trends in total factor productivity (TFP) are consistent with partial productivity measures, such as rate of yield growth. Pingali and Heisey (2001) provide a comprehensive compilation of TFP evidence for several countries and crops.

The returns to investments in high-yielding modern germplasm have been measured in great detail by several economists over the last few decades. These studies found high returns to the Green

Revolution strategy of germplasm improvement. The very first studies that calculated the returns to research investment were conducted at International Rice Research Institute (IRRI) for rice research investments in the Philippines (Flores-Moya *et al.*, 1978) and at CIAT (Centro International de Agricultural Tropical) in Colombia (Scobie and Posada, 1978). More detailed evidence on the high rates of return to public-sector investments in agricultural research was provided by the International Service for National Agricultural Research (ISNAR) (Echeverría, 1990) and the International Food Policy Research Institute (IFPRI) (Pardey *et al.*, 1992). For detailed synthesis of the numerous studies conducted across crops and countries, see Evenson (2001) and Alston *et al.*, (2000). Alston *et al.*, concluded from a review of 289 studies that there was no evidence that the rate of return to agricultural research and development has declined over time.

Widespread adoption of modern seed-fertiliser technology led to a significant shift in the food supply function, contributing to a fall in real food prices. The primary effect of agricultural research on the non-farm poor, as well as on the rural poor who are net purchasers of food, is through lower food prices.

Early efforts to document the impact of technological change and the consequent increase in food supplies on food prices and income distribution were made by Hayami and Herdt (1977), Pinstrup-Andersen *et al.* (1976), Scobie and Posada (1978), and Binswanger (1980). Pinstrup-Andersen argued strongly that the primary nutritional impact for the poor came through the increased food supplies generated through technological change.

Several studies have provided empirical support to the proposition that growth in the agricultural sector has economy-wide effects. One of the earliest studies showing the linkages between the agricultural and non-agricultural sectors was done at the village level by Hayami *et al.* (1978). Hayami provided an excellent micro-level illustration of the impacts of rapid growth in rice production on land and labour markets and the non-agricultural sector. Pinstrup-Andersen and Hazell (1985) argued that the landless labour did not adequately share in the benefits of the Green Revolution because of depressed wage rates attributable to migrants from other regions. David and Otsuka (1994), on the other hand, found that migrants shared in the benefits of the Green Revolution through increased employment opportunities and wage income. The latter study also documented that rising productivity caused land prices to rise in the high-potential environments. For sector level validation of the proposition that agriculture does indeed act as an engine of overall economic growth see Hazell and Haggblade (1993); Delgado *et al.* (1998); and Fan *et al.* (1998).

Although the favourable, high-potential environments gained the most in terms of productivity growth, the less favourable environments benefited as well through technology spillovers and through labour migration to more productive environments. According to David and Otsuka, wage equalisation across favourable and unfavourable environments was one of the primary means of redistributing the gains of technological change. Renkow (1993) found similar results for wheat grown in high- and low-potential environments in Pakistan. Byerlee and Moya (1993), in their global assessment of the adoption of wheat MVs, found that over time the adoption of MVs in unfavourable environments caught up to levels of adoption in more favourable environments, particularly when germplasm developed for high-potential environments was further adapted to the more marginal environments. In the case of wheat, the rate of growth in yield potential in drought-prone environments was around 2.5 per cent per year during the 1980s and 1990s (Lantican and Pingali, 2003). Initially, the growth in yield potential for the marginal environments came from technological spillovers as varieties bred for the high-potential environments were adapted to the marginal environments. During the 1990s, however, further gains in yield potential came from breeding efforts targeted specifically at the marginal environments.

## The Changing Locus of Agricultural R&D: From National Public to International Private Sector

In the decades of the 1960s through the 1980s, private sector investment in plant improvement research was limited, particularly in the developing world, due to the lack of effective mechanisms for proprietary protection on the improved products. This situation changed in the 1990s with the emergence of hybrids for cross-pollinated crops such as maize, etc. The economic viability of hybrids led to a budding seed industry in the developing world, but the coverage of seed industry activity has been limited to date, leaving many markets under served. The seed industry in the developing world was started by multinational companies based in the developed world, and then led to the development of national companies (Morris, 1998). Despite its rapid growth, the private seed industry continued to rely, through the 1990s, on the public sector gene banks and pre-breeding materials for the development of its hybrids (Morris and Ekasingh, 2001; Pray and Echeverría, 1991). The break between public and private sector plant improvement efforts came with the advent of biotechnology, especially genetic engineering. The proprietary protection provided for artificially constructed genes and for genetically modified plants provided the incentives for private sector entry.

The large multinational agro-chemical companies were the early investors in the development of transgenic crops. One of the reasons that agro-chemical companies moved into crop improvement was that they foresaw a declining market for pesticides (Conway, 2000). The chemical companies got a quick start in the plant improvement business by purchasing existing seed companies, first in industrialised countries and then in the developing world.

The amalgamation of the national private companies with the multinational corporations makes economic sense (Pingali and Traxler, 2002). The process of variety development and delivery is a continuum that starts at the upstream end of generating knowledge on useful genes (genomics) and engineering transgenic plants to the more adaptive end of backcrossing the transgenes into commercial lines and delivering the seed to farmers. The products from upstream activities have worldwide applicability, across several crops and agro-ecological environments. On the other hand, genetically modified crops and varieties are applicable to very specific agro-ecological and socioeconomic niches. In other words, spillover benefits and scale economies decline in the move to the more adaptive end of the continuum. Similarly, research costs and research sophistication decline in the progression towards downstream activities. Thus, a clear division of responsibilities in the development and delivery of biotechnology products has emerged, with the multinational providing the upstream biotechnology research and the local firm providing crop varieties with commercially desirable agronomic backgrounds (see Pingali and Traxler, 2002, for a more detailed discussion on this point).

The options available for public research systems to capture the spillovers from global corporations are less clear. Public sector research programmes are generally established to conform to state or national political boundaries, and direct country-to-country transfer of technologies has been limited (Traxler and Pingali, 2002). Strict adherence to political domains severely curtails spillover benefits of technological innovations across similar agro-climatic zones. The operation of the CGIAR germplasm exchange system has mitigated the problem for several important crops, but it is not clear whether the system will work for biotechnology products and transgenic crops, given the proprietary nature of the technology.

Moreover, in the case of biotechnology innovations, the national and international public sector, do not have the resources to effectively create an alternative source of knowledge and technology supply. To understand the magnitude of private sector investment in agricultural research today, one need only look at its annual research budget relative to public research targeted to the developing country agriculture. The world's top 10 multinational bioscience corporations' collective annual expenditure on agricultural research and development is nearly three billion US Dollars. In comparison the CGIAR, which is the largest international public sector supplier of agricultural technologies, spends less than 300 million US Dollars annually on plant improvement research and development. The largest public sector agricultural research programmes in the developing world, those of Brazil, China, and India, have annual budgets of less than half a billion dollars each (Byerlee and Fischer, 2001).

If we look at public expenditures for biotechnology alone, the figure comes out to be substantially smaller for the developing world as a whole. Public research expenditures on agricultural biotechnology (Table 10.1) reveal a sharp dichotomy between developed and developing countries. Byerlee and Fischer (2001) show that developed countries spend four times as much on public sector biotech research than developing countries, even when all sources of public funds— national, donor and CGIAR centres—are counted for developing countries. Developed countries also spend a higher proportion of their public sector agricultural research expenditures on biotech than developing countries or the CGIAR centers (Byerlee and Fischer, 2001).

## Table 10.1

*Estimated Crop Biotechnology Research*
*Expenditures (million US dollars)*

|  | Biotech R&D (million $/year) | Biotech as Share of Sector R&D |
|---|---|---|
| **Industrialised countries** | **1900-2500** |  |
| Private sector* | 1000-1500 | 40 |
| Public sector | 900-1000 | 16 |
| **Developing countries** | **165-250** |  |
| Public (own resources) | 100-150 | 5-10 |
| Public (foreign aid) | 40-50 | n.a. |
| CGIAR centres | 25-50 | 8 |
| Private sector | n.a. | n.a. |
| **World total** | **2065-2750** |  |

*Note*: * Includes an unknown amount of R&D for developing countries.
*Source*: Byerlee and Fischer, 2001.

The rapid growth of private sector investment in biotech research in developed countries means that private research expenditures now exceed public sector expenditures, both in absolute terms and as a share of total agricultural R&D expenditures. Comprehensive data on private sector biotech research in developing countries are not available, although partial evidence suggests that the private sector is less developed than in industrialised countries. Data for seven Asian countries show that private agricultural research is equivalent to about 10 per cent of total public sector agricultural research (Pray and Fuglie, 2000). If this ratio is applied to all developing countries (probably an upper bound), we can estimate private sector research expenditures at about $ 1, 150 million per year. If we assume that the share of biotech in total private R&D is the same as in developed countries (40 per cent, also an upper bound), this gives us an estimate of $ 458 million in annual private sector biotech research in developing countries. A lower-bound estimate could build on the fact that the share of total public sector research devoted to biotech in the developing countries is about 8 per cent. If we apply that ratio to the private sector expenditures, we get a lower-bound estimate of $ 92 million for private biotech in developing countries. Although it is likely that private sector investment is somewhere between these estimates, even the upper bound estimate is only about one-third the level of private sector investment in developed countries.

## Emerging Trends in Biotechnology Research, Development and Commercialisation in the Developing World

Only a few developing countries have highly sophisticated biotech research programmes, but growing numbers have the capacity to adopt and adapt innovations developed elsewhere. Only three countries—China, India and Brazil—have extensive research programmes in all areas of biotechnology, including advanced genomics and gene manipulation techniques (FAO, BioDeC). According to IFPRI (2004), 15 developing countries have significant and growing capacity for biotechnology research, but these are typically more advanced countries such as Brazil, Argentina, and Egypt. Most of the least developed countries, however, have no documented research experience with genetically modified organisms and many have limited capacity for agricultural research of any kind (FAO, BioDeC).

Many developing countries, including some higher-income countries, also lack regulatory capacity in the areas of intellectual property rights protection and biosafety procedures (food safety and environmental protection). Subsistence agriculture remains the dominant agricultural system in much of the developing world. The agricultural sectors of several more advanced developing countries exhibit a dualistic agricultural structure in which a few large very modern commercial farms coexist with many small subsistence farms. As a result, commercial markets for agricultural inputs and outputs remain weak, especially in the least developed countries, suggesting that the potential for commercial joint ventures between multinational biotech companies and local seed companies is limited to the more advanced developing countries.

## Commercial Cultivation of GM Crops in the Developing World

James (2004) reports that transgenic crops were commercially planted on 81 million hectares in 2004, in 17 countries, 12 of them developing. Developing countries accounted for 37 per cent of the total global transgenic crop area in 2004, having increased consistently from 14 per cent of 12.8 million hectares in 1997. Argentina, Brazil, and China are the largest developing country producers (Figure 10.2).

## Figure 10.1

*Global Area of GM Crops in 2004 (81.1 million ha)*

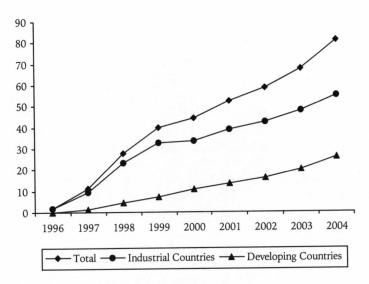

## Figure 10.2

*GM Crops by Country (2004)*

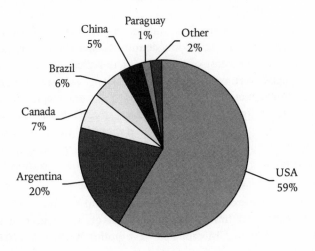

**Figure 10.3**

*Transgenic Crops, by Crop, 2004*

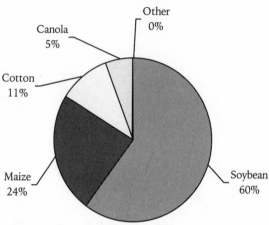

Source: James, 2004.

Herbicide tolerance and pest resistance remain the main GM traits that are currently under commercial cultivation and the main crops are soybean, maize, canola and cotton (Figure 10.3). In addition to these major crops, China also produces small quantities of virus resistant tomatoes and peppers, delayed ripening tomatoes and flower-colour altered petunias.

Comprehensive data are not available on the origin of the GM varieties being planted in developing countries; however, the available evidence suggests that most of the GM varieties grown in developing countries in 2004 were developed by multinational companies for the developed country markets of North America or were adapted locally from imported varieties. China is the exception. China is the only developing country to have developed transgenic varieties in the public sector from a locally developed genetic transformation construct (Pray and Naseem, 2003). In other countries, commercial GM crops are imported or locally adapted from imported varieties.

This evidence suggests that globalisation and the international transfer of technology have been essential factors in promoting the commercial spread of GM crops in developing countries. It also suggests that developing countries that lack strong public sector research systems and/or strong commercial seed sectors will be handicapped in the adoption of transgenic varieties.

## Accessing Biotechnology Knowledge and Products for the Poor

Unlike the Green Revolution technologies, transgenic technologies are transferred internationally primarily through market mechanisms, often through commercial relationships between the multinational bioscience firms and national seed companies. This system of technology transfer works well for commercially viable innovations in well-developed markets, but perhaps not for the types of innovations needed in developing countries: crops and traits aimed at poor farmers in marginal production environments. These 'orphan' technologies have traditionally been the province of public sector research. Given the dominance of private sector research in transgenic crop research and meagre resources being devoted to public sector research in most developing countries, it is unlikely that public sector research can play this role for transgenic crops.

The options available for public research systems in developing countries to capture the spillovers from global corporations are limited. Public sector research programmes are generally established to conform to state or national political boundaries, and direct country-to-country transfer of technologies has been rare (Pingali and Traxler, 2002). Strict adherence to political domains severely curtails spillover benefits of technological innovations across similar agro-climatic zones. The operation of the CGIAR germplasm exchange system has mitigated the problem for several important crops, but it is not clear whether the system will work for biotechnology products and transgenic crops, given the proprietary nature of the technology.

Although private sector agricultural research expenditures seem overwhelmingly large, the reality is that they are focused very narrowly on the development of biotechnology related plant varieties, and even that for a very small number of crops. A large part of the private sector investment is concentrated on just four crops: cotton, corn, canola, and soybeans. Private sector investment on the world's two most important food crops, rice and wheat, is insignificant in comparison. Moreover, all of the private sector investment is targeted towards the commercial production sector in the developed world, with some spillover benefits flowing to the commercial sector in the developing world. The public sector, with its increasingly meagre budget, is left to take care of the research and technology needs of the subsistence farming sector, as well as being the only source of supply for conventionally bred seed as well as crop and resource management technologies.

Will the poor benefit from any of the technological advances that are taking place today in the private sector? Private sector investments in genomics and genetic engineering could be potentially very useful for addressing the problems faced by poor farmers, particularly those in the marginal environments. Knowledge generated through genomics, for example, could have enormous potential in advancing the quest for drought tolerant crops in the tropics. The question that needs to be asked is whether incentives exist, or can be created, for public/private sector partnerships that allow the public sector to use and adapt technologies developed by the private sector for the problems faced by the poor. Can licensing agreements be designed that will allow private sector technologies to be licensed to the public sector for use on problems of the poor? Pingali and Traxler (2002) suggest that the public sector may have to purchase the right to use private sector technology on behalf of the poor.

Pingali and Traxler (2002) suggest three possible avenues for public sector institutions in developing countries to gain access to transgenic technologies: (i) directly import private- or public-sector transgenic varieties developed elsewhere; (ii) develop an independent capacity to develop and/or adapt transgenic varieties and (iii) collaborate on a regional basis to develop and/or adapt transgenic varieties. The second option is the most costly and requires the highest degree of national research capacity, while the first option depends on the availability of suitable varieties developed elsewhere. The third option would require a higher degree of cooperation across national boundaries than has typically characterised public sector research. Pingali and Traxler (2002) ask whether incentives exist or can be created for public/private partnerships that allow the public sector to use and adapt technologies developed by the private sector.

Before considering the prospects for partnerships for accessing technologies in the pipeline it is important to conduct a detailed inventory of all prospective biotechnology products characterised by crop and by agro-ecological environments. Followed by an *ex ante* assessment of the impact each of these technologies could have on the productivity and livelihoods of the subsistence producers. The above assessment would lead to the identification of a set of products with high pro-poor potential that public/private partnerships could be built around.

Even if public-private partnerships could be developed, will the resulting technologies ever get to the poor? Given that technologies that are on the shelf today (generated by conventional research methods) have not yet reached farmers' fields, there is no guarantee that the new biotechnologies will fare any better. Are there any policy interventions that will make the situation any better? Identifying small farmer constraints to technology access and use continues to be an issue that the development community ought to deal with. This suggests a need for a third wave of globalisation to ensure that international spillovers from the Gene Revolution make their way to the poor. Investments in biotechnology research capacity for the public sector will only be worthwhile if the current difficulties in delivering conventional technologies to subsistence farmers can be reversed.

# References

Alston, J.M., M.C. Marra, P.G. Pardey, and T.J. Wyatt (2000). "Research Returns Redux: A Meta-analysis of the Returns to Agricultural R&D", *Australian Journal of Agricultural and Resource Economics*, Vol. 44(2), pp.185-215.

Binswanger, H.P. (1980). "Income Distribution Effects of Technical Change: Some Analytical Issues", *South East Asian Economic Review*, Vol. 1(3), pp.179-218.

Byerlee, D. and P. Moya (1993). "Impacts of International Wheat Breeding Research in the Developing World, 1966-1990", International Maize and Wheat Improvement Center (CIMMYT), Mexico, D.F.

Byerlee, D. and K. Fischer (2001). "Accessing Modern Science: Policy and Institutional Options for Agricultural Biotechnology in Developing Countries", *IP Strategy Today*, No. 1, BioDevelopments–International Institute Inc, Cornell, Ithaca, NY.

Byerlee, D. and G. Traxler (2002). "The Role of Technology Spillovers and Economies of Size in the Efficient Design of Agricultural Research Systems", in J.M. Alston, P.G. Pardey and M.J. Taylor (eds.), *Agricultural Science Policy: Changing Global Agendas*, Johns Hopkins University Press, Baltimore, USA.

Conway, G. (2000). "Crop Biotechnology: Benefits, Risks and Ownership", Rockefeller Foundation, New York (Foundation News 03062000).

David, C., and K. Otsuka (eds.) (1994). *Modern Rice Technology and Income Distribution in Asia*, Lynne Rienner, Boulder.

Delgado, L.C., J. Hopkins, and V.A. Kelly (1998). "Agricultural Growth Linkages in Sub-Saharan Africa", *IFPRI Research Report* No. 107, International Food Policy Research Institute (IFPRI), Washington, DC.

Echeverría, R.G. (1990). "Assessing the Impact of Agricultural Research", in R.G. Echeverría (ed.), *Methods for Diagnosing Research System Constraints and Assessing the Impact of Agricultural Research*, Vol. 2, International Service for National Agricultural Research (ISNAR), The Hague.

Evenson, R.E. (2001). "Economic Impacts of Agricultural Research and Extension", in B.L. Gardner and G.C. Rausser (eds.), *Handbook of Agricultural Economics*, Vol. 1, North Holland.

Evenson, R.E. and D. Gollin (2003). "Assessing the Impact of the Green Revolution: 1960-1980", *Science*, Vol. 300, pp.758-762.

Fan, S., P. Hazell, and S. Thorat (1998). "Government Spending, Growth, and Poverty: An Analysis of Interlinkages in Rural India", *EPTD Discussion Paper* No. 33. International Food Policy Research Institute (IFPRI), Washington, DC.

FAO (2005). *FAOSTAT*.

———. (2005). *FAO-BioDeC* database, Unpublished.

Flores-Moya, P., R.E. Evenson and Y. Hayami (1978). "Social Returns to Rice Research in the Philippines: Domestic Benefits and Foreign Spillover", *Economic Development and Cultural Change*, Vol. 26(3), pp.591-607.

Hayami, Y. and R.W. Herdt (1977). "Market Price Effects of Technological Change on Income Distribution in Semi-subsistence Agriculture", *American Journal of Agricultural Economics*, Vol. 59(2), pp.245-256.

Hayami, Y., with M. Kikuchi, P.F. Moya, L.M. Bambo, and E.B. Marciano (1978). *Anatomy of a Peasant Economy: A Rice Village in the Philippines*, International Rice Research Institute (IRRI), Los Baños.

Hazell, P., and S. Haggblade (1993). "Farm-nonfarm Growth Linkages and the Welfare of the Poor", in M. Lipton and J. van de Gaag (eds.), *Including the Poor*, The World Bank, Washington DC.

IFPRI (2004). "To Reach the Poor: Results from the ISNAR-IFPRI Next Harvest Study on Genetically Modified Crops: Public Research and Policy Implications", *EPTD Discussion Paper* No. 116.

James, C. (2004). "Global Status of GM Crops", *ISAAA Brief* No 32.

Lantican, M. and P.L. Pingali (2003). "Growth in Wheat Yield Potential in Marginal Environments", in *Proceedings of the Warren E. Kronstad Memorial Symposium*, March 1-17, 2001, International Maize and Wheat Improvement Center (CIMMYT), Mexico City.

Maredia, M.K., D. Byerlee and C.K. Eicher (1994). "The Efficiency of Global Wheat Research Investments: Implications for Research Evaluation, Research Managers and Donors", *Staff Paper* No. 94-17, Department of Agricultural Economics, Michigan State University, USA.

Morris, M. (1998). *Maize Seed Industries in Developing Countries*, Lynne Rienner Publishers, Boulder, Colorado.

Morris, M. and B. Ekasingh (2001). "Plant Breeding Research in Developing Countries: What Roles for the Public and Private Sectors", in D. Byerlee, R. Echeverria (eds.), *Agricultural Research Policy in an Era of Privatization: Experiences from the Developing World*, CABI, Wallingford, UK.

Pardey, P.G., R.K. Lindner, E. Abdurachman, S. Wood, S. Fan, W.M. Eveleens, B. Zhang, and J.M. Alston (1992). *The Economic Returns to Indonesian Rice and Soybean Research*, Jakarta and the Hague: Agency for Agricultural Research and Development (AARD) and International Service for National Agricultural Research (ISNAR), Unpublished Report.

Pingali, P.L., and P.W. Heisey (2001). "Cereal-Crop Productivity in Developing Countries: Past Trends and Future Prospects", in J.M. Alston, P.G. Pardey and M. Taylor (eds.) *Agricultural Science Policy*, IFPRI and Johns Hopkins University Press, Washington.

Pingali, P.L. and S.R. Rajaram (1999). *World Wheat Facts and Trends, 1998/99*, CIMMYT Institute, Mexico, DF.

Pingali, P. and G. Traxler (2002). "Changing Locus of Agricultural Research: Will the Poor Benefit from Biotechnology and Privatization Trends", *Food Policy*, Vol. 27, pp.223-238.

Pinstrup-Andersen, P., N. Ruiz de Londoño and E. Hoover (1976). "The Impact of Increasing Food Supply on Human Nutrition: Implications for Commodity Priorities in Agricultural Research", *American Journal of Agricultural Economics*, Vol. 58(2), pp.131-42.

Pinstrup-Andersen, P. and P.B.R. Hazell (1985). "The Impact of the Green Revolution and Prospects for the Future", *Food Review International*, Vol. 1(1), pp.1-25

Pray, C.E. and R.G. Echeverria (1991). "Private Sector Agricultural Research in Less Developed Countries", in P.G. Pardey, J. Roseboom and J. Anderson (eds.), *Agricultural Research Policy—International Quantitative Perspectives*, Cambridge University Press, Cambridge.

Pray, C.E. and K.O. Fuglie (2000). "Policies for Private Agricultural Research in Asian LDCs", Paper presented at the XXIV International Conference of Agricultural Economists, Berlin, Germany.

Pray, C.E., A. Courtmanche and R. Govindasamy (2002). "The Importance of Intellectual Property Rights in the International Spread of Private Sector Agricultural Biotechnology", Presented at the 6th International Conference convened by ICABR, July 11-14, Ravello, Italy.

Pray, C.E. and A. Naseem (2003). "The Economics of Agricultural Research", *ESA Working Paper* 03-07, FAO.

Renkow, M. (1993). "Differential Technology Adoption and Income Distribution in Pakistan: Implications for Research Resource Allocation", *American Journal of Agricultural Economics*, Vol. 75(1), pp.33-43.

Scobie, G.M. and R.T. Posada (1978). "The Impact of Technical Change on Income Distribution: The Case of Rice in Colombia", *American Journal of Agricultural Economics*, Vol. 60(1), pp.85-92.

Traxler, G. and P.L. Pingali (1999). "International Collaboration in Crop Improvement Research: Current Status and Future Prospects", *Economics Working Paper* No. 99-11, International Wheat and Maize Improvement Center, Mexico City.

# 11

## Fragmenting Bottom and Consolidating Top

### India's Changing Food System and Implications for Smallholders

ASHOK GULATI

### Introduction

The structure of food system in India is rapidly changing due to economic growth, urbanisation, globalisation, emerging exports opportunities and more female participation in the work force. This has major ramifications for Indian agriculture which is dominated (and will continue to be dominated) by smallholders with less than 2 hectares of land, who fall into the bottom of the economic pyramid.[1] The structural changes in the economy are leading to a subtle change in the consumption basket with higher consumption of high value commodities like fruits and vegetables, livestock and fishery, and processed foods. The marketing chains are also getting compressed with growing consolidation in the form of scaling up and concentration by processors and retailers.

This is both an opportunity and challenge for smallholders. In India, as in most developing countries of Asia and sub-Saharan, the farm size is seeing a continuous process of fragmentation as landholdings continue to shrink. Some economists, like Maxwell (2004), portray a pessimistic view of these small farmers, arguing that small-scale, undercapitalised and often undereducated farmers will find it particularly difficult to meet the quantity, quality, timeliness and traceability requirements of the new supply chains. They further argue that small farmers with scale disadvantages will

---

1. The term "bottom of the pyramid" has been coined by Prahalad (2005) for the lowest income group of the population.

find it particularly difficult to participate in new technologies that are likely to involve mechanisation and capitalisation or require high levels of education, both of which may disadvantage smaller farms. While retailers and processors need to guard supply lines, small farmers need to respond to the consolidation in firms, if they are to move out of the poverty trap. Smallholders that are unable to meet the production and marketing demands will lose out, while participation would ensure a much higher income.

So, will the small farmers be left out of the emerging opportunities in the food systems? The evidence from Latin America suggests that smallholders have been largely left out of modern marketing chains but this chapter suggests that there is evidence in India which can bring about some optimism in this rather pessimistic scenario. The concurrence of fragmentation of farm holdings and consolidation among firms implies that linkages have to be developed to safeguard supply lines. And in ensuring their participation, this chapter argues for innovative sustainable solutions in institutions and infrastructure-delivery that are not government or subsidy-driven. As smallholders suffer from scale disadvantages, linkages with them involve high transaction costs. For smallholders to ride the wave, it is necessary to adopt new innovative institutions and to use infrastructure in such a way that it cuts transaction costs significantly. There is evidence of innovations that have been instituted to involve small farmers in emerging opportunities for high value agriculture. Though diverse, all the case studies have followed few fundamental principles to bring about innovation in delivery system. At the same time, it is necessary that the policy environment be conducive to promote innovations as well as provide the necessary infrastructure, so that small farmers can compete in this new environment.

### Fragmenting Bottom

Globally, the share of smallholders in number of holdings is opposite the share of smallholders in operated area—85 per cent of landholdings are less than 2 hectares whereas they occupy only 6 per cent of global farm area (Figure 11.1, Von Braun, 2003). However, the case is not true for India with 81 per cent of smallholdings occupying 37 per cent of farm area (Figure 11.2, Agricultural Census Division, 2000-01).

### Figure 11.1

*Farm Pyramids: Opposing Structures of Holdings and Area (Global)*

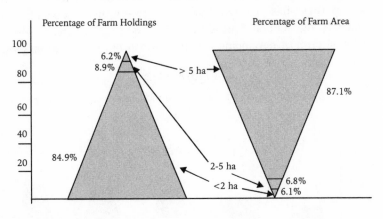

Source: von Braun 2003 (FAO)        Source: Gulati *et al.*, 2005 (FAO)

### Figure 11.2

*Farm Pyramids in India (2000-01)*

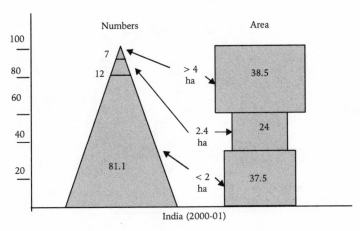

Source: Agricultural Census Division.

In the Indian case, the average farm size has been decreasing over time from 2.3 hectares in 1970 to 1.4 hectares in 1995-96, decreasing further to 1.37 hectares in 2000-01. The fragmentation of landholdings has been associated with a swelling up in the area operated by smallholders. While the number of holdings of less than 2 hectares is going up in percentage terms over time, the operated area of these has also gone up in relative terms (Figure11.3 of pyramids, Agricultural Census Division, 2000-01). This trend reflects the case of most developing countries which has been characterised

## Figure 11.3

*Expanding Base of Farm Pyramids in India Over Time*

**Area of Holdings-India**

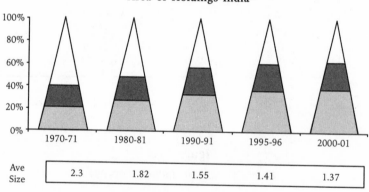

**Area of Holdings-India**

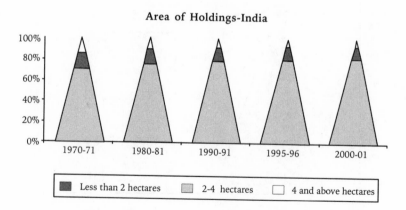

*Source:* Agricultural Census Division.

by fragmentation and swelling up of farm pyramid at the bottom. This is typically in contrast to the trend in developed countries where the average size of holdings has been increasing over time. It is expected that developing countries too would experience a turnaround point when the average farm size will start increasing instead of decreasing, as their income levels improve and GDP structure changes.

In India, this turnaround can be seen in some states like Punjab, Goa, Manipur and Sikkim. Being an agricultural state, the case of Punjab is especially notable as it has witnessed significant increase in state level per capita income in recent years, owing largely to gains from the Green Revolution. The average size decreased from

## Figure 11.4

*Export of Non-Traditional Crops in the 1980s and 1990s (US$ Million)*

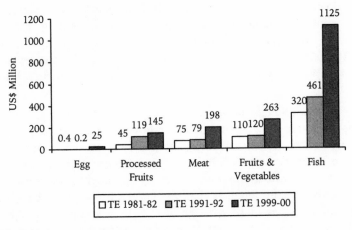

Source: Joshi *et al.*, 2003.

3.8 hectares in 1980-81 to 3.6 hectares in 1990-91. The turnaround was witnessed in 1995-96 when the average size increased again to 3.8 hectares and to 4 hectares in 2000-01. Concurrently the per capita net state domestic product in Punjab also increased (Figure 12.4, Indiastat 2006). The average size has also stabilised in Bihar, Orissa, Uttar Pradesh, Assam, Jammu and Kashmir, Arunachal Pradesh and Tripura, and these states might also witness a turnaround in the near future (Agricultural Census Division, 2000-01).

Still with 81 per cent of total holdings and 37 per cent of operated area in 2000-01, the question of smallholders is of utmost importance. They account for 41 per cent of foodgrain production in 1990-91 and the highest share of livestock in 1998-1999 (Narayanan and Gulati 2002). The incidence of hunger is 32 per cent among farmers will less than 0.5 hectares and incidence of poverty at 38 per cent in the same farm-size class. This incidence of hunger and poverty decreases to 12 per cent and 13 per cent respectively among farmers with more than 4 hectares (Singh 2004). Thus, smallholders will continue to remain a development priority in the future.

## Demand is Changing—Consumption Patterns, Exporting

Fuelled by rising income, urbanisation, female participation in work force, demand side factors are subtly transforming the food system in India. This is leading to a change in consumption patterns from staples to high value commodities. Rising exports in high value products is also providing impetus, albeit to a lesser extent.

Consumption patterns in India reveal that cereal consumption has fallen not only among the upper income group but also among people below the poverty line. In contrast, the consumption of high value products such as fruits and vegetables, milk, meat, fish and eggs has increased. The lower income group might have consumed less of high value products than the upper income group but there consumption has increased significantly with a rise of as high as 164 per cent in fruits and 50 per cent vegetables from 1983 to 1999-00. In contrast, the consumption of cereals declined for both income groups, a steeper decline for upper income group at 20 per cent (Table 11.1). Urbanisation has also influenced consumption patterns with urban areas consuming more high value commodities. But rural areas are not far behind in increasing their demand for high value crops. In fruits and vegetables, the consumption of fruits and vegetables increased by 35 per cent in rural areas as compared to 38 per cent in urban areas. In contrast, the consumption of

## Table 11.1

### Annual Per capita Food Consumption by Different Income Classes in India, 1983 and 2000

*(kg/person/annum)*

| Commodity | Bottom Income Group | | | Upper Income Group | | |
|---|---|---|---|---|---|---|
| | 1983 | 1999-00 | Change, % | 1983 | 1999-00 | Change, % |
| Total cereals | 147.1 | 132.4 | -10.0 | 194.3 | 154.6 | -20.4 |
| Pulses | 7.6 | 6.9 | -9.21 | 17.7 | 16.6 | -6.21 |
| Vegetables | 36.0 | 53.9 | +49.7 | 65.2 | 90.8 | +39.3 |
| Fruits | 1.6 | 4.2 | +162.5 | 6.4 | 18.2 | +184.4 |
| Milk | 15.7 | 20.5 | +31.0 | 89.7 | 117.2 | +30.7 |
| Meat, fish & Eggs | 1.9 | 3.8 | +100 | 4.8 | 10.6 | +121 |

*Note:* Bottom Group—Below poverty line

Upper Group—Above 150 per cent of poverty line

*Source:* Authors' calculations using data from National Sample Survey Organisation.

*Source:* Kumar and Mruthyunjaya (2002).

## Table 11.2

### Structural Change in Food Consumption in Rural and Urban Areas of India, 1983 and 1999-2000

| Commodity | Rural | | | Urban | | |
|---|---|---|---|---|---|---|
| | 1983 | 1999-00 | Change per cent | 1983 | 1999-00 | Change per cent |
| Annual per capita food consumption (kg) | | | | | | |
| Cereals | 181.5 | 157.3 | -24.2 | 141.7 | 131.1 | -10.6 |
| Pulses | 11.1 | 11.2 | +0.1 | 12.4 | 14.7 | +2.3 |
| Vegetables & fruits | 48.8 | 83.9 | +35.1 | 76.7 | 114.7 | +38 |
| Milk | 37.0 | 63.3 | +26.3 | 55.5 | 90.7 | +35.2 |
| Meat, fish & eggs | 3.9 | 6.7 | +2.8 | 1.4 | 9.5 | +8.1 |

*Source:* Kumar and Mruthyunjaya (2002).

cereals is higher in rural areas in 1999-00 but falling at a much higher rate of 24 per cent from 1983 to 1999-00 (Table 11.2).

Besides domestic demand, the exports situation has also picked up. Exports of high value agriculture, which were low in the 1980s, have picked up significantly in the late 1990s (Figure 11.4). The exports of fruits and vegetables more than doubled during the last two decades—from US $ 110 million in TE 1981-82 to US$ 263 million in TE 1999-2000. The exports of fish also shot up from $320 million in TE 1981-1982 to $1125 million by TE 1999-2000[2] (Joshi and Gulati, 2003).

This has led to a movement towards production of high value commodities and its share in the gross value of agricultural output has increased from 32 per cent in 1982-83 to 44 per cent in 2002-03,

### Table 11.3

*Composition and Growth of Agricultural Sector in India*

| Commodity | Share in Gross Value of Agricultural Output (%) | | | Compound Annual Growth (%) | |
|---|---|---|---|---|---|
| | TE 1982/83 | TE 1992/93 | TE 2002/03 | 1980/81 to 1991/92 | 1992/93 to 2002/03 |
| Crops | 77.3 | 74.3 | 70.9 | 2.8 | 2.5 |
| Rice | 14.6 | 15.1 | 12.9 | 4.0 | 1.5 |
| Wheat | 7.9 | 8.2 | 7.7 | 3.2 | 2.6 |
| Coarse cereals | 4.9 | 3.9 | 2.8 | 0.4 | -0.1 |
| Pulses | 5.6 | 4.6 | 3.3 | 1.2 | -.0.1 |
| Foodgrains | 33.0 | 31.8 | 26.8 | 2.8 | 1.4 |
| Oilseeds | 6.6 | 8.5 | 6.7 | 6.0 | 0.3 |
| Sugar | 6.0 | 5.9 | 6.4 | 3.5 | 4.4 |
| Fibre | 3.4 | 3.3 | 2.5 | 2.9 | -0.03 |
| Drugs and narcotics | 1.6 | 1.4 | 1.7 | 1.9 | 4.5 |
| Spices | 2.1 | 2.2 | 2.6 | 4.3 | 4.4 |
| Fruits and vegetables | 14.0 | 13.5 | 17.9 | 2.5 | 6.0 |
| Livestock | 20.0 | 22.7 | 25.1 | 4.5 | 3.8 |
| Dairy | 12.9 | 15.4 | 17.6 | 5.2 | 4.2 |
| Poultry | 1.6 | 2.2 | 3.2 | 6.8 | 6.3 |
| Red meat | 1.4 | 1.8 | 1.7 | 5.2 | 2.4 |
| Fish | 2.6 | 3.0 | 4.0 | 3.7 | 5.0 |
| Total agriculture | 100.0 | 100.0 | 100.0 | 3.2 | 2.9 |
| High-value | 32.5 | 35.9 | 44.4 | 4.1 | 5.0 |
| Rest | 67.5 | 64.1 | 55.6 | 2.7 | 1.5 |

*Note*: Includes livestock, fish and fruits and vegetables.

*Source*: Birthal *et al.*, Forthcoming.

2. The export value figures are in current US dollar terms.

growing at a compound annual rate of 5 per cent in decade from 1992-1993 to 2002-03 (Table 11.3, Birthal *et al.*, Forthcoming).

Will the demand for high-value agriculture help the small farmer? To answer this question, it is important to know that small farms have lower labour-related transaction costs and more family workers per hectare while large farms have lower capital- and land-related transaction costs. Hence, small farms have an advantage in developing countries which have a higher labour/land ratio and lower capital while large farms have an advantage in developed countries with more savings and capital (Fan and Chan-kang, 2003; Eastwood *et al.*, Forthcoming) Hence, it follows that the cultivation of high-value commodities suits the small farmers as it is a labour-intensive crop. For example, the average labour used in the cultivation of potato is 200 man days per hectare and 195 man days per hectare for tomato, as compared to 105 man days/

### Figure 11.5

*Average Labour Used for Cultivation of Cereals and Vegetables (man days/hectare)*

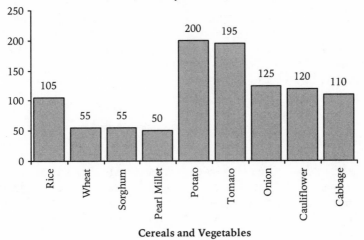

**Cereals and Vegetables**

Source: Joshi *et al.*, 2003.

hectare for rice and 55 for wheat (Figure 11.5, Joshi *et al.*, 2003). The small farms with their low labour-related costs are perfectly suited for the cultivation of high-value commodities and it has a potential for generating high farm employment in labour-abundant countries like

India, and a source for small farmers to augment their income significantly. In India, 15.3 per cent of farm households grow vegetables and 4.6 per cent grow fruits. Smallholders, despite limited access to land, participate more in cultivation of fruits and vegetables. Nearly 15.5 per cent of marginal and 16.6 per cent of small farm households grow vegetables, which is much more than the national average. The corresponding figures for medium and large farm households are 14.8

### Table 11.4

*Participation of Categories of Farm Households in Cultivation of Fruits and Vegetables*

|  | North | East | Northeast | South | West | India |
|---|---|---|---|---|---|---|
| | | | **Per cent Households** | | | |
| Vegetables | | | | | | |
| Marginal | 15.7 | 19.5 | 64.9 | 8.5 | 4.4 | 15.5 |
| Small | 16.3 | 27.9 | 66.9 | 6.8 | 7.5 | 16.6 |
| Medium | 15.3 | 29.0 | 75.9 | 8.0 | 8.3 | 14.8 |
| Large | 12.7 | 22.3 | 74.5 | 8.7 | 6.9 | 10.4 |
| All | 15.6 | 21.6 | 66.9 | 8.1 | 6.4 | 15.3 |
| Fruits | | | | | | |
| Marginal | 2.1 | 1.0 | 4.1 | 20.5 | 1.5 | 5.6 |
| Small | 2.7 | 1.5 | 5.5 | 8.1 | 1.4 | 3.2 |
| Medium | 2.0 | 1.9 | 6.1 | 6.7 | 1.3 | 2.7 |
| Large | 2.9 | 0.0 | 4.9 | 6.4 | 2.2 | 3.0 |
| All | 2.3 | 1.1 | 4.7 | 15.7 | 1.5 | 4.6 |
| | | | **Per cent of Gross Cropped Area** | | | |
| Vegetables | | | | | | |
| Marginal | 2.59 | 4.44 | 17.01 | 2.53 | 1.31 | 3.38 |
| Small | 2.00 | 3.44 | 11.85 | 2.19 | 1.39 | 2.56 |
| Medium | 1.67 | 2.78 | 10.28 | 1.63 | 1.05 | 1.80 |
| Large | 1.31 | 2.31 | 10.59 | 1.23 | 0.82 | 1.20 |
| All | 1.91 | 3.52 | 12.73 | 1.83 | 1.04 | 2.12 |
| Fruits | | | | | | |
| Marginal | 0.70 | 0.24 | 0.82 | 5.52 | 0.55 | 1.31 |
| Small | 0.60 | 0.21 | 0.83 | 2.39 | 0.37 | 0.74 |
| Medium | 0.39 | 0.37 | 1.03 | 2.56 | 0.29 | 0.67 |
| Large | 0.47 | 0.00 | 1.13 | 2.25 | 0.57 | 0.78 |
| All | 0.54 | 0.22 | 0.92 | 3.08 | 0.46 | 0.86 |

*Source:* Birthal *et al.*, Forthcoming.

and 10.4 per cent respectively. The proportion of households growing fruits is also higher among smallholders (Table 11.4, Birthal *et al.*, Forthcoming).

Not only do high value commodities have the potential to provide more employment for smallholders but this is truer for women. Dolan and Sorby (2003) document very high share of women labour in high-value food production in a number of countries. In Brazil, women comprise 65 per cent of labor force in fruit production. In Tanzania, Ecuador, Kenya and Uganda women comprise between 57-87 per cent of laborforce in fruits, vegetables

**Figure 11.6**

*Share of Women in Total Workers in Production of High-value Commodities and Grains, 1999/2000*

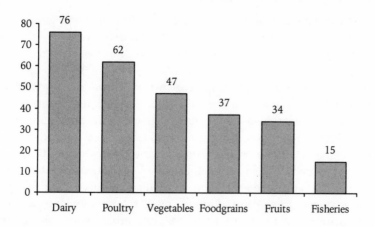

Source: Birthal *et al.*, Forthcoming.

and cut flower. In India also, women provide considerable labour to high-value production. The share of women employed in dairy is as high as 76 per cent of total workers as compared to 37 per cent for foodgrains (Figure 11.6, Birthal *et al.*, Forthcoming).

Thus, high-value agriculture represents an opportunity to raise income of small farmers, empower women and move them out of the poverty trap. But with opportunities, comes the constraints that farmers have to face, the obvious one being high transaction costs and risks associated with the perishability of high value agricultural commodities. With respect to transaction costs, Poulton *et al.*, (2005) argues that small farms have a competitive advantage over large farms in low labour-related transaction costs and intensive local knowledge, but their small scale leads to high unit transaction costs in almost all non-labour transactions. Besides access to inputs, credit and technology, the new frontier of scale economies is marketing, which is likely to be based on non-labour related transaction costs. Even if smallholders get access to credit and inputs and are thereby competitive at the farm level, they face the scale disadvantage in marketing owing to high transaction costs. This can be a special challenge when compared with the other development in the food system to do with consolidation on the firm side.

## Industry and Retail Changing

As fragmentation is happening on the farm side and growth of high value agriculture on the demand side, concurrently a gradual process of consolidation is happening in the firm side. The retail and processing sector is seeing an increasing level of scaling up and concentration of firms which can together be termed as consolidation in supply side factors in the firm side. Changes in consumption patterns as mentioned before, improvement in infrastructure, and growth of foreign direct investment (FDI) have led to a growth in the number of supermarkets, hypermarkets, etc. Growth in HVA and processed food has also led to an increase in operations of processing firms. The path to consolidation in retailing and processing follows three stages. In the initial stage, small retailers and processors dominate but with increasing income and urbanisation, change in food habits, and entry of FDI, firms scale up operations. New firms come in with new product differentiation and a constant process of churning out is observed. However, by the third and final stage, only the efficient firms that can adapt to the demands of the local market survive, thus, high level of concentration with few scaled up firms dominating the market.

The consolidation process is very developed in high-income countries, and growing at a fast rate in middle-income countries and urban areas of low-income countries. This trend has been observed in developed markets like the United States where in 2002, the 4 largest food retailers' share of grocery store sales was estimated at 31 per cent, up from 17 per cent in 1987; the 8 largest retailers' share was 41 per cent, up from 26 per cent; and the 20 largest retailers' share was 57 per cent, up from 37 per cent (ERS, USDA). Even in developing countries, especially middle-income countries, Table 11.5 shows that there is indeed a rising trend in consolidation of modern

### Table 11.5

*Market Shares and Concentration of Supermarkets and Processing Firms*

|  |  | *Past* | *Present* |
|---|---|---|---|
| Supermarkets | Brazil (top 10 supermarkets) | 24% (1994) | 47% (2000) |
|  | Chile (top 4 supermarkets) | 47% (1996) | 52% (2002) |
|  | South Africa (top 4 supermarkets) | 88% (1993) | 98% (2003) |
| Processing firms | Brazil (top 4 firms) | 17% (1993) | 18% (2000) |

*Source::* Brazil – Farina (2002); Chile – Faiguenbaum *et al.*, (2002); South Africa – Louw *et al.* (2004).

processors and retailers. For example, in Brazil the top 10 supermarkets control 47 per cent of the market share and the top 4 processing firms control 18 per cent. Table 11.6 shows the growth in retail share of processed/packaged food for different countries by

### Table 11.6

*Annual Average Growth in Retail Sales in Packaged Foods*

| Country Group[1] | Per Capita 2002 Retail Sales ($) | Total Retail Growth During 1996-2002 (%) | Per Capita Growth During 1996-2002 (%) |
|---|---|---|---|
| High income | 979 | 3.2 | 2.5 |
| Upper middle income | 298 | 8.1 | 6.7 |
| Lower middle income | 143 | 28.8 | 28.1 |
| Low income | 63 | 12.9 | 11.9 |

*Note:* 1. Country group classification follows the World Bank definition.
*Source:* USDA, 2005.

income groups with lower middle income countries showing the highest retail growth of 29 per cent between the years 1996-2002. The retail industry has seen a rapid growth due to the development of supermarkets. Foreign direct investment, income growth and urbanisation have accelerated this trend with supermarkets taking over 50 per cent of market share in some middle-income countries such as Philippines, and under 2 per cent in low-income countries such as Vietnam and Bangladesh (Table 11.7 and Gulati *et al.*, 2005). Even in food processing, some level of consolidation is observed in developing countries. In 1999, food processing industries accounted for 13 per cent of domestic manufacturing in Thailand and 18 per cent in India (Gulati *et al.*, 2005).

### Table 11.7

*Supermarket Share in National Food Retails Sales in Asia*

*(in Per cent)*

| Country | Share in 1999 | Share in 2001 |
|---|---|---|
| China (urban) | 30 | 48 |
| Indonesia | 20 | 25 |
| Korea | 61 | 65 |
| Malaysia | 27 | 31 |
| Philippines | 52 | 57 |
| Taiwan | 65 | 69 |
| Thailand | 35 | 43 |

*Source*: USDA, 2005.

In the case of India, the organised processing sector is not much developed with a substantial part of the agro-output still unprocessed. India produces 91 million tonnes of milk (highest in the world), 150 million tonnes of fruits and vegetables (second largest), 483 million tonnes of livestock (largest), 210 million tons of foodgrain (third largest), 6.2 million tonnes of fish (seventh largest) and is fifth in egg production. However, conservative estimates put processing levels in the fruits and vegetables sector at 2 per cent, meat and poultry at 2 per cent, milk by way of modern dairies at 14 per cent, fish at 4 per cent and bulk meat deboning at 21 per cent. Further, the value addition to raw produce by processing is 7 per cent in India, compared with as much as 45 per cent in

Philippines and 23 per cent in China (Government of India, 2005). Also, most of Indian agro-processing is concentrated in the unorganised sector. Within agro-industry, food processing is an important component with 37 per cent production units, 38 per cent employment and 53 per cent of gross value added, although it is dominated in the organised sector (Chadha and Gulati, Forthcoming).

Retailing in India is at present by and large unorganised, highly fragmented, predominantly small, and mostly family-owned. It has been estimated that there are 11.16 million retail outlets in the country in 2001, of which 33 per cent deal in food items (Table 11.8). The organised retailing accounts for less than 2 per cent of the food retailing

### Table 11.8

*Growth of Retail Outlets in India ('000)*

|  | 1996 | 1997 | 1998 | 1999 | 2000 | 2001 |
|---|---|---|---|---|---|---|
| Food retailers | 2769.0 | 2943 | 3123.4 | 3300.2 | 3480.0 | 3682.9 |
| Non-food retailers | 5773.6 | 6040 | 6332.2 | 6666.3 | 7055.5 | 7482.1 |
| Total retailers | 8542.6 | 8983.6 | 9455.6 | 9966.5 | 10535.5 | 11165.0 |
| Per cent of food retail to total outlets | 32.41 | 32.77 | 33.03 | 33.11 | 33.03 | 32.99 |

*Source:* Chengappa *et al.*, Forthcoming.

industry in India and of this, the share of supermarkets is approximately 2 per cent of total food retail (Table 11.9, Figure 11.7, Chengappa, Forthcoming).

### Table 11.9

*Share of Organised Food Retail in India*

|  | 1999 | 2002 | 2005* |
|---|---|---|---|
| Total food retail (USD Billion) | 159 | 180 | 225 |
| Organised food retail (USD Billion) | 1.1 | 3.2 | 7.0 |
| Per cent of organised food retail | 0.70 | 1.78 | 3.11 |

*Note:* * Estimated

*Source:* Chengappa *et al.*, Forthcoming.

### Figure 11.7

*Share of Organised Food Retail in India*

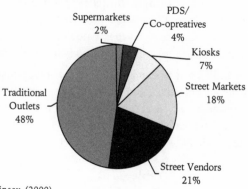

*Source:* McKinsey (2000).

## Dynamic Linkages—Institutions and Infrastructure Necessary

The growth of high value products and the emergence of modern marketing channels are linked in several ways. The perishability of high-value products necessitates health and hygiene requirements which result in high fixed costs, creating greater economies of scale in retailing. Also, consolidation requires that firms guard their supply lines and necessitates strong linkages with farmers to prevent post-harvest losses and reduce risk for buyers and sellers. The question of small farmers then becomes more relevant in this scenario. While smallholders have low labour-related transactions cost which is advantageous with high value agriculture, which has a high labour-capital ratio, they also have a scale disadvantage. With credit constraint and the scale disadvantage in marketing for the smallholders, according to Maxwell (2004), undercapitalised and undereducated small farmers will find it increasingly difficult to meet the quality, quantity, timeliness and traceability requirements of new supply chains. Opponents of this view like Lipton (2004) acknowledges that supermarkets, export horticulture and grades and standards as the 'three ugly sisters' of globalisation, but asserts that there are plenty of success stories of intermediation between small farmers and market institutions.

This chapter argues that there is reduced basis for concern. The possibility of aping the Latin American experience, where smallholders have been left out of the marketing chains, is less likely to happen in India as unlike Latin America, smallholders are preponderant in Asia and Africa. However, the continuing fragmentation in farm size, growth of high value products and consolidation at firm-level is leading to the emergence of new dynamic linkages with farmers, processors and retailers being the leading actors. Figure 11.8 presents the dynamics of the emerging

## Figure 11.8
### The Dynamics of Linkages

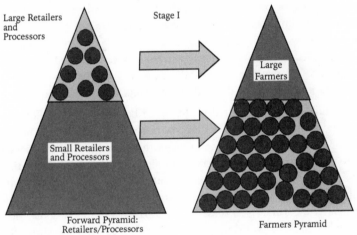

The Dynamics of Linkages: continued

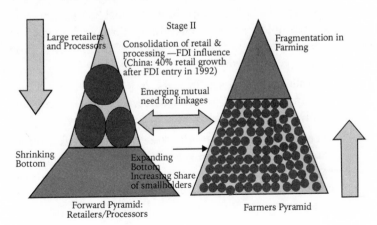

linkages. The left pyramid refers to the firms (processing and retail) and the right pyramid is the farmers pyramid. In the early stages, with lower fragmentation on the farm side and high dominance of small and informal processing and retailing the linkages are between similar entities from the firm and farm pyramids. Large farms link up with large firms and *vice versa*. Over time as fragmentation continues on the farm side, the bottom of the farm pyramid expands and within the expanded bottom the average sizes (represented by circles) tend to get smaller. The opposite happens on the firm and retail side with consolidation (scaling up and concentration). This leads to linkages between the consolidating firms and fragmenting farms. In the intermediate stage, a constant process of churning out will be observed with large-scale entry and exit of processing and retailing firms. But in the final stage, only a few consolidated firms will survive and will develop strong linkages with smallholders as due to fragmentation in farm holdings this represents the only possibility.

The linkages demonstrated in the figure between the consolidating firms and fragmenting farms can only be achieved if suitable institutions and infrastructure are created to facilitate these linkages. As mentioned before, linkages with smallholders entail high transaction and marketing costs. Thus, innovative institutions that cut down on costs for both firms and farms are necessary to make it profitable for firms to link with farmers. At the same time, these innovations have to follow some basic principles for the solutions to be sustainable. The solutions for improving the lot of the smallholders can broadly be classified into two categories: (i) institutional innovations in farming linkages with the smallholders; and (ii) innovations in the enabling environment that make smallholders more competitive (through provision of credit, information, etc). Few best practices in these firm-farm linkages can be generalised:

- In dealing with the smallholders, *creating scale is a necessity*. This implies that firms have to develop mechanisms that involve the smallholders as a group cumulatively.

- Secondly, all the *mutually beneficial* linkages involve competition on the firm side. To ensure that smallholders get reasonable benefits, it is important that the farmers continue to have an outside option.

- Investments in linking with the smallholders tend to have greater gestation lags. The returns increase with the scaling up as more farmers get linked and/or the small farmers over time transition to bigger farmers mainly by ploughing back their profits. Thus, success lies in *creating long term linkages* with repeated interactions which mitigates the adverse selection problem for firms.

- Finally, smallholders operate in an environment where publicly provided infrastructure and institutions are severely lacking thus *requiring compensatory actions* from the firms. This, in itself, accounts for greater gestation lags while doing business with smallholders.

Birthal *et al.,* (2005) analysed three contract farming arrangements in India—poultry by Venkateshwara Hatcheries in Andhra Pradesh, dairy by Nestle India Limited in Punjab, and fruits and vegetables by Mother Dairy Fruits and Vegetables Limited (MDFVL) in and around Delhi. High value agriculture like poultry, dairy and fruits and vegetables are highly prone to production and marketing risks that threaten the profitability particularly on small farms. These risks also affect the profitability of the firms. In order to minimise risks, Venkateshwara Hatcheries began integrating its activities with that of broiler production through contract farming beginning in the late 1980s and Nestle with milk suppliers starting in early 60s. Nestle follows a two-fold contracting arrangement. For those having more than 25 milch animals, it enters into a legal contract. For small producers, the milk is procured through the agents, with whom the firm has a legal contract. Venkateshwara Hatchery provides day-old chicks, feed and medicines to contract growers. The contract growers supply land, labour and other variable inputs. At the end of the production cycle, the farmer receives a net price. The firm monitors quality tightly with a company supervisor visiting the farmer daily. The net price received by the farmers fluctuates within a narrow band and the firm also provides insurance to farmers for mortality rates up to 5 per cent. MDFVL integrates fruits and vegetable production through retail chains in Delhi by procuring from 100 producers' associations that cover 18,000 growers. The study collected data from a primary field survey of contract and non-contract producers to study if contract farming arrangements exhibited systematic bias against smallholders, if these arrangements benefit the smallholders and whether they are mutually beneficial or the firms exploiting small farmers given the large difference in bargaining powers.

It was found that the net profit for the contract dairy farmer was more than double than non-contract milk farmers, 78 per cent higher for vegetable farmers and 13 per cent higher for poultry farmers. The costs of milk production of contract farmers were less by approximately 21 per cent in milk and 26 per cent in vegetable than those of non-contract farmers. The lower total costs can be attributed to lower transaction costs. The share of transaction costs in total cost for non-contract farmers was 20 per cent for milk and 21 per cent for vegetables, while it was around 2 per cent for contract farmers. For poultry, the estimated costs savings for contract growers from cheaper feed and medicine (provided by the firm) equal approximately Rs. 1.9 per kg of bird, a saving of nearly 8 per cent. The inputs chicks, medicines and feed accounted for about 75 per cent in the total cost of broiler production and were the critical inputs for productivity and profitability. The firm bears mortality risk of 5 per cent, and remaining is to be borne by the producer. This means that broiler contract farmers were enjoying indirect credit for important inputs without any interest and, transferring some risks to the firm. This was beneficial to the firm too as it gets an assured and timely supply of the desired raw material and helps the firm in having a better control over its operational and fixed costs and minimising the risk on account of underutilisation of its capacity, thus eventually minimising the cost of processing. It also enables the firm to improve its market reputation. Such a win-win situation was found to have remarkably increased farmers' participation in contract farming in niche areas and commodities with 56 per cent of broiler farmers had expanded their scale of operation between 1990 and 2000. The distribution of smallholders in the sample also clearly showed that they were well represented in the contractual arrangements in the three case studies (Birthal *et al.*, 2005).

Another study was done by Rao (Forthcoming) on contract farming models for gherkins in Andhra Pradesh. The company Global Green has adopted contract farming model for procuring the produce from farmers. It has also set up two processing plants and four production centres/growing regions that feed the processing plant in the state. Under this model, the company is providing technical guidance and inputs to farmers and the farmers in turn are supplying quality produce to company. The farmer gets seed, fertilisers and pesticides on credit and the firm recovers the loan from payments to the farmers' for the final output. If the crop fails before harvest, the company encourages farmers to take up another crop of gherkin and extents the repayment period of the first crop. It also provides extension services like technical guidance on agronomic practices and appropriate use of fertilisers and pesticides and effective management to augment productivity and reduce unit cost of production to become more competitive.

Gherkins is a short duration crop (60-70 days only) and the study shows that farmers are realising a net income of Rs. 6000 to 7000/acre/crop with the option of cultivating a second crop or growing alternative crops. The returns over variable costs are about 30 per cent higher per acre/annum for farmers growing at least one gherkin crop during the year. In contrast to popular belief, a large number of small and marginal farmers are involved in production of gherkins. Family labour is engaged all throughout the crop period and women are getting on an average 100-120 women days of employment per crop/acre during harvest period. The area under gherkin contract farming at present is 3500 ha and is expected to double in the next 2-3 years (Rao, forthcoming).

To summarise the firms, which fit the profile of firms with a strong need to secure their supply lines and protect their investments, have formed linkages with farmers that has a fair degree of representation by smallholders. The linkages formed by these firms have been mutually beneficial to the contractor and the contracted and follow several institutional innovations that relate to the unifying principles listed above:

1. Both are addressing scale disadvantages in dealing with smallholders.

2. In presence of credit market imperfections, both have provided inputs on credit to the farmers.

3. Both are mutually beneficial linkages that are providing

benefits to both firm and farm, thus assuring sustainability of the innovation.

## The Role of Policy

The discussion in the last section has shown that there exists scope for firms to do business with the BoP in a mutually beneficial manner. What is needed is a new way of doing business, a new approach based on innovative institutions that can cut transaction and marketing costs for both firms and farms. The need is for scaling up of success stories like the Indian cooperative movement in dairy and for this, it is necessary to identify the problems that are associated with the scaling up of success stories. While innovative solutions have to be market-based, mutually profitable ones, that are not subsidy-driven, they do require a complementary role of the government through the building of appropriate infrastructure and institutional support. Government has to work as a facilitator in enabling the dynamic linkages between the firms and farms, which has been enumerated above, to function in a mutually beneficial manner. Institutional bottlenecks require significant policy changes to induce efficiency. For example, the taxation on processed foods is one of the highest in the world. Rao (forthcoming) states that the net tax level is 21-23 per cent on food items with India being the only country to levy excise duty on machinery and equipment for processed foods. Comparative tax burden is 10 per cent in Philippines, Indonesia and Malaysia, 14-15 per cent in Netherlands and UK, 17 per cent in China and Ireland (Rao, Forthcoming). It is necessary that a uniform value added tax is imposed in all states to facilitate growth.

An adequate supply chain, backed by improved infrastructure, is essential. For example, in the case of fruits and vegetables, which are perishable products, just 2 per cent processing levels leads to a high level of wastage and shrinkage. If smallholders are to reap the benefits, what is needed is the development of the entire value chain from farms, processing firms to retail outlets. What is clear is the need for investment in both processing and retail industry. While FDI is allowed in processing, it is restricted in retailing and this has repercussions on both food retail and food processing industries. Corporate houses like ITC, Pepsi Foods, Bharti, etc. have started food processing initiatives, and more investment from private players is expected in the future. Putting food processing in priority sector in the recent budget has given another significant boost to this sector, especially with regards to access to priority-sector lending. For private sector to invest more vigorously in the food processing sector, it is essential that all restrictions on scale in the food processing industry is removed which implies that eliminating all remaining reservations for small-scale industries.

To promote investment from private players, it is also essential to remove all restrictions on processors buying directly from farmers which necessitate significant improvements in agricultural marketing, especially in amending the Agricultural Produce Marketing Committee (APMC) Act. Several states have started the work on amending the Act and this is crucial for market reform. The Ministry of Agriculture had formulated a model law on agricultural marketing in consultation with state governments which enables establishment of private markets/yards, direct purchase centres, consumers/farmers markets for direct sale, and promotion of public-private-partnership (PPP) in management and development of agricultural markets. Regulation and promotion of contract farming arrangement is also part of this legislation. This is a step in the right direction and it is imperative that state governments adopt this amended Act.

Besides this, it is necessary to remove all limitations in the private sector developing their state-of-the-art markets for perishable products including developing infrastructure such as cold storage, processing plants, etc. Initiative has been taken by the National Institute of Agricultural Marketing (NIAM) to promote public-private-partnership (PPP) in establishment of state-of-the-art terminal markets for fruits, vegetables and other perishables in important urban centres. It is also essential that investments in agro-based infrastructure be treated as priority sector. In the recent Economic Survey, the government has also listed four central sector schemes that have been introduced for development of marketing infrastructure: (i) developing a Marketing Research and Information Network (MRIN); (ii) a scheme with 25 per cent back-ended subsidy component for construction of rural godowns; (iii) strengthening of agricultural marketing infrastructure, grading and standardisation in those states that have amended the AMPC Act on the lines of the Model Act; and (iv) Venture Capital Assistance scheme by Small Farmers' Agri-Business Consortium (SFAC) to promote agribusiness projects (Economic Survey 2005-06).

Compared to food processing, private investment in retail is quite low. In the past, inefficient supply chain had led to the failure of the Nanz supermarkets that had been promoted by the Escorts Group. But corporate houses have started taking the plunge with the Pantaloon group operating 37 food supermarkets called Food *Bazaar* in India. A significant big player to jump the fray is the Reliance Industries which plans to invest $ 3.4 billion to open about 1575 stores. These will be in the form of hypermarkets or supermarkets selling food, consumer electronics and clothes (IHT, 2006). While domestic investment is coming in, albeit at a slow rate, foreign direct investment still has a long way to go. Recently FDI in single brand retail has been allowed but more is needed for the food retail sector. It is necessary to remove restrictions on scale in retailing which implies opening FDI for retail. Policy options, like opening FDI in retailing with some domestic sourcing clause, need to be investigated.

Policy must also be directed in creating the enabling environment for small farmers to integrate into the system. Among the enabling factors, access to credit is the most important. Kisan Credit Card Scheme was an innovation in this regard and although credit through this scheme has increased, other instruments for credit outreach must be explored. One such channel can be Non-Banking Financial Intermediaries (NBFIs) like contract farming entities that have pre-established links to the small farmer. Credit can be channelled through NBFIs at a rate that is advantageous for small farmers, compared to local informal rates, and also factor in a margin for the firm.

It is clear that Indian agriculture is going through a dynamic phase which has positive implications for the smallholders. What is needed is the creation of a policy environment to facilitate the process of change. It is evident that policies are being created to facilitate this dynamism but is the pace fast enough? As Indian agriculture moves into this new phase of development, it is essential that changes in the policy environment keeps pace of the structural changes in the economy and do not impede the process of development.

# References

Agricultural Census Division (2000-01). Ministry of Agriculture, Government of India, New Delhi.

Birthal, P., P.K. Joshi, D. Roy and A. Thorat (Forthcoming). *From Plate to Plough: Patterns and Determinants of Diversification Towards High Value Agriculture in India*. Report for the Ford Foundation project "Plate-to-Plough: Agricultural Diversification in India and Implications for Small Holders", International Food Policy Research Institute, Washington, DC.

Birthal, P., A. Gulati and P.K. Joshi (2005). "Vertical Coordination in High-Value Food Commodities: Implications for Smallholders", *MTID Discussion Paper* No. 85. International Food Policy Research Institute, Washington, DC.

Chadha, G.K. and A. Gulati (Forthcoming). "Performance in India's Agro-Industry in Recent Years: Emerging Issues and Prospects", International Food Policy Research Institute, Washington, DC.

Chengappa, P.G., L. Achoth, A. Mukherjee, B.M. Reddy and P.C. Ravi (Forthcoming). "Evolution of Food Retail Chains in India", International Food Policy Research Institute, Washington, DC.

Dolan, C.S., and K. Sorby (2003). "Gender and employment in high-value agriculture industries. Agriculture and Rural development", *Working Paper* 7, The World Bank, Washington, DC.

Eastwood, R.K, M. Lipton, and A.T. Newell (Forthcoming). "Farm Size", in R. Evenson and P. Pingale (eds.), *Handbook of Agricultural Economics*, Vol. 3.

Faiguenbaum, S., Julio Berdegue and Thomas Reardon (2002). "The Rapid Rise of Supermarkets in Chile: Effects on Dairy, Vegetable, and Beef Chains", *Development Policy Review*, Vol. 20(4), pp.459-471.

Fan, S. and C. Chan-Kang (2003). "Is Small Beautiful? Farm Size, Productivity and Poverty in Asian Agriculture", Plenary paper prepared for the 25th International Conference of Agricultural Economists, July 17, Durban, South Africa.

Farina, E.M.M.Q. (2002). "Consolidation, Multinationalisation, and Competition in Brazil: Impacts on Horticulture and Dairy Products Systems", *Development Policy Review*, Vol. 20(4), pp.441-457.

GoI (Government of India) (2005). *Food Processing Policy 2005*, Ministry of Food Processing Industries, Government of India, New Delhi, India.

Gulati A., N. Minot, C. Delgado and S. Bora (2005). "Growth in high-value agriculture in Asia and the emergence of vertical links with farmers", *mimeo*, International Food Policy Research Institute.

Indiastat (2006). *http://www.indiastat.com/default1.asp*. Accessed in March.

International Herald Tribune (2006). *Indian Shoppers, Meet Reliance*, March 8, *http://www.iht.com/articles/2006/03/07/bloomberg/sxreliance.php*

Joshi, P.K. and A. Gulati (2003). "From Plate to Plough: Agricultural Diversification in India", Paper presented at the JNU-IFPRI workshop on the Dragon and the Elephant: A Comparative Study of Economic and Agricultural Reform in China and India, March 25-26, New Delhi, India.

Joshi, P.K., A. Gulati, P.S. Birthal and L. Tewari (2003). "Agricultural Diversification in South Asia: Patterns, Determinants and Policy Implications", *Discussion Paper No. 57*. Market and Structural Studies Division, November, International Food Policy Research Institute, Washington D.C.

Kumar, P. and Mruthyunjaya (2002). "Long-term Changes in Food Basket in India", Paper presented in an International workshop on *Agricultural Diversification in South Asia*, jointly organised by MoA, Bhutan, NCAP and IFPRI, Paro, Bhutan, 21-23 November.

Lipton, M. (2004). *New Directions for Agriculture in Reducing Poverty: The DFID Initiative*, Available at: *http://dfid-agriculture-consultation.nri.org/launchpapers/michaellipton.html*

Louw, A., H. Madevu, D. Jordaan, and H. Vermeulen (2004). *Regoverning Markets: Securing Small Holder Producer Participation in Restructured National and Agri-food System*, RSA Country Report, International Institute for Environment and Development.

Maxwell, S. (2004). *Launching the DFID Consultation: New Directions for Agriculture in Reducing Poverty*, available at: *http://dfid-agriculture-consultation.nri.org/launchpapers/simonmaxwell.html*

McKinsey and Company (2000). *MGI Retail Report*, McKinsey Global Institute.

Ministry of Finance (2006). *Economic Survey (2005-06)*, Government of India, New Delhi.

Narayanan, S. and A. Gulati (2002). "Globalization and the Smallholders: A Review of Issues, Approaches and Implications", *Discussion Paper* No. 50, Market and Structural Studies Division, International Food Policy Research Institute, November Washington D.C.

Prahalad, C.K. (2005). *Fortune at the Bottom of the Pyramid. Eradicating Poverty through Profits*, Wharton School Publishing.

Poulton, C., A. Dorward and J. Kydd (2005). "The Future of Small Farms: New Directions for Services, Institutions and Intermediation", Paper prepared for *The Future of Small Farms Workshop*, Imperial College, June 26-29, Wye, UK.

Rao, P. (Forthcoming). "Revitalizing Agriculture Sector in Andhra Pradesh: Role of Agricultural Diversification and Agro-Processing", Report for USAID Project *Agricultural Diversification in Andhra Pradesh*, International Food Policy Research Institute, Washington, DC.

Singh, P. (2004). "Agricultural Policy: Vision 2020", Background Paper No. 24 prepared for *Vision 2020*, Planning Commission, Government of India, Indian Agricultural Research Council, New Delhi.

USDA (2005). "New Directions in Global Food Markets", (Regmi, A., and Gehlhar, M eds) *Agriculture Information Bulletin* No. 794, United States Department of Agriculture.

————. Economic Research Service.

von Braun, J. (2003). "Agricultural Economics and Distributional Effects: Shaping Agricultural Policy for Improved Outcomes", Presidential Address. 25th Conference of the International Association of Agricultural Economists (IAAE) on *Reshaping Agriculture's Contribution to Society*, August 16-22, Durban, South Africa.

My sincerest gratitude to Saswati Bora and Devesh Roy for their invaluable contribution and comments on this paper. This paper borrows heavily from an upcoming IFPRI discussion paper on "Making business with smallholders: How can innovative institutions help?" by Ashok Gulati, Devesh Roy and Saswati Bora.

# Editors / Contributors

*Editors:*

## S. Mahendra Dev

Prof. S. Mahendra Dev is currently Director, Centre for Economic and Social Studies, Hyderabad. He did his Ph.D. from the Delhi School of Economics and his Post-doctoral research at the Economic Growth Centre, Yale University and was faculty member at the Indira Gandhi Institute of Development Research, Mumbai for 11 years. He was Senior Fellow at Rajiv Gandhi Foundation (1996-97) and Visiting Professor at University of Bonn, Germany (1999). He has written extensively on agricultural development, poverty and public policy, food security, employment guarantee schemes, social security, farm and non-farm employment. He has more than 70 research publications in national and international journals. His co-edited books include: *Social and Economic Security in India* (published by Institute for Human Development), *Towards A Food Secure India: Issues & Policies* (published by Institute for Human Development (IHD) and Centre for Economic and Social Studies (CESS), *Andhra Pradesh Development: Economic Reforms and Challenges Ahead* (published by CESS) and *Rural Poverty in India: Incidence, Issues and Policies* (published by Indira Gandhi Institute of Development Research (IGIDR)). He has been a consultant and advisor to many international organisations like the UNDP, UNICEF, World Bank, International Food Policy Research Institute, ESCAP. He has been a member of several government Committees including Prime Minister's Task Force on Employment. He is also a member of the Committee on Financial Inclusion chaired by Dr. C. Rangarajan.

## K.S. Babu

K.S. Babu is a Faculty Member (Reader) at the Centre for Economic and Social Studies (CESS) in Hyderabad. He has M.A. in Anthropology from the Andhra University, Visakhapatnam and Ph.D. from the University of Delhi, Delhi. In the past he has worked on healthcare, health insurance, tribal development and child labour issues. He was the project director of the study "Yanadi Development Plan" submitted to Government of Andhra Pradesh. He has presented a paper on NGOs in the Third International Convention of Asia Scholars (ICAS3), Singapore in 2003. His current research focuses on NGOs and rural development. He was local co-ordinator for three international conferences held in collaboration with CESS in Hyderabad besides other national seminars. He has authored over a dozen research papers in various professional journals.

*Contributors:*

## André Béteille

Professor André Béteille assumed the office of the chairman of the Indian Council of Social Science Research (ICSSR) on 29 March 2005. Prof. Béteille is a Sociologist who is known world-wide for his contribution to the comparative study of social inequality. With Indian society as his focus he has examined the nature and types of inequality in human societies in general. He has lectured in many universities, and his books and papers have been widely appreciated in India and abroad. He is a corresponding Fellow of the British Academy and an Honorary Fellow of the Royal Anthropological Institute. Prof. Béteille had his education mainly in Kolkata where he took an M.Sc. degree in Anthropology from University of Calcutta, later taking Ph.D. degree in Sociology from the University of Delhi. After a brief stint at the Indian Statistical Institute, he joined the faculty of the Department of Sociology at the Delhi School of Economics in 1959 and taught there until his retirement in 1999. Later he became a National Fellow of the Indian Council of Social Science Research.

Prof. Béteille is Chancellor, North-Eastern Hill University, Shillong and Chairman, Centre for Studies in Social Sciences, Kolkata. In addition, he is a Trustee of the Sameeksha Trust, the Institute of Economic Growth, the National Foundation for India and the New India Foundation. He was awarded the Padma Bhusan by the President of India in 2005.

## Jayati Ghosh

Jayati Ghosh is a professor of economics at the Centre for Economic Studies and Planning, School of Social Sciences, Jawaharlal Nehru University, New Delhi. Among others, she has co-authored (with Prof. C.P. Chandrasekhar) the books: *Crisis as a Conquest: Learning from East Asia, The Market that Failed: A Decade of Neoliberal Economic Reforms in India* and *Work and Well-being in the Age of Finance*. She is a regular columnist for *Frontline* magazine and *Businessline* financial daily. She is involved in managing several public information websites including, *http://*

*www.macroscan.org* and *http://www.kisanwatch.org* and also runs the secretariat and *website http://www.networkideas.org* of International Development Economics Associates (IDEAS). She is a member of several government Committees/Commissions including the recently constituted Knowledge Commission. She was the Chairperson of the Commission on Farmer's Welfare in 2004 constituted by Andhra Pradesh Government.

## Ashok Gulati

Prof. Ashok Gulati is currently IFPRI Director in Asia based in IFPRI's New Delhi Office, India. He joined IFPRI as Director of the Markets, Trade and Institutions Division (formerly called Markets and Structural Studies Division) in January 2001 until February 2006. His special areas of research include: analysis and policy advice on issues related to agricultural markets, trade liberalisation and its impact on producers and consumers, WTO and trade negotiations in agriculture; globalisation and the small holders, vertical linkages between farms and firms, pricing and institutional reforms in input markets, especially fertilisers, power and canal irrigation, and their efficiency and welfare impact, and the role of infrastructure and institutions in making markets function efficiently. Before joining IFPRI, Ashok Gulati was a NABARD Chair Professor at the Institute of Economic Growth in Delhi, India, and a member of the Economic Advisory Council of the Prime Minister of India. In 2004, he was named a fellow of the National Academy of Agricultural Sciences. Prof. Gulati received his M.A. and Ph.D. in economics from the Delhi School of Economics, University of Delhi.

Current Research: 1) Agricultural Diversification and Vertical Coordination in South Asia. 2) Grain Marketing Parastatals in Asia. 3) The Dragon and the Elephant: A Comparative Study of Economic and Agricultural Reforms in China and India, and 4) WTO, Agricultural Negotiations and Developing Countries.

## Jayaprakash Narayan

Dr. Jayaprakash Narayan is a physician by training, a public servant by choice, and a democrat by conviction. He joined the Indian Administrative Service in 1980 in the aftermath of Emergency and the failure of the Janata Experiment. During his 17 years of distinguished public service in various capacities, he acquired a formidable reputation in the State of Andhra Pradesh. Rehabilitation of 8000 youth from displaced families of Visakhapatnam Steel Plant, designing the reconstruction of drainage and irrigation network in Krishna and Godavari deltas, strengthening the credit cooperatives and making them independent of government control, and several major policy initiatives including empowerment of parents in schools, speedy justice through rural courts, economic reform and restructuring of Andhra Pradesh, developing the Infocity in Hyderabad, and empowerment of local governments and stake holders are among his outstanding accomplishments in Andhra Pradesh. Among other things, he served as Secretary to both Governor and Chief Minister. Dr. Narayan's experience in government fully convinced him that what India needs today is not merely periodic change of players, but a fundamental change in the rules of the game. In order to translate his vision into practical reality, he resigned from the Indian Administration Service (IAS) from the post of Secretary to the government in 1996, and worked with like-minded colleagues for the formation of Lok Satta and is currently its National Coordinator.

## Deepak Nayyar

Deepak Nayyar is Professor of Economics at Jawaharlal Nehru University, New Delhi. Earlier, he has taught at the University of Oxford, the University of Sussex, and the Indian Institute of Management, Calcutta. He was, until recently, Vice Chancellor of the University of Delhi. He served as Chief Economic Adviser to the Government of India and Secretary in the Ministry of Finance. He was educated at St. Stephen's College, University of Delhi. Thereafter, as a Rhodes Scholar, he went on to study at Balliol College, University of Oxford, where he obtained a B. Phil and a D. Phil in Economics. He has published several books and articles in professional journals. He has received awards for his contribution to research in Economics. He has been a Member of the World Commission on the Social Dimension of Globalization. He is an Honorary Fellow of Balliol College, Oxford. Professor Nayyar is Chairman of the Board of Governors of the UNU World Institute for Development Economics Research, Helsinki, a Member of the Board of Directors of the Social Science Research Council in the United States, and Chairman of the Advisory Council for the Department of International Development, Queen Elizabeth House, University of Oxford. He is a member of the recently constituted National Knowledge Commission in India. He is also Vice President of the International Association of Universities, Paris.

## Prabhu Pingali

Prof. Prabhu Pingali is the Director of the Agricultural and Development Economics Division of the Food and Agriculture Organisation of the United Nations. He is also the President of the International Association of Agricultural Economists (IAAE) for the 2003-2006 time period. He was the Vice-President of the IAAE from 1997-2000 and chairman of the programme committee for the 24th International Conference of Agricultural Economists. He co-chairs the Millennium Ecosystem Assessment Panel's working group on Future Scenarios. He is also the editor of the newly established e-Journal of Agricultural and Development Economics (e-JADE). Prof. Pingali has over 25 years of experience in assessing the extent and impact of technical change in developing country agriculture in Asia, Africa and Latin America. An Indian national, he earned a Ph.D. in Economics from North Carolina State University in 1982. He was Director of the Economics Program at CIMMYT, Mexico from 1996-2002. Prior to joining CIMMYT, he worked at the International Rice Research Institute at Los Baños, Philippines from 1987 to 1996 as an Agricultural Economist, and prior to that at the World Bank's Agriculture and Rural Development Department from 1982-1987 as an economist. He was a visiting scholar at Stanford University, Food Research Institute, and an Affiliate Professor at the University of the Philippines at Los Baños. Prof. Pingali has authored 6 books and over 90 refereed journal articles and book chapters on technological change, productivity growth and resource management issues in Asia, Africa and Latin America. He has received several international awards for his work, including two from the American Agricultural Economics Association: Quality of Research Discovery Award in 1988 and Outstanding Journal Article of the Year (Honorable Mention) in 1995.

## Bhanoji Rao

Prof. Bhanoji Rao had his early education at the Municipal High School and Maharajah's College, Vizianagaram. He has a B.A. (Honours) in Economics from the Andhra University, Visakhapatnam and a Ph.D. from the University of Singapore. In 1967, he left for Singapore where he worked for 27 years as an academic at the Singapore Polytechnic, University of Singapore and the National University of Singapore. He was away from Singapore during 1979-1985 and served the World Bank as an Economist at Washington and Jakarta. After returning home in early 2001, he served as Visiting Faculty, Centre for Public Policy, IIM-B and Honorary Research Professor, GITAM Institute of Foreign Trade, Visakhapatnam. Since August 2004, he is Professor Emeritus, GITAM Institute of Foreign Trade (GIFT), Visakhapatnam and also a Visiting Professor of ASCI, Hyderabad. His Consultancy clientele included, Singapore Airlines, IBM-Singapore, IDRC -Canada, UNESCAP, the World Bank and most recently ADB. His publications included 15 books, 37 chapters in books, 62 papers in refereed international and regional journals and 12 monographs. His most recent books are: *East Asian Economies: The Miracle, A Crisis and the Future* (Published by McGraw-Hill, Singapore in 2001) of which he is the sole author and *Visakhapatnam Development Report* (Published by the GITAM Institute of Foreign Trade, Visakhapatnam, 2003) of which he is the coordinator. Dr Rao writes a regular fortnightly column in *Hindu Business Line*.

## M. Govinda Rao

Prof. M. Govinda Rao is the Director, National Institute of Public Finance and Policy, New Delhi, India (since January 2003). He is also a Member, Economic Advisory Council to the Prime Minister. His past positions include Director, Institute for Social and Economic Change, Bangalore (1998-2002) and Fellow, Research School of Pacific and Asian Studies, Australian National University, Canberra, Australia (1995-1998). After completing his doctoral degree in Economics in India, Dr. Rao undertook his post-doctoral research at University of Maryland, College Park, Md. He has had visiting assignments at University of Maryland, College Park, University of California, Santa Cruz, University of Toronto and University of Montreal.

Prof. Rao has a number of advisory roles, besides being a Member of the Economic Advisory Council to the Prime Minister. These include, Member, International Advisory Panel on Governance, UNDP Regional Office, Bangkok, Member, Expert Committee on Multilevel Planning, Planning Commission, Government of India, Chairman, Expert Group on Taxation of Services (2000-01), Chairman, Technical Experts Committee on VAT, and Member, Consultative Group of Inter-State Council, Government of India. He is also a Member of the Taxation Policy Group in the Initiative for Policy Dialogue led by Prof. Joseph Stiglitz of Columbia University. He is also a member of Steering Committee for the South Asia Network of Economic Research Institutions (SANEI). Dr. Rao's research interests include public finance and fiscal policy, fiscal federalism and state and local finance. He has published technical articles extensively in a number of reputed journals besides 12 books and monographs on various aspects of Public Finance.

## Gerry Rodgers

Dr. Gerry Rodgers is Director of the International Institute for Labour Studies, Geneva. Prior to this position he was Director of the Policy Integration Department of the International Labour Office, which carries out research and policy development on integrated approaches to work and employment. At the ILO he has been responsible for policy development on the decent work agenda in the Director-General's Office; was Technical Director of the Secretariat for the World Commission on the Social Dimension of Globalization; directed the ILO's Multi-disciplinary Technical Team for the Southern Cone of Latin America for several years; and has directed programmes of research and action on training systems, on labour markets and labour institutions and on population issues. His publications include work on poverty, inequality, social exclusion, employment, labour markets, child labour, population growth and economic development, including empirical work in South and Southeast Asia, in Latin America and in Europe.

### T.N. Srinivasan

T.N. Srinivasan is a Ph.D. from and Samuel C. Park, Jr. Professor of Economics at Yale University. Formerly a Professor, and later Research Professor, at the Indian Statistical Institute, Delhi (1964-1977), he has taught at numerous universities in the US. His research interests include International Trade, Development, Agricultural Economics and Microeconomic Theory.

He recently authored *Federalism and Economic Reform: International Perspectives,* with Jessica Seddon Wallack (Cambridge University Press, 2006) as well as *Reintegrating India with the World Economy* with Suresh D. Tendulkar (Washington: Institute for International Economics, 2003) and edited the volume *Frontiers in Applied General Equilibrium Modeling: Essays in Honor of Herbert Scarf* (Cambridge University Press, 2005) with Timothy J. Kehoe and John Whalley and Trade, Finance and Investment in South Asia (New Delhi: Social Science Press, 2001). He is also the author of *Developing Countries and the Multilateral Trading System* (Boulder, CO: Westview Press, 1998).

He is a Fellow of the American Philosophical Society, the Econometric Society and the American Academy of Arts and Sciences, and a Foreign Associate of the National Academy of Sciences. He was named Distinguished Fellow of the American Economic Association in 2003.

### K. Subbarao

Prof. K. Subbarao was until recently a lead economist in the Africa Region of the World Bank, responsible for research and operations in social protection, poverty and vulnerability. He is currently a consultant on safety nets and social protection for the South Asia Region of the Bank. Prior to joining the Bank, he was a professor of economics at the Institute of

Economic Growth, Delhi, and a visiting research fellow at the University of California at Berkeley. At the Bank, Dr. Subbarao played a major role in analytical and policy work on poverty, particularly in the domain of safety nets. He has published extensively on the subject, and is the lead author of *Safety Net Programs and Poverty Reduction: Lessons from Cross Country Experience*, and *Reaching Out to Africa's Orphans: A Framework for Public Action*. His recently completed work and current research interests include ageing and poverty in Africa and the role of social pensions, understanding risk and vulnerability in rural Kenya, social protection of orphans and vulnerable children in Africa, and food aid and food security policies in Asia and Africa. Dr. Subbarao's past research spanned a variety of issues bearing on India's agricultural price policy and income distribution, equity and efficiency of farm price and input subsidies, public distribution system, and other anti-poverty programmes. He has authored or co-authored 8 books and over 50 research papers in various professional economic journals.

# Index